THE PLAINS POLITICAL TRADITION

VOLUME 4

SOUTH DAKOTA
HISTORICAL SOCIETY
PRESS
25
YEARS OF
PUBLISHING

THE PLAINS POLITICAL TRADITION

• • •

ESSAYS ON SOUTH DAKOTA POLITICAL CULTURE

VOLUME 4

EDITED BY

JON K. LAUCK AND

PAULA M. NELSON

SOUTH DAKOTA

HISTORICAL SOCIETY PRESS

PIERRE

The South Dakota Historical Society Press gratefully acknowledges the University of South Dakota for its help in funding this project.

Library of Congress Cataloging-in-Publication Data available

The paper in this book meets the guidelines for permanence and durability of the committee on Production Guidelines for Book Longevity of the Council on Library Resources.

Text and cover design by Rich Hendel
Cover photograph by the South Dakota Department of Tourism

Please visit our website at sdhspress.com

Printed in the United States of America
22 21 20 19 18 1 2 3 4 5

To our long-time friend and coeditor John E. Miller,

1945–2020.

CONTENTS

Introduction 1
Jon K. Lauck and Paula M. Nelson

1 | The Origins and Distribution of South Dakota's Non-Indigenous Population, 1870–1890 12
Greg Rose

2 | Printing History in the Making: Political Culture in South Dakota's German-Language Press, 1880–1915 39
Randi Ramsden

3 | General William H.H. Beadle: Abolitionist, Soldier, Statesman, Educator 60
Justin Blessinger

4 | Safeguarding the Interests of the People: Governor Peter Norbeck and Conservative Reform 77
Daryl Webb

5 | William J. Bulow: The Conservative Democrat Who Time Passed By 97
Tonnis H. Venhuizen

6 | The Eastern Establishment on Trial: Congressman Karl Mundt, 'Inland' Republicanism, and the Hiss Case 126
Sean J. Flynn

7 | Two Senators and South Dakota Politics in Comparative Perspective: Lyndon Baines Johnson versus Francis Case 148
Paul Higbee

8 | The Political Strategies of George Mickelson 170
Paul Wilson

9 | Political 'Nobodies' Out of Political 'Nowhere':
From Where Have South Dakota's Political Leaders Come? 199
Marshall Damgaard

10 | The Politics of the South Dakota Budget Process 222
Michael Card

Contributors 253

Index 257

JON K. LAUCK AND PAULA NELSON

INTRODUCTION

TWO DECADES OF *THE PLAINS POLITICAL TRADITION*

• • •

In April 2020, we were busily sending emails back and forth, sorting through the various proposals that had come in during the early stages of this volume. We debated whether topics were worthy of study, whether enough primary source material was available to explore them, and whether they had been missed by previous historians or had been the subject of frequent analysis. This is a familiar process for those involved in selecting authors and chapters for an edited volume. Then the news came. Our longtime collaborator, who had been involved in this book series for twenty years, had died. On 1 May 2020, John E. Miller died of a heart attack in his kitchen in Brookings, South Dakota, as he was preparing to go golfing early one morning. Perhaps no other person had done more in their life to advance the cause of studying South Dakota history. Over three decades of teaching at South Dakota State University, John had written many key chapters of South Dakota's political history and had helped students develop their ideas and courses of study that produced important published works. We all are the poorer for not having John's experience and learning brought to bear on this volume about the state's political culture.

John was present at the creation of this series. In 2004, as a major U.S. Senate race was brewing in South Dakota, the *New York Times* called a South Dakota State University professor to get some perspective. They wanted to know how to explain and summarize the nature and trajectory of South Dakota's politics in their reporting about the Senate race. The recipient of the *Times* call, Jon Lauck, soon received a visit from then-retired Miller, who frequently stopped by the office to talk history, baseball, and travel plans for history conferences. Soon after yellow legal pads were being filled with notes, outlines were being generated, and email chains of ideas were circulating. The geographer of South Dakota, Ed Hogan, joined the discussion and in short order an article was being contemplated and then drafted. The result was entitled "The Contours of South Dakota Political Culture" by Jon Lauck, John Miller, and Edward Hogan, which was published in the Summer 2004 issue of *South Dakota History*.

The idea behind "Contours" was to transcend the details of vote totals and specific elections to say something broader about the setting for political activities in South Dakota, or to explain the more general political culture of the state. In "The Contours of South Dakota Political Culture," in very broad general strokes, the authors suggested that South Dakota was characterized by a "moderate republican political culture." The emphasis in this phrase was on the philosophical political tradition that animated the form of eighteenth-century, anti-monarchical thinking that undergirded the battles of the Revolutionary generation and the work of the Founding Fathers who later wrote the American Constitution. Small-"r" republicanism in fact traced back to Renaissance Florence and earlier and emphasized citizen participation, public virtue, limits on government power, and egalitarianism. This was the political and philosophical tradition that had germinated in the American colonies and grew in the young American republic and that had been planted in South Dakota.

This tradition of American republicanism was shaped by the particulars of the South Dakota setting. Most prominently is the overwhelming influence of farming and ranching, economic sectors which have dominated the state since its beginning. The unique division of the state is also important. South Dakota was not simply a replica of farming Iowa, but was about half Iowa-oriented with another half welded on west of the Missouri River that approximates a Wyoming or Montana. The divide between "East River" and "West River" remains a recognizable demarcation line in the state.[1] South Dakota is also out in the middle of the country, far-removed from Manhattan and Los Angeles, a position that fosters regionalist inclinations, or a desire to be independent and not be dominated by the coasts. The mix of people in South Dakota is also unique. In addition to the Sioux who were here long before statehood and what Frederick Manfred called the "lingering . . . Anglo-Saxon imprinting" of the American settlers who moved in, mostly from the Midwest with their republican traditions, South Dakota also saw a large influx of immigrants. This group included Germans, both from Germany proper and from German settlements in

Russia, along with Scandinavians, Dutch, Irish, Czechs, and others.[2] As a place with a strong agrarian grounding and few cities and located far from the coasts, it is also true that left-wing activism has historically been weak in South Dakota.

Nineteenth-century republicanism and the unique setting of South Dakota are linked to a more tangible political reality in the state in the form of the prominence of the Republican Party. In the 1850s, as the first settlers were just beginning to trickle into what would become the Dakotas, the newly formed and vehemently anti-slavery GOP swept the Midwest. Many Republican midwesterners and young Civil War veterans from the Midwest migrated to Dakota Territory to become farmers and made the emerging young state heavily Republican from the time of the territorial era in the 1860s. Democrats did not elect a governor in South Dakota until 1926, as Tony Venhuizen explains in this volume, and he was a conservative who defeated a troubled incumbent and benefitted from running against a GOP which was deeply divided. GOP dominance in South Dakota has been accentuated in recent years. Since 2008, Democrats have not won a statewide race here. This is saying something since there are thirteen offices elected by statewide votes in South Dakota. As of this writing, the legislature is made up of ninety-four Republicans and eleven Democrats.

While these broad outlines hold true, there are important exceptions and nuances to consider. During the 1890s, for example, the Populist Party, led and supported by many Republicans, found success in South Dakota. The success of the Populists in the 1890s is not unrelated to other forms of populism, especially conservative varieties, that became more prominent in American politics in the decades after World War II and in more recent years. The reform era of the early twentieth century also witnessed some unique political machinations in South Dakota. During the Progressive Era, some Republicans such as Peter Norbeck were active leaders in progressive politics, but, as Daryl Webb shows in this volume, their reforms were generally conservative or moderate in orientation. The dominance of farming in South Dakota history can also lead to moments when the normal conservative propensities of the state are overcome by the pain in farm country. During the Great Depression, for example, the Democrats had a surge of success, as they did all around the country. By World War II, this surge had sputtered out and the state returned to GOP domination.

The Democrats saw another surge in the 1970s, led by George McGovern's organizing in farm country, and this upswing benefitted Democrats into the 1990s.[3]

When attempting to explain the prevalence of the GOP in South Dakota and the exceptions and deviations from this norm we have tried to stay attuned to a wider canvas of events and the broader political environment, or what is known as political culture. Throughout this series our understanding of political culture has remained an eclectic one, encompassing elements of both thought and behavior. In addition to attitudes, beliefs, assumptions, values, and ideology, it includes roles, symbols, practices, procedures, habits, traditions, organizations, and institutions, among other things. We include public opinion, political leaders and organizations, campaign rhetoric, and policy positions, along with any number of other factors, in our definition of politics. Starting from these broad-stroke observations, writers in our first three volumes filled in many of the details with analyses of politics and religion, education, transportation, women's issues, immigration, ethnicity, Native Americans, economic development, and other subjects. Studying literature, environmentalism, war and peace, local government, U.S. Senate and gubernatorial elections, business, farm organizations, planning, and geography, our authors probed many of the nooks and crannies of South Dakota's political culture and greatly added to our knowledge of the assumptions, ideas, mechanisms, organizations, and processes of statewide politics. Biographical studies of people such as Ben Reifel, William Janklow, Karl Mundt, Coe I. Crawford, and Laura Ingalls Wilder exemplified the wide variety of options and paths that have been carved by the state's political actors.

The chapters in this volume build on these earlier insights. In chapter 1, Greg Rose explains how the original immigrants to a state form the backbone of its political traditions. While noting the continuing presence of South Dakota's Indigenous population, Rose outlines how the foundation of the state's current cultural and political characteristics was established by the Euro-American immigrants who arrived in large numbers during the late nineteenth century. According to the 1880 census, the Midwest provided the largest number of immigrants to the state's territory, notably from Wisconsin, Iowa, Illinois, and Minnesota (beyond the region, New York also supplied many settlers). Scandinavians, especially Norwegians but also Swedes and Danes, were nearly as common among the immigrants as were Germans, particularly if those born in Germany are combined with the greater number of Russians, nearly all of whom were ethnically German, known as Germans from Russia. The distribution of nativity groups by county reveals that certain settlement groups tended to cluster in areas within South Dakota, sometimes with other ethnic groups, sometimes separately. The culture and ethnicity of the Scandinavians and the Germans from Russia (religiously diverse and occasionally living in isolated, inward-looking colonies) remained deeply within them, affecting their settlement associations, religion, language, and politics. Midwesterners brought with them a northern outlook, as most had northern origins, and the locally developed Midwestern cultural characteristics of their home states. At least some Midwestern cultural influence also likely affected foreign immigrants (and certainly their U.S. born children) who stopped in the Midwest on their way to South Dakota. Clearly, South Dakota's unique immigration and ethnic history—Midwestern, Scandinavian, Germanic—represents a significant factor in the development of its political culture.

As Rose explains, South Dakota became home to thousands of European immigrants who arrived between the territorial days and the early twentieth century. According to the 1900 Federal Population Census, as Randi Ramsden explains in her chapter, nearly 20 percent of South Dakota's foreign-born population originated from the many states now known as Germany. Others arrived from German expatriate colonies in Russia. In search of a better life with religious, political, and economic freedoms in South Dakota, they contributed to a patchwork of German-speaking immigrant communities with varying cultural and political backgrounds. As they settled, many continued to celebrate their traditions and speak their native language, and as more and more Germans arrived, South Dakota developed its very own German-language newsprint culture. The newspapers of German immigrant communities not only recorded everyday life through the reporting of local news, cultural events, and entertainment, but they also reflected and reinforced the linguistic, political, and social identity of their readers. Some newspapers revealed their community's attempts and successes at political integration and assimilation, while others functioned as a driving force of isolation and the preservation of Germanity in linguistic and cultural islands throughout the state.

Finally, some newspapers depicted how the growing German-reading population was a major part of the local economy and highlighted how editors sought to increase profits by way of finding a wider audience. All in all, German-language news publications provide insight into the ways in which, over time, German-speaking immigrants found their place in the existing South Dakota political landscape.

Another helpful lens through which one can view South Dakota political culture is via the stories of prominent political leaders such as William Henry Harrison Beadle, Peter Norbeck, William Bulow, Karl Mundt, Francis Case, and George Mickelson. As Justin Blessinger demonstrates in his chapter, Beadle exerted more influence on Dakota Territory and the fledgling state of South Dakota than perhaps any other individual. He surveyed and described the massive territory, wrote the codified laws, shaped the constitution to protect school lands, and led the Madison Normal School, now Dakota State University, during its precarious first decades. But the character that Beadle brought to these many roles was shaped by the service of his youth, on both sides of the law, as he both helped escaped slaves avoid the law and bounty hunters and as he served the Union throughout the entire Civil War, continuing his service even after as a member of the Freedmen's Bureau. These formative years help us better understand the man who so significantly shaped South Dakota.

Governor and later U.S. senator Peter Norbeck earned a reputation as a *progressive* reformer both among contemporaries and with later biographers and historians, says Daryl Webb. But in his chapter, Webb argues that a more accurate representation of the man would be as a *conservative* reformer. Norbeck's understanding of the world around him and the issues facing him as a public official was largely shaped by his background in an America that was quickly vanishing. For him, progressive policies such as public ownership were ways of heading off even more radical forms of reform, like those being advocated by the Industrial Workers of the World and the Nonpartisan League that had invaded the state from across the border in North Dakota. Norbeck thus took his place with other conservative reformers—most importantly, Theodore Roosevelt—who strategically viewed moderate reform as a path to conservative stability.

In 1926, William J. Bulow was elected governor of South Dakota. He was the first Democrat to hold that office, and his election, as Tony

Venhuizen explains, came as the era of Peter Norbeck progressivism was on the wane. Bulow, a folksy and charismatic lawyer from Beresford, considered himself a Jeffersonian Democrat, and emphasized limited government, a balanced budget, and a common sense and nonpartisan approach. He would veto the general appropriations bill to force the legislature, controlled by Republicans, to balance the budget. After two terms as governor, Bulow was elected to the U.S. Senate amidst the early days of the Great Depression. In Washington, he soon found himself in opposition to President Franklin D. Roosevelt, whose New Deal of government spending and control of the economy were contrary to Bulow's Jeffersonianism. In South Dakota, though, FDR's election brought a wave of Democrats into state government, led by Governor Tom Berry. Berry, a friend of Bulow's, soon became an enthusiastic supporter of Roosevelt's, administering New Deal programs in the state. In the Senate, Bulow joined Democratic senators in opposing Roosevelt's court packing plan, leading to FDR's first major legislative defeat. An isolationist, Bulow resisted Roosevelt's interventionism in the early days of World War II, until the Japanese attack on Pearl Harbor made entering the war a necessity. By 1942, Bulow's Jeffersonianism was out of step with a Democratic Party remade in FDR's image. He lost the Democratic primary for U.S. Senate to Governor Berry, who ran as a Roosevelt ally against Bulow, and Berry lost the general election during a period of GOP resurgence. Bulow's unlikely career had begun during the days of the progressive Peter Norbeck Republicans, and as it ended Karl Mundt was the ascendant conservative figure in the Republican Party. Bulow's Jeffersonian approach, which had enabled him to win every statewide general election he entered, had been abandoned by the Democratic Party.

A more liberal, FDR-oriented national Democratic Party would have to contend with another rising figure in South Dakota politics. In his chapter, Sean J. Flynn shifts readers' attention to Congressman Karl E. Mundt of South Dakota, who was first elected to Congress in 1938. Mundt became a leader on the House Committee on Un-American Affairs (HUAC) and a skilled cross-examiner of the witnesses who appeared before HUAC during their investigations of the prominent New Dealer, Alger Hiss, and his accuser, Whittaker Chambers, in 1948. Motivated by the eastern intelligentsia's ridiculing of rural culture and by New Dealers' accusations that Midwestern Republicans were reactionary and unreasonably "obsessed" with Communism, Mundt, who by World War II had developed a national reputation as a spokesperson for the "Midwestern viewpoint," used his HUAC seat to expose how the lax screening policies of the Roosevelt administration threatened national security. As he chronicles Mundt's pursuit of Hiss and other New Deal officials who collaborated with Soviet spy rings, Flynn illustrates how the congressman embodied South Dakotans' reasonable suspicions about the loyalties of Ivy League elites who filled the offices of the burgeoning federal bureaucracy during the Roosevelt era. From the perspective of Mundt and his constituents, Hiss's snobbery, prevarications and lies, and treasonous acts during the Roosevelt presidency accentuated the divide between eastern urban and "inland" rural political cultures. Yet by discrediting Hiss in a methodical and judicious manner, Mundt confirmed that South Dakota voters' concerns about Communist moles, despite charges by the eastern establishment that they were exaggerated, were legitimate and utterly sensible.

Mundt's GOP colleague in Congress, Francis H. Case, is examined by Paul Higbee in his chapter. Case, who took his seat in the U.S. House of Representatives the cycle before Mundt was elected, can be viewed as an architect of the state's modern Republican party. Case was elected the same year as Congressman Lyndon B. Johnson, a Democrat from Texas. Despite the partisan divide between Case and Johnson, and the fact that they were opposites in personality (Case low-key and retiring, Johnson gregarious and domineering), common concerns often put them on the same page. They fought for water projects to benefit the semi-arid Great Plains. Both favored a strong national defense, abhorred Communism, and expressed concern about too-powerful organized labor hindering industry. In South Dakota, those positions remained central to Republican thinking throughout the twentieth century, and still resonate today. By using a comparative approach and highlighting Johnson's approach to politics, Higbee explains the career of Francis Case and what it reveals about South Dakota political culture.

Both Mundt and Case served during the same time that George T. Mickelson was governor of South Dakota (1947–1951). In his chapter, Paul Wilson explains how Mickelson's son, George S. Mickelson, became successful politically by adopting new campaign tactics, advertising modes, technologies, and organizational principles for winning elections. Wilson offers a case study in how politicians in South Dakota were affected by trends and developments that were sweeping across the nation. The piece also speaks to the particular qualities and practices of the Mickelson organization and what it did to succeed. Mickelson became acquainted with farmers, who could play a supporting role in his television ads; enlisted the entire Republican leadership of the House and Senate, who likewise played roles in his political ads; organized door-to-door campaigning; and, in general, used cutting-edge techniques to "spin" his candidacy and to identify himself more closely with the voting public.

Moving beyond the stories of particular political leaders, Marshall Damgaard offers a more synthetic picture of the state's political culture by analyzing the process of leader selection. While certain individuals, such as Richard Pettigrew, Peter Norbeck, Karl Mundt, George McGovern, Bill Janklow, Jim Abdnor, Jim Abourezk, Tom Daschle, and John Thune, stand out in people's minds when they think about the state's political culture, a broader survey of who the leaders are and where they come from reveals some important insights into the political culture of the state. Dynastic succession plays a relatively small role in South Dakota politics, although we have had the Herseth and Mickelson families represented for two or three generations in important official positions. The names "McGovern" and "Johnson" have not been enough to help other hopefuls rise to a high position. Many, if not most, of the state's political leaders have risen from modest circumstances and come from rural or remote locations. Sioux Falls, surprisingly, has not netted many governors or other high-ranking officials. South Dakotans respect and elect officials not for what they are but for who they are and the state's political culture is remarkably non-judgmental and egalitarian.

Finally, in his chapter, Michael Card examines the nature of South Dakota's conservative leanings by way of the state budget process. South Dakota conservativism, according to Card, represents an individualistic political culture where government is seen as a means to respond efficiently to citizen demands through the encouragement of private initiative and efforts to improve the marketplace. Earlier in its history, the state's populist and progressive leanings represented a moralistic political culture, where government is the mechanism for resolving disputes, competitive in terms of ideas, principles, and issues, and paying one's fair share based on one's ability to pay. Perhaps the clearest distinction is that the moralistic political culture favors direct government action and the individualistic political culture favors enhancing the marketplace. South Dakota's conservativism has a pragmatic side to it. The state legislature enacted an income tax in 1933 with bipartisan support to replace declining revenue from the state's tax levy on property due to the decade-old farm price depression, rural credits debt, and the worsening drought. When the income tax failed to produce enough funds to support state government, the legislature enacted a sales tax, also with bipartisan support, and increased the rate as more funds were needed to support state government services. Today, there is little support for candidates favoring a personal income tax or ballot initiatives that might lead in that direction. However, the stability of the sales tax and the funding of local government with property taxes means that the moralistic principle that one pay his fair share of the cost of government based on their ability to pay, Card believes, is compromised.

Story by story, episode by episode, and subject by subject, the political culture of South Dakota becomes more nuanced and complex. The generally conservative and republican nature of the phenomenon remains persuasive as an interpretation, but counter-themes and more detailed descriptions make our understanding of that culture more complete and instructive. The mixture of broad themes and particular nuances yields the kind of history John Miller appreciated. To him, this volume is dedicated.

Finally, we must extend a special and heart-felt thank you to President Sheila Gestring and Provost Kurt Hackemer at the University of South Dakota for extending their generous financial support of this volume. Without their assistance, our exploration and discussion of South Dakota's long political history would not be possible.

Jon K. Lauck
Paula Nelson
October 2021

NOTES

1. On the Midwest/plains West divide see Jon K. Lauck, ed., *The Interior Borderlands: Regional Identity in the Midwest and Great Plains* (Sioux Falls: Center for Western Studies, 2019).

2. Art R. Huseboe, "From Feikema to Manfred, from the Big Sioux Basin to the Northern Plains," *Great Plains Quarterly* 21 (Fall 2001): 313.

3. Jon K. Lauck, "George S. McGovern and the Farmer: South Dakota Politics, 1953–1962," *South Dakota History* 32 (Winter 2002): 331–53; Jon K. Lauck, "'It disappeared as quickly as it came': The Democratic Surge and the Republican Comeback in South Dakota Politics, 1970–1980," *South Dakota History* 46 (Summer 2016): 95–140.

GREGORY S. ROSE

1 | THE ORIGINS AND DISTRIBUTIONS OF SOUTH DAKOTA'S NON-INDIGENOUS POPULATION, 1870–1890

• • •

The characteristics or culture of a place reflect in large part the characteristics or culture of its people. Who was there originally? Where did others come from within the United States, elsewhere in the Americas, or overseas? What changes occurred over time in the leading origin sources as new immigrants arrived? How did their cultural baggage impact the economic and social development of their new homes; their support for public education; their attitudes regarding societal structures; their religious activities; the agricultural associations they created; their level of public engagement; their political preferences; how they viewed the role of government; and more?[1] For South Dakota, which underwent rapid population growth during the late nineteenth century and considerably slower expansion subsequently, the impact of the first Euro-American settlers remains particularly significant.

Geographers and others have mapped, in broad strokes, the general features of South Dakota's cultural characteristics that built upon the state's unique late nineteenth century mix of immigrants and Native Americans. South Dakota's eastern half lands within the Upper Middle West traditional culture area, its major sources of culture stemming from New England Extended (New York and the northern Midwest), nineteenth-century Europe, and Canada. The state falls within the Upper Middle Western (predominantly Protestant) religious region, according to Wilbur Zelinksy.[2] Additionally, Zelinksy describes South Dakota's "Dominant Political Culture" as "moralistic" and "individualistic."[3] A deeper understanding of South Dakota's early immigration history can illuminate the impact of its distinctive ethnicity on the state's developing cultural characteristics.

Drilling down into census records reveals details regarding the origins and distribution of South Dakota's population during the crucial territorial and very early statehood period, thereby establishing a base line for examining how South Dakota's Euro-American settlers influenced the development and evolution of the state. In 1850, for the first time in U.S. Census history, canvassers asked inhabitants to identify their "nativity," meaning their state or country of birth.[4] Information supplied by the respondent was not checked against any other documentation but simply recorded on sheets that canvassers carried from house to house as they collected answers to other questions such as the names and ages of everyone in the residence, their gender, race, occupation, and value of their property. Nativity information was published in statewide tables for 1850 and 1860, in county-based tables for the states and countries supplying the largest numbers of birthplaces in 1870 and 1880 and in county tables for 1890, but only for the leading foreign birthplaces.

The Euro-American settlers who began appearing in the mid-nineteenth century and arrived in droves during the "Boom Decade" from the late 1870s through the late 1880s were not the first to occupy what became South Dakota.[5] That distinction fell to Indigenous peoples who had been present on the continent for millennia but were largely displaced and decimated by diseases and social disruptions from centuries of Euro-American contact. They experienced more of the same after the mid-1800s from the new arrivals to South Dakota. While Native Americans were the first peoples to establish a continuing presence in the state, the wave of Euro-Americans set the sociocultural environment and political structures that remain dominant today.[6]

With the end of the Civil War, migration within the United States and immigration from foreign countries experienced renewed vigor and expanded into new territory. In an unusual twist, some of this migration headed inland and eastward from the Pacific Coast but, as had been most common for decades if not centuries, the more typical flow expanded westward from areas where the Indigenous Americans already had been displaced by Euro-Americans. Just west of the Old Northwest and prior to the Civil War, Iowa had achieved statehood in 1846 and had a population of almost 1.2 million in 1870, while Minnesota's statehood had been granted in 1858 and it contained 440,000 people in 1870. By then, all of eastern Iowa and the southeastern corner of Minnesota had reached population densities of eighteen persons per square mile, a level associated with the establishment of successful agricultural settlement.[7] For some less sociable pioneers, this level of settlement drove them toward open land elsewhere. For others—families just starting, young people lower in the sibling order unlikely to inherit the family farm, domestic and foreign immigrants of limited means—inexpensive and available land beyond the comparatively "old" states of Iowa and Minnesota beckoned.[8] Not so long previously, Iowa and Minnesota were new and Illinois and Wisconsin were old; not long before that Illinois, Michigan, and Wisconsin were new, and Indiana and Ohio were old. And so it went. Dakota Territory was the next lure for many of these settlers.

Following Minnesota's statehood, the remaining portions of what had been Minnesota Territory—basically west of Minnesota to the Missouri River—fell into an unorganized territorial status; beyond the Missouri River remained Native American territory.[9] Through the Treaty of Yankton in 1858, the Sioux Nation ceded much of eastern South Dakota to the U.S. government. Three years later, Dakota Territory, incorporating a swath of land west of Minnesota including today's South and North Dakota, much of Montana, and the northern half of Wyoming, became an official entity. According to the 1860 Census, the population of Dakota Territory neared 5,000, almost all concentrated in the southeast. The Fort Laramie Treaty of 1868 established the Great Sioux Reservation west of the Missouri River, and reduced Dakota Territory to what became South and North Dakota plus a small chunk of Nebraska. By 1870, the population of Dakota Territory was just over 14,000; later calculations assigned 11,776 of them to what became South Dakota.[10] By 1880, Territorial inhabitants numbered about 135,000, with 98,268 in the South Dakota area. After the division of the territory into two states in 1889, the combined population reached almost 540,000, with nearly 350,000 in South and 191,000 in North Dakota.

Although significantly dispossessed of much territory and reduced in numbers during 1860 to 1890, the Indigenous peoples remained an important element of the state's population. The Census Bureau categorized Native Americans in two basic ways, using similar terms in different years for each category.[11] Native Americans on reservations were variously listed as "In Tribal Relations," "Retaining their Tribal Character," "Sustaining Tribal Relations," "Reservation Indians," or "Not Taxed" as they were members of theoretically sovereign nations. Native Americans living outside of the reservation system were termed

Table 1. Native American Populations in Dakota Territory (1860–1880) or South Dakota (1890)

	Off Reservations or Taxed	*Tribal or On Reservations*	*Reservation Populations, 1890*	
1860	2,261	39,664	Cheyenne River	2,823
1870	1,200 (387 in South Dakota area)	26,320	Crow Creek	1,058
1880	1,391 (795 in South Dakota area)	27,168	Lower Brule	1,026
1890	782	19,068	Lake Traverse	1,522
			Pine Ridge	5,533
			Rosebud	5,381
			Yankton	1,725

Source: *Report on Indians Taxed and Indians Not Taxed, 1890*; 17, 18, 22, 23, 26, 27, 573

"Out of tribal relations," "Off reservations, self-supporting and taxed," or simply "Taxed," subject to taxation by governments as were all others living independently; sometimes the latter group was listed using the now-questionable terms "Domesticated Indians" or "Civilized Indians." Instructions for the 1850 Census specifically indicated that Native Americans were not to be counted, but a special census of tribal population conducted in 1853 by the Commissioner of Indian Affairs determined that at least 21,000 Native Americans lived in Minnesota Territory, including the future South Dakota.[12]

Starting in 1860 and expanding through 1890, the categories into which the Census Bureau placed Native Americans determined whether they were counted among the general population (if "Taxed") or listed separately (if "Not Taxed"), although tables enumerating both "Taxed" and "Not Taxed" Native Americans were published in the census.[13] (Table 1) Of the 1,200 Native Americans counted as "Out of tribal relations" in 1870, 999 were born in the United States (765 in Dakota) and 201 had foreign birthplaces (two hundred in Canada); data for 1870 in the 1890 census indicated that 387 of the 1,200 non-reservation Native Americans lived in the future South Dakota.[14] In 1880, 1,229 of the 1,391 "Taxed" individuals outside of reservations had U.S. birthplaces and 102 were from foreign countries; a later analysis placed 795 of those in the "Taxed" category in South Dakota.[15] In addition to the 782 Native Americans living off reservations in 1890, another four were "in prison, not otherwise enumerated," bringing the total to

786.[16] The 1890 census also counted those residing on each of South Dakota's seven reservations, some territorially larger than others and some within counties also inhabited by Euro-Americans. Populations ranged from 5,381 Native Americans on the Rosebud Reservation along the south central border to 1,026 living on the Lower Brule Reservation in the state's center.[17]

In the censuses from 1870 to 1890, at least a few "Taxed" Native Americans were listed among the general population in most counties. While over the course of this era new counties were organized within South Dakota and existing boundaries changed, a handful of counties, often located near or partially within reservations undergoing establishment or modification during 1870 to 1890, accounted for most of the non-reservation residences of Native Americans.[18] Counties with the largest number of "Taxed" Native Americans across the three censuses included Stanley in the center of the state, overlapping the Lower Brule Reservation (102 in 1880 and 392 in 1890); Moody in the east (221 in 1880 and 147 in 1890); Charles Mix in the southeast, including the Yankton Reservation (117 in 1870; 95 in 1880; 28 in 1890); Brookings in the east (145 in 1870, none in subsequent years); Hughes, part of the Crow Creek Reservation, in the center (129 in 1880 and 13 in 1890); and Gregory in the southeast, across from the Yankton Reservation (109 in 1890).[19]

African Americans represented another non-Euro-American population group responsible for the early growth and development of South Dakota, both as soldiers and as voluntary settlers.[20] A table in the 1890 census of "Native and Foreign Born and White and Negro Population" provided numbers for South Dakota and its counties; a footnote indicated the "Negro" category "includes all persons of negro descent."[21] Seventy African Americans were counted in what became South Dakota in 1870, 288 in 1880, and 541 in 1890. Elsewhere in the document, another table titled "Native Colored Population" listed 1,306 persons but a footnote indicated that it comprised "persons of negro descent, Chinese, Japanese, and civilized Indians."[22]

African Americans resided in about half of South Dakota's few counties in 1870, were then more sparsely distributed in 1880, but again lived in about half of the state's counties in 1890.[23] Some, but not all, African American populated counties contained towns or villages, but because South Dakota's urban centers were too small, they were not listed separately in published census tables. In 1870, eighteen African Americans lived in unorganized territory predominantly west of the Missouri River and nineteen resided in Yankton County, including the river town of Yankton, which was an early African American settlement center.[24] In 1880, the largest number of African Americans, 97, lived in Lawrence County, including the towns of Deadwood and Lead where gold mining attracted them and many others.[25] As Yankton County's African American population rose to 55 in 1880, 25 lived in Minnehaha County (Sioux Falls), and 21 in Charles Mix County. Although the census counted only five African Americans in Sully County in 1880 and seven in 1890, it may have held more since it was identified as a successful late nineteenth century Black settlement.[26] In 1890, Pennington County, including Rapid City, held more African Americans than any other county, 116, followed by 63 in Lawrence County, 62 in Yankton County, 40 in Meade County (Sturgis), and 35 in Fall River County.[27] According to the "Native Colored Population" table, which included native Americans, a majority of the U.S. birthplaces for the "Colored" population were in the South.[28] Minnesota, with 100 birthplaces, accounted for the most individuals, followed by Missouri (97), Alabama (38), Tennessee (37), Virginia and West Virginia together (28), and Kentucky (27); Iowa provided twenty, Ohio and Texas both accounted for nineteen each, and Wisconsin eighteen.

County-based listings of two other non-Euro-American population groups—natives of China and of Japan—also appear in a section of the 1890 Census focused on minority populations in 1870, 1880, and 1890.[29] While no Japanese natives were identified in South Dakota during any of the three census years and no Chinese natives appeared in the 1870 Census, by 1880, 230 immigrants from China were present and 195 in 1890. The largest number by far resided in Lawrence County, which included the settlements of Deadwood and Lead: 220 in 1880 and 152 in 1890. Newspapers identified these two towns as destinations for Chinese immigrants joining the gold rush, with the first "arriving in the Black Hills by the winter of 1875-1876."[30] Ten natives of China resided in Pennington County in 1880, with Rapid City as the major settlement; fourteen were there in 1890. Seven inhabitants born in China appeared in Hughes County, which included Pierre. Initially, most Chinese immigrants mined placer deposits, but over time, the majority engaged in service occupations (often laundries) and ex-

Table 2. Leading Sources, by Percent of Immigrant Population, in Minnesota Territory (1850) and Dakota Territory (1860, 1870, 1880)

Rank	*1850*	*Percent*	*1860*	*Percent*	*1870*	*Percent*	*1880*	*Percent*
1	Canada	31.5	Canada	44.9	Norway and Sweden	12.9	Norway and Sweden	14.0
2	New York	10.8	Minnesota	14.8	New York	10.5	Wisconsin	10.0
3	Maine	8.1	Wisconsin	10.7	Iowa	8.6	Canada	9.1
4	Wisconsin	6.7	Norway	4.0	Canada	7.5	New York	7.8
5	Ireland	6.0	New York	3.6	Ireland	7.3	Minnesota	7.5
6	Ohio	5.4	Michigan	3.4	Pennsylvania	5.5	Iowa	6.7
7	Pennsylvania	5.0	Missouri	2.5	Illinois	5.3	Russia	5.5
8	Illinois	3.7	France	1.7	Ohio	5.3	Germany	5.1
9	Germany	3.2	Iowa	1.7	Germany	4.7	Illinois	3.9
10	Vermont	2.2	Illinois	1.5	Minnesota	3.0	Pennsylvania	3.7
11	Massachusetts	2.0	Ohio	1.4	Indiana	2.1	Ireland	3.5
12	Missouri	2.0	Pennsylvania	1.4	England	2.1	Ohio	3.2

Sources: 1850, 1860, 1870, and 1880 Published Census Volumes

tended these services into other communities. As they "cultivated a social and economic niche, an 'ethnic oasis,' in the predominantly white region," they sometimes faced resentment and discrimination, as did other minority groups.[31]

The leading state or country birthplaces from 1850 through 1880 for the larger territories that encompassed South Dakota are displayed in Table 2. For the 1850 census, only areas east of the Missouri River that became the Dakotas fell within Minnesota Territory, while the 1860, 1870, and 1880 enumerations included the entire Dakota Territory. Minnesota Territory's population in 1850 was 6,077, two-thirds of whom had U.S. birthplaces. Canada was the largest single source of immigrants, foreign or domestic, with 1,417 settlers accounting for over 30 percent of those not born in Minnesota.[32] Secondary sources suggest that some may have been French Canadians or Métis hunters and trappers associated with fur trading posts.[33] New York was the leading supplier of incoming settlers born in the U.S., accounting for 488 or 10.8 percent of all immigrants, followed by Maine (365 natives and 8.1 percent), Wisconsin (301 and 6.7 percent), Ireland (271), Ohio

(241), Pennsylvania (227), and Illinois (168). Germany was ninth among the sources of non-Minnesota born inhabitants, providing 146 or 3.2 percent of immigrants, with Vermont (100 or 2.2 percent) in tenth place. This mix basically represented the population characteristics of Minnesota as areas west of what became the state remained in Native American possession and no civil subdivisions existed within which population could be counted.[34]

Minnesota had become a state by the June 1 collection date for the 1860 census, but the eastern half of the Dakotas remained without territorial designation. By the 1864 publication date for the 1860 data, Dakota Territory had been established and had a population of 4,837, compared to 172,023 in Minnesota.[35] Most Dakotans in 1860 lived in eastern areas, with the largest single group consisting of 1,586 individuals born in Dakota Territory.[36] Immigrants to the Territory were nearly evenly divided between those born in the U.S. and those born in foreign countries. Canada again was the largest supplier, with 1,458 natives accounting for more settlers than in 1850 and comprising nearly 45 percent of immigrants. The 480 Minnesotans, nearly 15 percent of immigrants, formed the second leading group and represented a new population at least in name, since the state was now separated from Dakota Territory. Wisconsin supplied 347 immigrants (10.7 percent of the total), New York 117, Missouri 82, and France 56; Ohio and Pennsylvania accounted for the same number and percent (47 and 1.4). Michigan (110), and Iowa (54) were two other new sources of Dakota Territory settlers. Footloose pioneers and young families arriving in an adjacent new frontier like the Dakotas from nearby states like Minnesota, Iowa, and Wisconsin were common features of nineteenth-century migration, as was the tendency to migrate along latitude lines.[37] The appearance of 129 Norwegians reflected their growing emigration to the United States.[38] The 22 German natives in 1860 were considerably fewer than the 146 living in Minnesota Territory in 1850. However, Germans formed a major element in Minnesota's population and its elevation to statehood and separate enumeration focused their count there, leaving few behind in the Dakotas; for similar reasons, the number of Irish also declined, from 271 to 42.[39]

By 1870, Norway and Sweden (combined in the census but with Norwegians comprising 80.7 percent of the territory-wide total) had become the top supplier of immigrants, accounting for 1,559 individuals and nearly 13 percent of inhabitants not born in Dakota Territory.[40] Since 1860, the number of New York increased ten-fold, to 1,273, or 10.5 percent of immigrants, and the many newly arriving Iowans lifted them to the third largest group (1,044 and 8.8 percent of immigrants), followed by Canada at 7.5 percent (906 residents, and Ireland (898 or 7.3 percent).

In 1880, Norwegians and Swedes increased their proportion of immigrants to 14 percent and remained the largest group. Although natives of Wisconsin were not among the top twelve sources in 1870 (that table included only five domestic sources rather than ten listed in 1880), they numbered 11,685 in 1880, forming the second largest supplier of immigrants, with 10 percent of the total.[41] Canada, at a larger percentage than in 1870, and New York, at a lesser percentage, filled the third and fourth places on the list. Minnesota represented a significantly more important source in 1880, providing nearly nine thousand settlers and rising from tenth rank in 1870 (3.0 percent) to fifth in 1880 (7.5 percent). Russia made its first appearance on the birthplace list that year, accounting for 5.5 percent of immigrants.

Although the South Dakota area's proportion of Dakota Territory population slipped below 75 percent in 1880 (from over 80 percent in 1870), nativity information in Table 2 roughly approximates its ethnic origins. However, it is possible to deeply examine the data to extract South Dakota's specific nativity. Using maps of the evolving county boundaries every census year from 1860 through 1890, the future state's civil divisions can be separated from those in the remainder of Dakota Territory (estimation is needed for a few cross-border counties or unorganized territory) and county-based nativity information applied.[42] In 1870, only the area east of the Missouri River, ceded by Native Americans in 1868, had been divided into counties. Even within that portion, most established counties were confined to a range or two along both the southeastern border with Nebraska and a range along the eastern border with Iowa and Minnesota. The primary exception was Buffalo County, which then included most of the east central area. The remainder of the Dakota Territory was "unattached" to any civil divisions.[43] By 1880, as future South Dakota's population surged, only a comparatively small area in the northwest corner of future South Dakota remained "unattached" to any county, although newly formed counties in north central and especially south central

Table 3. Leading Sources, by Percent of Immigrant Population, for South Dakota (Area of State in Territory or State)

Rank	*1870*	*Percent*	*1880*	*Percent*	*1890*	*Percent*
1	Norway and Sweden	15.2	Norway and Sweden	11.8	Wisconsin	11.5
2	New York	10.6	Wisconsin	10.8	Norway and Sweden	11.0
3	Iowa	10.0	New York	8.5	Iowa	10.6
4	Canada	6.1	Iowa	7.9	Germany	7.4
5	Illinois	6.0	Russia	7.6	Illinois	7.3
6	Ireland	5.5	Minnesota	6.4	New York	7.0
7	Pennsylvania	5.4	Canada	5.0	Minnesota	6.3
8	Ohio	5.3	Germany	4.9	Russia	5.1
9	Germany	3.6	Illinois	4.7	Canada	3.9
10	England and Wales	1.7	Pennsylvania	4.0	Ohio	3.7
11	Austria	1.6	Ohio	3.6	Pennsylvania	3.0
12	Bohemia	1.5	Ireland	3.2	Michigan	2.9
13	Denmark	1.0	England and Wales	2.1	England and Wales	2.4
14	Scotland	0.6	Michigan	1.8	Indiana	2.0
15	France	0.4	Indiana	1.7	Ireland	1.9

Sources: 1870, 1880, and 1890 Published Census Volumes compared to County Boundaries for South Dakota

and southwestern areas overlying Native American reservations were supposedly unpopulated by non-indigenous peoples.[44] County outlines east of the Missouri River displayed their current format by 1890, and while west of the river some boundary changes and new divisions were to come, counties containing the reservations continued to be listed as unpopulated.[45]

The rankings and origin percentages of the leading states and countries providing immigrants to South Dakota in 1870, 1880, and 1890 are noted in Table 3. Across these decades, some sources remained generally consistent providers, new sources of immigrants appeared, and other sources became less significant as new settlers arrived. Norway and Sweden, combined in county level census data for 1870 and 1880, together were the first or second leading source of immigrants across the decades. While data limitations make it impossible to determine which country's settlers dominated in each county, Norwegians represented over 70 percent of the combination throughout South Dakota in those two years, as they did when separately counted in 1890.[46] Wisconsin was not among the leading sources in 1870, but it jumped to second in 1880 and first in 1890. Iowa's placement was third or fourth each year. Germany was a lesser source in 1870 and 1880 but rose to fourth in 1890, with the significant German element in Wisconsin's early population likely helping expand their influence in South Dakota.[47] New Yorkers and Canadians were more significant among immigrants in 1870 but less so by 1890.

Immigrants comprised nearly 90 percent of the South Dakota population in 1870. Settlers originating within the United States formed 63 percent of the immigrants while only about fourteen hundred inhabitants had Dakota Territory birthplaces. Norway and Sweden together represented largest group, providing 15.2 percent of immigrants. New York accounted for 10.6 percent, followed by Iowa at 10.0 percent, Canada at 6.1 and Illinois at 6.0. Ireland provided 5.5 percent of those born outside of South Dakota, with Pennsylvania (5.4), Ohio (5.3), and Germany (3.6) next in order. England and Wales together supplied 1.7 percent of the settlers; likely most were from England based on the British Isles detail in the 1890 census. Austria, Bohemia, Demark, Scotland, and France each provided between 1.6 and 0.4 percent of immigrants.

Of the nearly one hundred thousand people living in South Dakota in 1880, well over 83,000 (85 percent) were immigrants, an eight-fold increase from 1870. The 40 percent of immigrants born in foreign places constitutes a modest proportional increase from 1870—leaving 60 percent hailing from within the United States but outside South Dakota. Norway and Sweden again provided the largest percentage of the immigrant population, 11.8 percent, proportionally less than in 1870 but numerically more (9,849 compared to 1,580). Wisconsin, not among the top ten sources in 1870, supplied the second largest immigrant percentage (10.8), followed by New York (8.5), Iowa (7.9), and Russia (7.6). Too few immigrants from Russia were present in 1870 to be included among the leading birthplaces in the county tables, but 6,315 were in residence by 1880. Minnesota, also new on the list, accounted for 6.4 percent of the immigrants, followed by Canada (5.0), Germany (4.9), Illinois (4.7), and Pennsylvania (4.0). For Ireland, Ohio, and Illinois, immigrant percentages fell considerably between 1870 and 1880, although the number of settlers coming from each source increased.

By 1890, as South Dakota matured, the length of the Euro-American settlement period extended, and the "Boom Decade" of immigration receded. Proportionally more of its population had in-state birthplaces than in previous censuses. Not quite 75 percent of inhabitants were immigrants, more than a 10 percent drop from 1880, and just over 37 percent of immigrants had foreign birthplaces, a more modest decline from 1880. Wisconsin provided the largest group of immigrants, 11.5 percent, rising from second in 1880 to surpass Norway and Sweden combined (11 percent). Iowans increasingly emigrated to South Dakota, becoming the third ranking source at 10.6 percent. The fourth, fifth, and sixth spots were closely grouped, with Germany supplying 7.4 percent of immigrants, Illinois at 7.3, and 7 percent coming from New York. Rounding out the top ten sources were Minnesota, accounting for 6.3 percent of immigrants, followed by Russia (5.1), Canada (3.9), and Ohio (3.7).

Many researchers have focused on elements or aspects of South Dakota's Euro-American population history using genealogical, family history, and local history sources, often accompanied by high level census data. Two comprehensive, detailed examinations of South Dakota's early population appeared in 1936 and 1937 in publications from the South Dakota State University Agricultural Extension Service.[48] These papers included a mix of census-based assessments, primarily from the 1890s, 1910, and 1930 enumerations, a review of secondary sources, and some maps of the distribution of immigrant groups and their children. Other population history resources cover the full range of ethnic groups or just certain groups in the state, including teacher's guides to South Dakota immigration resources, bibliographies, documents held at cultural centers at universities, websites tied to the state's history, and various popular and scholarly publications.[49]

Mapping county concentrations of South Dakota's major foreign and domestic immigrant groups in the late nineteenth century is possible using nativity data from the censuses of 1870, 1880, and 1890 and the historical boundaries of civil divisions from those years.[50] However, an important caveat applies when comparing the 1890 nativity percentages to those of 1870 and 1880. In 1870 and 1880, county-level tabular data published in census volumes listed the leading birthplace sources of U.S. and foreign born immigrants, with "immigrants" defined as inhabitants not born in the Dakotas. These data permit calculation of the nativity percentages for each group of immigrants in each county by subtracting the population born in South Dakota. However, the 1890 tables listed county-by-county numbers only for foreign born residents. The absence of 1890 data for U.S. born inhabitants, including South Dakotans, makes it impossible to determine the number and percentage they represented among each county's immigrants. Another factor to consider is that 1870 pre-dates South Dakota's boom years. Therefore, to establish a consistent picture of the distribution of late nineteenth-century immigrant groups across South Dakota, 1880 census data will be used for mapping their locations. Otherwise, a potentially confusing shift of perspective would occur, with the distribution of specific ethnic groups by county in 1870 and 1880 considering their relative presence among just the immigrant population but the county proportions for 1890 comparing their relative presence to the total population. Because 1890 data are available for foreign immigrants, occasional reference will be made to changes from 1880 to 1890 in the locations of these settlers. A potential alternative path to 1890 data for domestic immigrants in each county—examining the manuscript schedules—is closed to researchers due to the destruction of nearly all of these documents in a 1921 fire.[51]

The distribution of South Dakota's Euro-American ethnic groups reflected the areas available to them in the late nineteenth century. Lands reserved for Native Americans largely restricted settlement by others to South Dakota's eastern half, a belt across the center, and the western quarter, although pressure to "open" the reserved territory regularly reduced its extent.[52] Eastern South Dakota, the agricultural area first available to immigrants, was the most heavily populated. Some counties there displayed both large numbers and high percentages of certain immigrant groups. The Black Hills region in the southwest also was more heavily populated, as the lure of gold and economic opportunities presented by the miners attracted settlers. Some immigrant groups were relatively evenly distributed across the available parts of South Dakota. In other instances, even comparatively smaller numbers of immigrants in a sparsely populated county resulted in a high proportion being recorded. Overall, these county-based maps of immigrant distributions indicate concentrations of certain immigrant groups, places where their unusual numbers could have had unusual influence on the development and character of those areas. Some of these locations may be well known due to the research work of local historians and genealogists, but the confirmation provided by census data highlights the impact of these ethnic groups. And mapping the distribution of birthplace concentrations occasionally reveals the presence of groups not researched previously. Examining the ebb and flow of different ethnic groups and their changing geographic distribution over the earliest decades of the state's history contributes to greater understanding of South Dakota's past.

Norway and Sweden (listed as a unit in 1870 and 1880) together formed the largest source of settlers not born in South Dakota, accounting for 11.8 percent of immigrants. Counties with immigrant percentages notably higher than the statewide average were grouped tightly along the southern two-thirds of the state's eastern border. (Map 1) Clay County's 1,125 Norwegians and Swedes comprised 32.3 percent of immigrants while Minnehaha County counted 1,834 Scandinavian immigrants, or 26.3 percent, and the 562 living in Deuel County represented 26.2 percent. Two counties toward the center of the state, Buffalo and Hand, also contained above average percentages of Norwegian and Swedish immigrants. The same general distribution patterns for these settlers occurred in 1890, with a notable increase in their presence in two counties in the northeast. In Day County, 21.1 percent of the total population reported birthplaces in Norway and Sweden and in Marshall County 12.8 percent had been born there. Secondary sources identified Norwegians in Brule, Clay, Lincoln, Minnehaha, Union, and Yankton counties, and Swedes in the same locations plus Day, Brown, and Grant counties.[53]

Wisconsin natives formed the second largest group of immigrants in 1880, accounting for 10.8 percent and tending to cluster in the eastern third of South Dakota. (Map 2). They appeared in highest numbers and percentages in two groups of counties, a more northerly set—Codington (531 natives representing 25.8 percent of immigrants), Spink (115 and 24.7 percent), and Hamlin (157 and 23.3 percent)—and a more southerly set—Hansen (254 and 20.8 percent), Davison (231 and 19.5 percent), and Lake (490 and 19.6 percent). Minnehaha and Brookings counties contained the largest number of Wisconsin natives in 1880, with each housing nearly 800 at above average proportions of 11.3 and 17.4 percent, respectively. According to a study of Sanborn County (the western half of Miner County after 1883), the

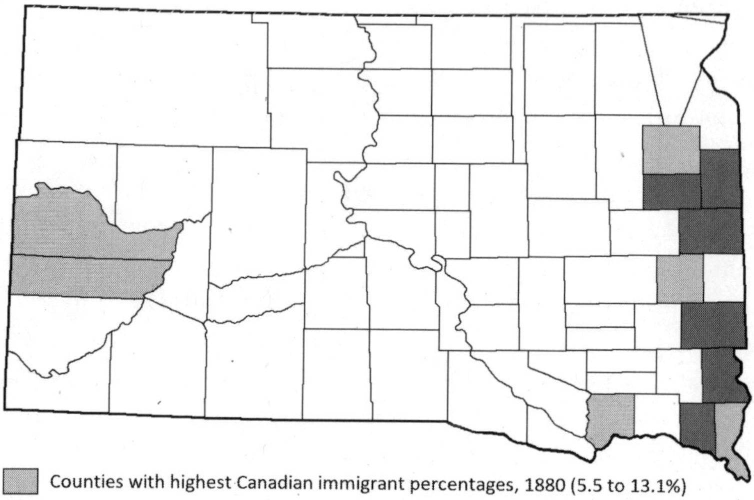

Counties with highest Canadian immigrant percentages, 1880 (5.5 to 13.1%)

Counties with highest Norwegian and Swedish immigrant percentages, 1880 (21.4 to 32.2%)

Map 1

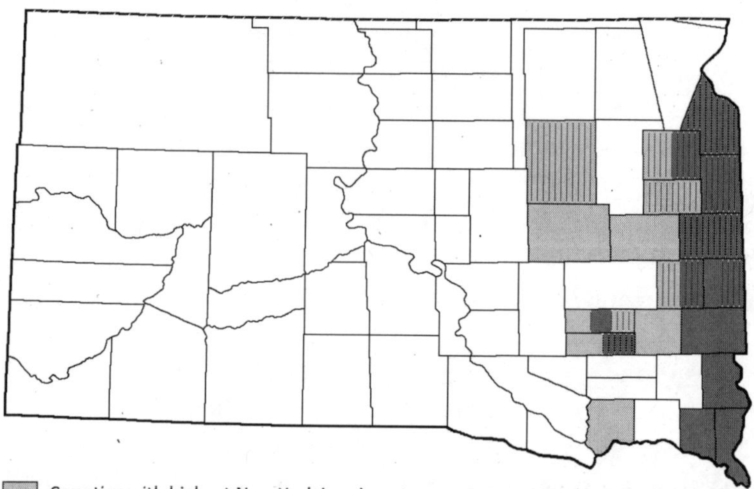

Counties with highest New York immigrant percentages, 1880 (11.3 to 13.9%)

Counties with highest Wisconsin immigrant percentages, 1880 (19.5 to 25.8%)

Counties with highest Iowa immigrant percentages, 1880 (12.0 to 13.4%)

Counties with highest Minnesota immigrant percentages (14.4 to 22.3%)

Map 2

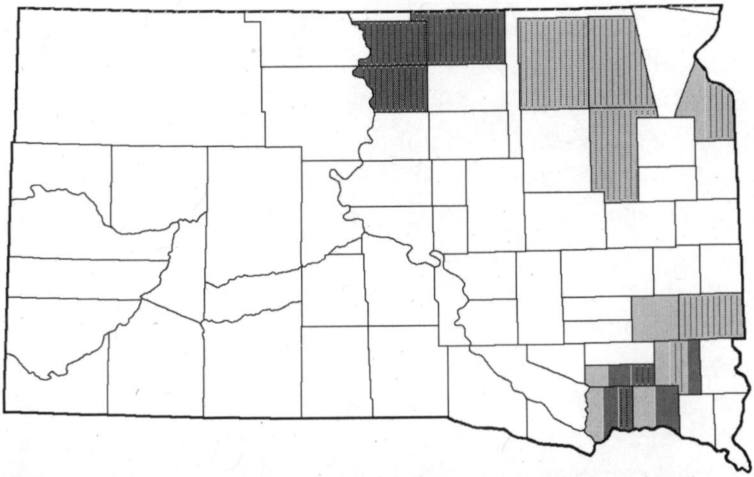

Counties with the highest German immigrant percentages, 1880 (5.6 to 9.8%)

Counties with the highest Russian immigrant percentages, 1880 (13.2 to 64.1%)

Counties with the highest German immigrant percentages, 1890 (14.6 to 23.0%)

Counties with the highest Russian immgirant percentages, 1890 (13.4 to 49.2%)

Map 3

64 natives of Wisconsin present in 1880 (18.6 percent of immigrants) came from the state's south central area, perhaps characteristic of the former locations of other Wisconsinites.[54]

Immigrants from New York, the nation's most populous state, ranked third in South Dakota in 1880 and represented 8.5 percent of immigrants. Although concentrating heavily in the east, they appeared in most South Dakota counties open to settlement by non-indigenous peoples. (Map 2) The top counties with more than one hundred New Yorkers comprising at least 10.5 percent of immigrants included five in the east: Davison (13.9 percent), McCook (13.0), Hanson (12.5), Beadle (12.4), and Kingsbury (11.3). Exceptions to the eastern orientation appeared in the western side of the state, including Pennington County, where the percentage of New York immigrants was 10.5, and Lawrence County just to the north which contained 1,200 New Yorkers (9.4 percent of immigrants), numerically the most in any county.

Settlers born in Iowa formed 7.9 percent of South Dakota's immigrants in 1880. (Map 2) Most lived in the state's eastern part along or a few counties away from the Iowa border. Counties with the largest number and highest percentage of Iowans concentrated in the southeastern corner directly west of Iowa, including Lincoln (608 Iowans comprising 13.4 percent of immigrants), Union (619 and 13.2 percent), Davison (152 and 12.8 percent), and, with the most Iowa natives, Minnehaha (869 and 12.5 percent of immigrants). In the same area, Clay and Moody counties both housed over four hundred settlers from Iowa, representing about 12 percent of immigrants. A study of the thirty-four Iowans living in Sanborn/Miner County (9.9 percent of immigrants in 1880) revealed that they came from across Iowa but mostly from its eastern half.[55]

According to the 1870 census, only four Russian natives were among the inhabitants of Dakota Territory, but 563 Germans lived there. The 1880 census reflected a major realignment, counting 6,493 Russians and 5,925 Germans living in Dakota Territory; within what became South Dakota were 6,315 Russian and 4,083 German residents.[56] Local histories clearly identify the Russians residing in the Dakotas as Germans from Russia, German Russians, or Black Sea Germans, collectively peoples of German ethnicity but Russian birth from families invited in the 1700s to settle in Russia (notably the Ukraine), largely in distinctive colonies often defined by religious adherence.[57] Assuming those born in Russia responded literally to the census canvasser's nativity question, their birthplaces were accurately recorded. Under the same assumption, Germans also accurately submitted their brithplaces, despite the lack of a unified Germany prior to unification in 1871.[58] However, in this instance, the mixture of Germans from Western Europe and Germans from Russia complicates simple reliance on census-based nativity as a cultural indicator. A comment in the 1880 census hints at this difficulty, noting that Dakota Territory contained the second largest number of "Russians (predominantly Mennonites)" and Mennonites typically were of German background.[59] Germans and Russian Germans both adhered to a variety of religious groups—Lutherans, Roman Catholics, Baptists, Mennonites, and Hutterites—adding another layer of complexity. Additionally, Germans and Russians, distinguished by their reported birthplaces, overlapped in parts of South Dakota and lived separately in others.

Following the influx of Russian Germans beginning about 1873, Russian natives increased to comprise 7.6 percent of South Dakota's immigrants in 1880, becoming South Dakota's fifth largest group.[60] By 1890 they had fallen to eighth place among immigrants, at 5.1 percent. Russians were unevenly distributed across the state in 1880, highly clustering in limited areas. (Map 3) They exceeded the 1880 statewide average in only four southeastern counties but did so greatly, accounting for 64.1 percent of immigrants (2,957 individuals, numerically the most) in Hutchinson, 27.7 percent in Bon Homme, 26.7 percent in Turner, and 14.1 percent in Yankton. By 1890, in addition to their continuingly strong presence in Hutchinson County (3,305 or 31.5 percent of immigrants), a new area with high concentrations of Russian Germans appeared along the north central border in counties on or just one away from North Dakota, notably in McPherson (home to 2,922 Russians forming 49.2 percent of immigrants), Campbell (1,265 and 36 percent), and Walworth (288 and 13.4). None of the latter three counties contained Russians in 1880.

Individuals indicating birthplaces in Germany represented the eighth largest source of South Dakota's immigrants in 1880, or 4.9 percent of the total. By 1890 they had become the fourth largest group at 7.4 percent. Although the various German provinces were unified in 1871, ethnic, linguistic, and religious differences among these immigrants resulted in more diversity than being "German" suggests.[61]

A table of birthplaces for Dakota Territory in 1880 included thirteen units within the "German Empire" plus "Prussia (not specified)," the latter was both the largest sector and contained elements scattered across Germany beyond its primary northeastern location.[62] Prussians represented 2,598 of the 5,925 Germans and those from "Germany (not specified)" numbered 2,181; three other provinces—Bavaria, Hanover, and Wurttemberg—provided about two hundred immigrants each.

In 1880, southeastern South Dakota counties contained the highest proportions of German immigrants (Yankton was 9.2 and Turner was 7.8). (Map 3) Grant County in the northeast was 9.1 percent German. Germans above the statewide mean also appeared in a strip of generally sparsely populated counties extending north-south across the center of the state, from Boreman (Corson County by 1890), where 28 Germans represented 11.4 percent of immigrants, to Meyer (Mellette and Todd counties by 1890). In the southwest, Lawrence County's German immigrant percentage fell just below the statewide average but it held the largest number of Germans, 582. Nearby in Custer County, Germans formed 5.1 percent of immigrants. A major enlargement of the German population of South Dakota occurred during the 1880s, more than quadrupling from just under 4,100 in 1880 to almost 18,200 in 1890. Their growth was especially notable in the northeast, where four counties contained unusually large German percentages within the total population: Brown (23.0 percent and 1,161 individuals), Spink (15.1 percent), Day (14.9), and Grant (14.6). These counties were not heavily populated by Russians. Germans remained in high proportions in the southeast, notably in Minnehaha, Turner, and Yankton counties, areas that also had high concentrations of Russians. In far western South Dakota, 455 Germans in Lawrence County formed 9 percent of immigrants.

Although counties where Germans exceeded the statewide average were more broadly distributed than those with Russians, their respective locations display both similarity, suggesting settlement among people of shared ethnicity, and separation, suggesting ethnic clustering. (Map 3) By 1880, notable overlap occurred between high concentrations of Germans and Russian Germans in parts of southeastern South Dakota (Bon Homme, Hutchinson, Turner, and Yankton counties). For some Russians, settling near fellow ethnic Germans might have eased the transition to Dakota life; for others who formed colonies or intentionally isolated settlements that might have been less important. Even in the overlap counties, Russians represented a higher proportion of the two groups, accounting for 60 to 92 percent of their combined total. In 1880 and 1890, the Germans, not Russians, were prevalent a bit farther north in McCook and Minnehaha counties. By 1890, the geographic divergence of the two groups was even more pronounced. In the northeastern corner where Germans concentrated (Brown, Day, Clark, and Grant counties), they accounted for 79 to 100 percent of the two groups. In the predominantly Russian counties in the north-center (Campbell, McPherson, and Walworth), Russians comprised 69 to 93 percent of both. Reviewing the locations of Russian German settlements described in two volumes of histories reveals twenty-five to thirty-one settlements in Bon Homme, Campbell, Hutchinson, Turner, McPherson, Walworth, and Yankton counties; in the German counties of Brown, Day, Grant, McCook, Minnehaha, and Spink, one source includes just two Russian German settlements and the other lists only one.[63]

Natives of Minnesota comprised 6.4 percent of South Dakota's immigrants in 1880. (Map 2) As with Iowans, settlers from Minnesota appeared in above average proportions in eastern parts of the state. Minnesotans were the most concentrated in six counties either on or one county west of the shared South Dakota border. Grant County held 650 Minnesota natives, accounting for 22.3 percent of immigrants, with Brookings (918 and 20.2 percent) and Deuel (412 and 19.2 percent) next in order. Three other top counties were Moody, where 657 Minnesotans comprised 18.7 percent of immigrants, Lake with 377 or 15.1 percent, and Codington with 297 or 14.4 percent. Twenty-four Minnesotans in Sanborn/Miner County (7 percent of immigrants) left former homes in its southeastern corner, perhaps an example of the source of other Minnesotans.[64]

Canadians, the Irish, and natives of England and Wales (the latter two combined in the census) were distributed similarly across South Dakota. (Map 1) Statewide in 1880, those born in Canada accounted for 5 percent of immigrants, while the Irish formed 3.2 percent and settlers from England and Wales represented 2.1 percent. Most counties east of the Missouri River held concentrations of Canadians, Irish, and English and Welsh above each group's averages. High numbers and percentages of immigrants born in Canada were found in Union

County in the southeastern corner (613 and 13.1 percent), which contained the town of Jefferson. Nearby, Bon Homme County housed 265 Canadians (6.1 percent of immigrants). While Minnehaha County's percentage did not exceed the average, 203 Canadians lived there. Farther north, Canadians in Codington County formed 11.8 percent of immigrants. Irish natives gathered in Union, Clay, Yankton, Bon Homme, and Moody counties in the southeast which, in addition to Hanson, Lincoln, and Minnehaha, were also the leading counties for settlers born in England and Wales. The distribution pattern of Canadian, Irish, and English and Welsh natives largely reappeared in 1890 with a new focus in northeast counties, such as Brown and Spink. In both 1880 and 1890, high concentrations of natives from all three groups appeared in Lawrence County on the western border (Canadians at 7.1 percent of immigrants in 1880, Irish 5 percent, and English and Welsh 4.9 percent). And all three groups were in above average percentages next door in Pennington County in both years. These Black Hills gold extraction counties—Deadwood was within Lawrence—attracted Cornish and Welsh miners.[65]

Counties with Illinois natives exceeding their average immigrant percentage of 4.7 were broadly distributed across South Dakota in 1880, rarely reaching 9 percent in any county. They were present in the largest numbers and percentages in five southeastern counties: Clay, with 254 representing 7.3 percent of immigrants, Lincoln and Union (both at 6.2 percent with nearly three hundred natives each), and 377 settlers in Minnehaha County comprising 5.4 percent of immigrants. Lawrence County in the Black Hills region contained the largest number of Illinoisians—677—who formed 5.4 percent of immigrants. Fifteen Illinois immigrants living in Sanborn/Miner County in 1880, perhaps typical of others, came predominantly from the north central part of the state.[66] Other, smaller groups of immigrants concentrated in locations around South Dakota. Among Europeans, Bohemians (or Czechs) clustered in 1890 in Bon Homme (numbering 1,032), Brule (532), and Yankton counties. Danes were found in 1890 in Clay (338 settlers), Kingsbury (336), and Turner (884) counties, while natives of Scotland congregated in Lawrence and Minnehaha counties.[67] Immigrants from Indiana (320 in 1880) and Michigan (376 in 1880) gathered in Lawrence County.

The foreign ethnic origins of South Dakota's late nineteenth century population were predominantly Scandinavian (Norway, Sweden, and Denmark accounted for 11,141 settlers in 1880 and 31,282 in 1890) and Germanic (if all born in Russia are considered ethnically German, then they plus those with German birthplaces totaled 10,398 in 1880 and 30,586 in 1890). Wisconsin, Iowa, New York, Illinois, and Minnesota were the leading states among the U.S. born. Combined, these ten sources accounted for over 60 percent of South Dakota's immigrants in 1880 and 1890, lending them outsized importance in the state's cultural, social, and political development. Over time, though, midwesterners formed the largest collection of settlers. In 1880, 36.8 percent of all immigrants came from the seven Midwestern states. The same percentage came from the top eight foreign birthplaces, with South Dakota's source countries in general alignment with those then supplying states across the U.S. But by 1890, the Midwest's percentage among all immigrants increased to 42.6 while the foreign percentage fell to 34.5. The Midwest was the leading region for immigrants born in the United States, accounting for 61.4 percent in 1880 and 70.2 percent in 1890. The next largest sources were New York and Pennsylvania, which together supplied 20.7 percent of U.S. immigrants in 1880 and 15.9 percent in 1890. Southerners were rare among the settlers.

Each Midwestern state was largely built on immigration from farther east. The Old Northwest's settlers came from the Northeast and some but fewer from the upland South; for more westerly Midwestern states, settlers often arrived from other parts of the Midwest.[68] Wisconsin's primary population sources were New York, Ohio, Pennsylvania, and Illinois. Illinois, New York, Pennsylvania, and Indiana supplied Iowa; Ohio, New York, Indiana, Pennsylvania, and Kentucky were leading sources for Illinois. Minnesota's settlers came from New York, Wisconsin, Illinois, Pennsylvania, and Ohio. Ohio's settlers predominantly came from Pennsylvania, Virginia, and New York. Many of Indiana's settlers (who came from Ohio, Pennsylvania, and Kentucky) eventually immigrated to South Dakota.

Midwesterners arriving in South Dakota already were imbued with the predominantly Northern-based and locally developed Midwestern cultural characteristics of their home states.[69] At least some Midwestern influence also might have affected foreign immigrants (and certainly their U.S. born children) who stopped in the Midwest on their way to South Dakota, but the influence of their foreign ethnic origins remained deeply within them in their settlement associations, religion, language, and politics, notably among conservative Germans.[70] Clearly, South Dakota's unique immigration and ethnic history—Midwestern, Scandinavian, Germanic—is a significant factor in the development of its political culture.

NOTES

1. Jon K. Lauck, *Prairie Republic: The Political Culture of Dakota Territory, 1879–1889* (Norman: University of Oklahoma Press, 2010).

2. Wilbur Zelinsky, *The Cultural Geography of the United States* (Englewood Cliffs, N.J.: Prentice-Hall, 1973), pp. 97, 117–20, 128–29.

3. Raymond D. Gastil, *Cultural Regions of the United States* (Seattle: University of Washington Press, 1975), p. 57.

4. Gregory S. Rose, "Information Sources for Nineteenth Century Midwestern Migration," *Professional Geographer* 37 (Feb. 1985): 66–72.

5. Lauck, *Prairie Republic*, pp. 6–9; Gary D. Olson, "A Dakota Boomtown: Sioux Falls, 1877–1880," *Great Plains Quarterly* 24 (Winter 2004): 17–30.

6. Zelinsky, *Cultural Geography*, pp. 13–14.

7. John Fraser Hart, "The Middle West," *Annals of the Association of American Geographers* 62 (June 1972): 260–61.

8. Frederick C. Leubke, "Ethnic Group Settlement on the Great Plains," *Western Historical Quarterly* 8 (Oct. 1977): 405–30.

9. William Thorndale and Willim Dollarhide, *Map Guide to the U.S. Federal Censuses, 1790–1920* (Baltimore: Genealogical Publishing, 1987), pp. 169–72, 259.

10. Richard L. Forstall, ed., *Population of the States and Counties of the United States: 1790–1990* (Washington D.C.: Government Printing Office, 1996), p. 142.

11. James P. Collins, "Native Americans in the Census, 1860-1890," *Prologue* 38 (Summer 2006): 1–3; Margaret M. Jobe, "Native Americans and the U. S. Census: A Brief Historical Survey," *Journal of Government Information* 30 (Spring 2004): 66–80; Department of the Interior, Census Office, *Report on Indians Taxed and Indians Not Taxed in the United States (Except Alaska) at the Eleventh Census: 1890* (Washington D.C.: Government Printing Office, 1894), pp. 22, 23, 26, 573.

12. *The Seventh Census of the United States: 1850* (Washington D.C.: Robert Armstrong, Public Printer, 1853), pp. iv, xxii, xciv; Jobe, "Native Americans," 66–80.

13. *Population of the United States in 1860* (Washington D.C.: Government Printing Office, 1864), pp. 551, 605; *Report on Indians Taxed*, pp. 22, 23, 26, 573; *The Statistics of the Population of the United States, 1870. Ninth Census—Volume 1*

(Washington D.C.: Government Printing Office, 1872), pp. xii, xvii; 328–42; *Report of the Population of the United States at the Eleventh Census: 1890, Part 1* (Washington D.C.: Government Printing Office, 1895), p. 448; Collins, "Native Americans," 1–3.

14. *Report of Indians Taxed*, p. 22; *Statistics of the Population, 1870*, pp. xvii; 328–42; *Report of the Population, 1890*, p. 448.

15. *Report on Indians Taxed, 1890*, p. 23; *Report of the Population, 1890*, p. 448.

16. *Report on Indians Taxed*, pp. 26, 573.

17. Ibid., p. 573; Raymond J. DeMallie, ed., *Handbook of North American Indians: Plains, Volume 13, Parts 1 and 2* (Washington D.C.: Smithsonian Institution, 2001), pp. 259, 778.

18. Barry M. Pritzker, *A Native American Encyclopedia: History, Culture, and Peoples* (New York: Oxford, 2000), pp. 317–19, 329–30, 334, 335.

19. *Report on the Population, 1890*, p. 448; *Handbook of North American Indians*, pp. 259, 778.

20. Sara L. Bernson and Robert J. Eggers, "Black People in South Dakota History," *South Dakota History* 7 (Fall 1977): 242–49; Jakob K. Friefeld, Mikal Brotnov Eckstrom, and Richard Edwards, "African American Homesteader 'Colonies' in the Settling of the Great Plains," *Great Plains Quarterly* 39 (Winter 2019): 11–37; Betti Van Epps-Taylor, *Forgotten Lives: African-Americans in South Dakota* (Pierre: South Dakota State Historical Society, 2008); "Black History," *History in South Dakota Blog*, https://historysouthdakota.wordpress.com/for-further-reading/black-history/.

21. *Report on the Population, 1890*, pp. 427–28.

22. Ibid., pp. 576–79.

23. Ibid., pp. 427–28.

24. Bernson and Eggers, "Black People in South Dakota," pp. 250–51; VanEpps-Taylor, *Forgotten Lives*, pp. 54–59.

25. Bernson and Eggers, "Black People in South Dakota," pp. 243–45; VanEpps-Taylor, *Forgotten Lives*, pp. 71–73; Liping Zhu, "Ethnic Oasis: Chinese Immigrants in the Frontier Black Hills," *South Dakota History* 33 (Winter 2003): 296–97.

26. Bernson and Eggers, "Black People in South Dakota," p. 249; Friefeld, Eckstrom, and Edwards, "African American Homesteaders," pp. 18–19; Van Epps-Taylor, *Forgotten Lives*, pp. 10, 94–98.

27. Bernson and Eggers, "Black People in South Dakota," pp. 247–49.

28. *Report on the Population, 1890*, pp. 576–79.

29. Ibid., pp. 440, 443.

30. Zhu, "Ethnic Oasis," pp. 289–329; 289, 290, 292, 296; Daniel Liestman, "The Chinese in the Black Hills, 1876-1932," *Journal of the West* 27 (Jan. 1988): 74–75; Grant K. Anderson, "Deadwood's Chinatown," *South Dakota History* 5 (Summer 1975): 266–85.

31. Zhu, "Ethnic Oasis," pp. 291, 291–310; Liestman, "Chinese in the Black Hills," 75–77 Anderson, "Deadwood's Chinatown," pp. 270–74.

32. *Seventh Census, 1850*, Table XV, pp. xxxvi–xxxvi (sic.), xxxvi–xxxvii.

33. Tim E. Holzkamm, "Eastern Dakota Population Movements and the European Fur Trade: One More Time," *Plains Anthropologist* 28 (Aug. 1983): 225–33; J. P. Hohansen, "Immigrant Settlements and Social Organization in South Dakota," *Bulletins* (June 1937): 6–7.

34. John G. Rice, "The Old-Stock Americans," in *They Chose Minnesota: A Survey of the State's Ethnic Groups*, ed. June Drenning Holmquist (St. Paul: Minnesota Historical Society Press, 1981), pp. 57–65.

35. *Population of the States and Counties: 1790–1990*, pp. 142, 146.

36. *Population of the United States in 1860*, pp. 616–23.

37. John C. Hudson, "Migration to an American Frontier," *Annals of the Association of American Geographers* 66 (June 1976): 253; Fred Kniffen, "Folk Housing: Key to Diffusion," *Annals of the Association of American Geographers* 55 (Dec. 1965): 560; D. W. Meinig, *The Shaping of America: A Geographical Perspective on 500 Years of History: Volume 2: Continental America, 1800–1867* (New Haven, Conn.: Yale University Press, 1986), pp. 221–36; Zelinsky, *Cultural Geography*, p. 81.

38. Jon Gjerde, *From Peasants to Farmers: The Migration from Balestrand, Norway to the Upper Middle West* (Cambridge: Cambridge University Press, 1985).

39. Kathleen Neils Conzen, *Germans in Minnesota* (St. Paul: Minnesota Historical Society Press, 2009); Hildegard Binder Johnson, "The Germans," in *They Chose Minnesota: A Survey of the State's Ethnic Groups,* ed. June Drenning Holmquist (St. Paul: Minnesota Historical Society Press, 1981), pp. 153–84; Ann Regan, *Irish in Minnesota* (St. Paul: Minnesota Historical Society Press, 2002).

40. *Statistics of the Population, 1870*, p. 348.

41. *Statistics of the Population of the United States at the Tenth Census, 1880* (Washington D.C.: Government Printing Office, 1883), p. 500.

42. Thorndale and Dollarhide, *Map Guide*, pp. 260–64, 306–10.

43. Ibid., p. 307.

44. Ibid., p. 308.

45. Ibid., p. 310.

46. *Report of the Population, 1890*, pp. 655–56; Hohansen, "Immigrant Settlements," 9.

47. Hildegard Binder Johnson, "The Location of German Immigrants in the Middle West," *Annals of the Association of American Geographers* 41 (Mar. 1951): 1–41.

48. J. P. Johansen, "Immigrants and Their Children in South Dakota" *Bulletins* (May 1936).

49. Gerald F. De Jong, "Dakota Resources. A Preliminary Guide for Study-

ing European Ethnic Groups in South Dakota: A Bibliographic Essay," *South Dakota History* 15 (Spring/Summer 1985): 66–114; South Dakota Germans from Russia Cultural Center, https://sdgfr.org/; Harry Thompson, "Guide to Collections Relating to South Dakota Norwegian-Americans" (Sioux Falls: Center for Western Studies, 2007), http://www.augie.edu/sites/default/files/norwegian-americanguide2006-07.pdf; https://historysouthdakota.wordpress.com/; Luebke, "Ethnic Group Settlement on the Great Plains," 405–30; Rex C. Myers, "An Immigrant Heritage: South Dakota's Foreign-Born in the Era of Assimilation," *South Dakota History* 19 (Spring 1989): 134–55.

50. Thorndale and Dollarhide, *Map Guide*, pp. 261–64, 307–10.

51. Robert Dorman, "The Creation and Destruction of the 1890 Federal Census," *The American Archivist* 71 (Fall 2008): 350–83.

52. Alan J. Neville and Alyssa Kaye Anderson, "The Diminishment of the Great Sioux Reservation: Treaties, Tricks, and Time," *Great Plains Quarterly* 33 (Fall 2013): 237–51.

53. Hohansen, "Immigrant Settlements," 8–16, 16–17.

54. John C. Hudson, "Two Dakota Homestead Frontiers," *Annals of the Association of American Geographers* 63 (Dec. 1973): 443.

55. Ibid.

56. *Statistics of the Population, 1880*, pp. 493, 495.

57. LaVerne J. Rippley, "Introduction" in Richard Sallet, *Russian-German Settlements in the United States*, trans. LaVerne J. Rippley and Armand Bauer (Fargo: North Dakota Institute for Regional Studies, 1974), pp. 8–16; Sallet, *Russian-German Settlements*, pp. 19–62; George Rath, *Black Sea Germans in the Dakotas* (Freeman, S.Dak.: Pine Hill Press, 1974), pp. 1–29.

58. Frank B. Tipton, *A History of Modern Germany Since 1815* (Berkeley: University of California Press, 2003), p. 29.

59. *Statistics of the Population, 1880*, p. 469; Anthony H. Richter, "A Heritage of Faith: Religion and the German Settlers of South Dakota," *South Dakota History* 21 (Spring 1991): 155–72.

60. Hohansen, "Immigrant Settlers," pp. 29–44.

61. Tipton, *A History of Modern Germany Since 1815*, pp. 3, 50–55, 103.

62. *Statistics of the Population, 1880*, p. 493.

63. Rath, *Black Sea Germans*, pp. 86–132; Sallet, *Russian-German Settlements*, pp. 19–62.

64. Hudson, "Two Dakota," p. 443.

65. Arthur Cecil Todd, *The Cornish Miner in America: The Contribution to the Mining History of the United States by Emigrant Cornish Miners, the Men Called Cousin Jacks* (Norman: University of Oklahoma Press, 1995).

66. Hudson, "Two Dakota," p. 443.

67. Hohansen, "Immigrant Settlements," pp. 17–29, 44.

68. Hart, "The Middle West," pp. 259–60, 264; John C. Hudson, "Yankeeland in the Middle West," *Journal of Geography* 85 (Oct. 1986): 195–200; Lauck, *Prairie Republic*, pp. 9, 28.

69. Zelinsky, *Cultural Geography*, pp. 117–19, 128–29; Lauck, *Prairie Republic*, pp. 31–32.

70. Hohansen, "Immigrant Settlements," pp. 12, 24; Hudson, "Migration," pp. 242–64.

RANDI RAMSDEN

2 | PRINTING HISTORY IN THE MAKING: POLITICAL CULTURE IN SOUTH DAKOTA'S GERMAN-LANGUAGE PRESS, 1880–1915

• • •

South Dakota became home to thousands of European immigrants from its territorial days until the 1920s. These newcomers helped shape the state's political culture as well as its economic growth. Among them were German-speaking settlers from the many states that made up Germany, and those who remigrated after many years of settlement in Russia. Immigration, which often arose from a desire to improve family economics and religious and political freedoms, also brought challenges of assimilation: culture shock and the navigation between old and new cultures, struggles with one's place in the political sphere of the new home, and potential family disruption as the new generation began to Americanize but their elders continued to maintain old home ways.

Soon after their arrival, literate German-speaking immigrants turned to local German-language publications. Newspapers were a lifeline which provided a connection to the old world. They offered the comfort of the native language while helping the new arrivals make sense of their unfamiliar surroundings. The press brought information, entertainment, and education right into the homes of its readers, catering to shared interests, cultural traditions, and linguistic identities. It functioned as an informant as much as it reflected its community and leadership. As it played such a significant role in the literate community, however, it could also be used or abused as a powerful tool to influence opinions, persuade, and shape its readership.

Historically, the American press has been highly political. Throughout the country, even small towns were typically home to multiple newspapers, which oftentimes aligned themselves with the ideals of differing political parties. German immigrant publications were no different. By 1910, more Germans called South Dakota home than any other ethnic group and they printed a variety of newspapers in their native language.[1] The early publications prior to World War I especially are a well of information about political, religious, and cultural affiliations. Moreover, they provide insight into the ways German-speaking immigrants navigated the existing political landscape. Some reflected communities' political integration; some functioned as a driving force of isolation; and other existing publications attempted to benefit by reaching the German audience from the outside.

The first wave of German immigrants arrived in South Dakota in 1873.[2] A group of Lutheran Germans from Russia first settled in the northern part of Yankton County.[3] Turner County became home to at least two hundred Mennonites in 1874 and Hutterites established communal colonies in Bon Homme and Hutchinson counties.[4] These groups shared a unique history of immigration which had started over a century prior. Following the invitation of Catherine the Great in 1762 and 1763, a significant number of Germans settled along the Volga River in the Russian Empire.[5] The Empress allowed them to farm land while remaining mostly independent. She granted them religious freedom and exempted them from military service. In contrast to their living conditions and the political turmoil they were facing in their German home states, Catherine's offer made the prospect of making a new home in the East attractive. In 1804, Alexander I invited even more Germans to settle by the Black Sea. By 1860, Russia was home to more than three hundred colonies of German immigrants who established and ran their own schools, churches, businesses, and newspapers.[6] In their self-governing colonies, they were able to maintain their native language and develop a shared German identity. Circumstances changed in 1874 when reforms demanded Germans become Russian Orthodox and extended military service to the German settlers.[7] Identifying as strict pacifists, many decided to leave Russia and seek a new home in the New World. Hence the Germans from Russia who arrived in South Dakota were no strangers to living in isolated colonies and establishing their own infrastructure in their own language.

In 1874, Yankton was on the cusp of a new era. Nestled on the northern bank of the Missouri River, the territory's capitol welcomed many new arrivals onboard a steamboat. In addition, the Southern Dakota Railway had just recently expanded to reach the town, boosting its accessibility. The English-literate population could follow the news of the commencement of Custer's exploration of the Black Hills that year in the *Yankton Press and Union and Dakotaian*, but the newly arriving

Germans struggled with the language that was foreign to them. The logistics of publishing a newspaper in these early days were fairly simple. Anybody with access to a printing press could start their own publication and with little or, in the case of the German-language press, no competition; a readership desperate for news that they could understand was almost guaranteed. Bernhard Quinke founded the first German-language newspaper, the *Dakota Freie Presse*, in 1874. In its first five years in business, it gained a good reputation, not only among its German immigrant readership, but also among the members of the English-speaking publishing world. In 1878, the *Daily Press and Dakotaian* reported: "The Dakota Freie Press [*sic*], the German newspaper of this city, commenced its 5th volume with the issue of the 24th. The Freie Press [*sic*] is a well conducted newspaper, and the fact that in entering upon the fifth year of its existence its size has been increased to a nine column folio is sufficient evidence that it is a financial success."[8]

In the summer of 1880, the *Dakota Freie Presse* reported a growing number of settlements in South Dakota. The growing population went hand in hand with the establishment of new newspapers, which now included over fifty publications, including eight dailies.[9] It remained, however, the sole provider of news in German and was about to welcome even more potential readers who arrived in the territory in the 1880s. East Frieslanders, or Germans from northwest Germany, began settling in Turner and Lincoln counties and another wave of Germans from Russia arrived. They settled in Roscoe, Hosmer, and Eureka counties.[10]

As the diversity among Germans in South Dakota grew, the *Dakota Freie Presse* identified itself as specifically catering to Germans from Russia under the leadership of Johann Christian Wenzlaff in 1886.[11] In Russia, German settlements had relied on German-language newspapers published in a central location to be circulated to reach their somewhat scattered settlements. The *Presse* adopted a similar model and became the voice of Russian Germans throughout the Dakotas, as well as the rest of the United States, Canada, and South America. It even made its way back to the colonies of remaining Germans in Russia.[12] Later, the newspaper's masthead would claim to be "the oldest and most widely distributed newspaper for Germans from Russia in the entire world." Wenzlaff himself had emigrated from Alt-Arcis, near Odessa on the Black Sea, in 1874, but the newspaper did not dedicate itself to informing Black Sea Germans specifically until Friedrich Sallet took possession in 1903 and the *Presse* became "the organ for the Black Sea Germans from Russia."[13] At that point, the publication was no longer the sole provider of German-language news content in the area and a more targeted approach made sense to differentiate itself from the competition.

While still living in Russia, a rivalry had emerged between the better-off Black Sea Germans, who had been carefully vetted to meet the emperor's requirements for immigration, and the Volga Germans, who, for the most part, were farmers and artisans and whose educational and professional background had not been as important of a factor in their move to Russia. The rivalry stemming from these class differences continued as the Germans from Russia settled in South Dakota and it also became apparent in the newspapers they published.[14] Besides class, religion distinguished the different German-speaking communities. They identified as Lutherans, Catholics, Mennonites, and Hutterites.[15] Political leadership was oftentimes taken on by ministers, but newspapers proved to be just as influential.[16]

The limited number of publications allowed for newspapers to establish a quasi-monopoly, giving editors and publishers a forum for their political views. Salomon Wenzlaff, who had taken over the *Dakota Freie Presse* from his father in 1886, was described as "a potent force in molding public thought and shaping public action."[17] He used his publication to "shape the political history as well as the general interests of the German-American citizens" in the northwest.[18] Wenzlaff had been politically active for most of his life. As a teenager, he had already campaigned for the Republican Party and had later served as treasurer for Bon Homme County. His political affiliation was no secret in the community, and he did not conceal it in his journalistic work either. On the contrary, for over a decade, the *Dakota Freie Presse* became his tool in the advancement of "Republican interests among the German-American population of the state."[19]

As Wenzlaff's health began to decline, he decided to retire from the news business. The ownership of the *Dakota Freie Presse* changed in 1899, but the new editor, Herman Ellermann, whose name is often changed to Ellerman in English, promised to continue to foster the Republican political stance of the publication.[20] Wenzlaff's and Ellermann's identification with the Republican Party agenda was not out of the norm. In general, Protestant German immigrants tended to support the Republican Party, while many German farmers supported Populist political ideals.[21] Therefore, counties with a larger Russian German population proved to be the most anti-populist.[22] The *Dakota Farmers' Leader* would later describe Ellermann as "a radical Roosevelt Republican" who was "among the champions of reform."[23]

Although Ellermann continued to publish the *Dakota Freie Presse* with the goal of furthering Republican ideals among Germans, he only did so until 1903 before selling to Sallet, whose stance on the role of party politics in the press differed immensely. Two years later, the newspaper officially declared its political independence.[24] In the following years, the *Presse* functioned as a medium for "personal exchange" and the preservation of "the cohesiveness of the entire ethnic group."[25] Traveling reporters would write about Germans from Russia anywhere and submit their articles for publication in Yankton. Through the shift in content, it became apparent that the *Presse* valued German identity and cultural conservation over political affiliations.

Having lost an important mouthpiece for his party, Ellermann regretted his decision to sell and began formulating plans for a new competing German-language newspaper, which would strictly follow party lines and would be published in Aberdeen. When Sallet heard about these plans, he offered to sell him back the *Presse* instead. Ellermann accepted and Sallet joined the *Nachrichten-Herold* in Sioux Falls. In his 1907 address to his readers, Sallet declared his work to be solely in the service of German culture: "Without an honest, purposeful press, the German element is politically and socially helpless in the hands of party dictators and fanatic nativists as a means to a selfish end."[26] Whether his statement was a direct reference to Ellermann and his associates or not, their conflicting views on what role political parties should play in the press resulted in a strained personal relationship, which escalated the same year. The *Herold* reported in detail on what unfolded next in a supplement on 6 September 1907. It accused Ellermann of defaming Sallet in his publication and of using the *Presse* solely for the purpose of furthering his political power. In the statement, Sallet argued that Ellerman could not possibly be truly invested in the Yankton community because he ran the paper from his home two hundred miles away in Aberdeen.[27] The following year, Sallet once again gained possession of the *Presse* and, by 1909, he had not only moved it to Aberdeen, but also reached an important milestone: the *Presse* claimed more subscriptions than any local English-language newspaper.[28]

While some editors disagreed about the role and ethics of partisanship in the press, the *Süd Dakota Nachrichten* became a model of political independence. The newspaper was first published in 1890 by Hermann Butikofer and Paul B. Meyer. Editor Butikofer was a Swiss immigrant who had arrived in the United States as a young man in 1882.[29] Stepping into his father's footsteps, Butikofer was a merchant before he decided to start publishing the news in German. Although he was not a German compatriot himself, his knowledge of the language enabled him to run a newspaper dedicated to a German cause in South Dakota. During its early years, its masthead read "Unparteiisch, zum Besten des Deutschthums" (Nonpartisan for the benefit of Germanity).[30]

The *Nachrichten* was the answer to those immigrants who refused to integrate into the existing political landscape and wished to expand it instead. To them, party politics were a distraction and would slowly diminish the role of their language, culture, and identity in an environment of rapid immigration and growing Americanization. Although usually discussed in the context of World War I, anti-German sentiment existed prior to the conflict and newspapers were one way of building and strengthening solidarity among the immigrant community. German immigrants in South Dakota experienced the hostility against them first-hand, which led the *Nachrichten* to invite its readers to gather and protest the anti-German sentiment, anti-German motivated attacks, and the anti-immigration movement in the spring of 1899.[31] The protest was scheduled for Pentecost Monday, a date specifically picked due to the holiday's importance in German cultural heritage, which usually celebrates it with family getaways or excursions.

Beyond public protest, the *Nachrichten* encouraged readers to take pride in their heritage and demonstrate it in their daily lives. As a news outlet, it printed local current events, as well as news from Germany, Austria, Switzerland, and Russian German colonies, but it also asked readers to continue to speak German. Between 1900 and 1901, the local news shorts section oftentimes began with the call to readers to embrace their native language before listing any community happenings: "Sprecht Deutsch!" (Speak German!). The publication's advertisement

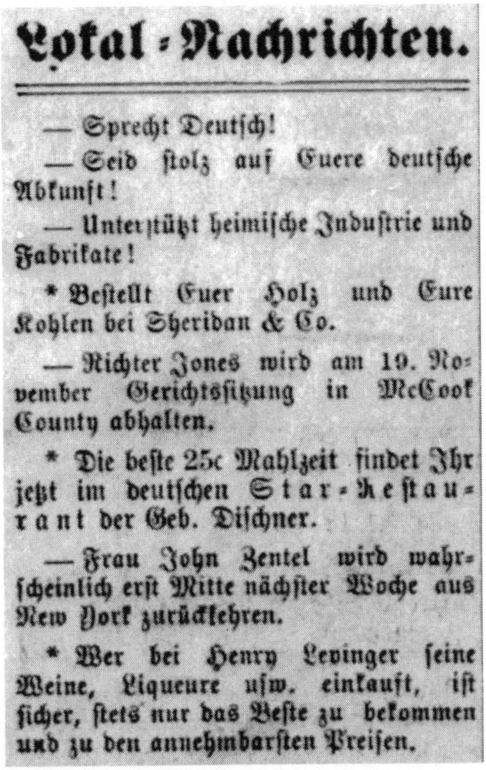

Lokal-Nachrichten.

— Sprecht Deutsch!

— Seid stolz auf Euere deutsche Abkunft!

— Unterstützt heimische Industrie und Fabrikate!

* Bestellt Euer Holz und Eure Kohlen bei Sheridan & Co.

— Richter Jones wird am 19. November Gerichtssitzung in McCook County abhalten.

* Die beste 25c Mahlzeit findet Ihr jetzt im deutschen Star-Restaurant der Geb. Dischner.

— Frau John Zentel wird wahrscheinlich erst Mitte nächster Woche aus New York zurückkehren.

* Wer bei Henry Levinger seine Weine, Liqueure usw. einkauft, ist sicher, stets nur das Beste zu bekommen und zu den annehmbarsten Preisen.

A local news section of the 15 November 1900 edition of the Herold *encouraged readers to speak German. Chronicling America*

sections also made it easy to identify German-owned businesses and those who welcomed German customers. The National Union Company, for example, directly addressed readers as Germans: "Deutsche! Achtung! Spart Geld!" (Germans! Attention! Save Money!).[32]

In 1900, when Hans Demuth took over the newspaper, which had moved from Mitchell to Sioux Falls, he promised that the *Nachrichten* was to remain a tool to educate and raise the next generation of Germans, as well as to preserve the German language and culture. Moreover, he described the publication's role as the "Verteidigung der deutsch-amerikanischen Interessen" (the defense of German-American interests) indicating a shift from the mere pursuit of preservation of German culture to an active defense of a cultural, linguistic, and ideological identity.[33]

Although the *Nachrichten* aimed to establish and maintain a German subculture, it did not exist in an echo chamber. Americanization in some form or another was inevitable. As time went on, the printed

German language changed. German phrases and idioms morphed with their American counterparts; the spelling of some German words changed mimicking English terms; and English words were adopted.[34] What remained mostly untouched, however, was the print culture. German-language newspapers were printed in Fraktur, a "broken script" typeface commonly associated with German-language print prior to World War II. The typeface derived from hand-written scripts of the Middle Ages and was commonly used to print texts in the German language since the development of Gutenberg's printing press in the fifteenth century.[35] Contrasted to Antiqua typeface, commonly used for English and many other non-German languages, Fraktur became the "visual embodiment of German identity since the days of Luther."[36] The continuation of this printing tradition impacted the physical printing process in the New World, as well as offering the reader a sense of home, belonging, and the comfort of the known.

While other European countries had adopted Antiqua typefaces as a standard, the Germans' insistence on Fraktur strongly suggests reasons beyond an emotional tie. Fraktur is especially efficient for printing German language texts. The stark contrast between the bold letters of the blackletter typeface against the white page allows for letters to be much closer together and requires less space between lines without compromising legibility.[37] Fraktur was the most efficient way to fit as many of the lengthy German words as possible on the page. Moreover, the typeface provides different versions of letters to visualize different pronunciations.[38] Hence, by importing their print culture, German immigrants also imported a tool to preserve their spoken language for literate community members.

The use of Fraktur was also a continuation of an ideological and political identity in the New World. When Germans began to settle in the United States, they did not come from a united nation, but different German states. Immigrants likely identified with their home state or their religious background rather than a common German national identity. In Europe, as political tension between German states and France had grown throughout the nineteenth century, Fraktur had become a printed manifestation of a shared national identity. During times of conflict such as the German Campaign against Napoleon (1813–1814), or the Franco-Prussian War (1870–1871), Fraktur had become the "German type," a symbol of nationalism in the fight against a foreign enemy.[39] Later in South Dakota, the use of Fraktur in German-language newspapers also caused them to visually stand out against English-language publications, which made them easily identifiable and helped develop a German print identity outside of the German states and colonies in Russia.

Textually, the *Nachrichten* likewise reflected its readership's identity. News from Germany (usually listed individually by state to offer more space for details and easier navigation for those readers who were particularly interested in their home region), Switzerland, and Austria took up a large portion of the paper and were titled "Lokalnachrichten" (local news). The common use of words such as "Vaterland" (Fatherland) and "Heimat" (homeland) further highlights the connection readers felt towards Germany. Interestingly, a spike in the usage of both terms can be seen after the turn of the century. In 1911, "Heimat" in proximity to the word "Deutsch" (German) was printed on at least 54 pages.[40] This is partially due to a campaign run by the newspaper arguing why readers should continue subscribing to their publication.[41] However, it also suggests a growing nostalgic longing for Germanity as more generations of German Americans were born in South Dakota. The use of "Vaterland" in proximity to "Deutsch" spiked in 1915, when it was printed on at least forty-nine pages. It can be found in serialized fiction and poetry in the entertainment sections, as well as the early coverage of conflicts in Europe and the beginning of the Great War. The incidence of the term rapidly declined thereafter. The following year, it was printed only on eleven pages; by 1918, usage was down to three pages. This decline of declarations of German affiliation is not surprising. The United States had declared war against Germany in the spring of 1917, challenging German loyalty, pride, and identity.

Under Demuth in 1900, the *Süd Dakota Nachrichten* was merged with the *Dakota Herold* to form the *Süd-Dakota Nachrichten und Herold*. As they had both aimed to preserve German culture and identity in the same community, the publishers believed that there was no need for two German-language newspapers. The *Dakota Herold* had had a Republican following, but once merged, Demuth claimed political independence: "The German is intelligent and knows right from wrong without lengthy editorials."[42] Political independence, however, did not mean that the content of the newspaper was apolitical. In his address to his readers, Demuth called for the fight against restrictions on

German immigration, against Prohibition, and for German American interests. He prioritized strengthening the working class, supporting German farmers, and aiding the oppressed.[43]

This declaration was very much in line with the opinions printed prior. In 1896, an article reported on prohibitionists coming from Canton to Tea to lecture a local tavern owner about the Germans' beverage of choice: beer. The newspaper complained about hypocrite outsiders coming from towns where alcohol, especially whiskey, was secretly consumed in large quantities. Arguing that "the foaming beer demands freedom, candor and light," the article was as much a political anti-prohibition piece as it was a love letter to the German brewing tradition and the "barley nectar."[44]

Leading up to the midterm election in 1898, the *Nachrichten* helped literate Germans understand the ballot and made voting recommendations based on German values and interests. Pointing out that literate Germans would be able to easily read the names of the candidates, the column focused on the three ballot measures voters would encounter on election day. The newspaper suggested memorizing the order of the measures and the appropriate vote, especially if readers were not fluent in English. The first measure addressed woman suffrage. Here, according to the *Nachrichten*, 99 out of 100 Germans would vote "No." The second measure proposed the state control of liquor: "Nobody should forget to mark the 'No' with a cross here." Finally, Germans should vote "Yes" to the creation of an initiative and referendum process in South Dakota if they cared about true democracy.[45]

Earlier that year, the newspaper had in length argued against woman suffrage, claiming that women were not physically capable of fulfilling all duties related to law enforcement, such as serving as police officers, sheriffs, or prison wardens, making them unfit to partake in the voting process altogether.[46] This belief continued into the new century. In a 1913 issue, readers could find an anti-woman suffrage poem, which called women involved in the movement "Verrückten Suffragetten" (crazy suffragettes).[47]

As German-language publications became inherent parts of their communities, publishers became aware of the potential political power of their readership. Appealing to communal "German interests" and the importance of "the German vote," the *Nachrichten* encouraged the formation of a voter block and the transformation of a shared cultural identity into voting power. Editors were in an influential position, calling on "every German voter" to vote against the interests of railroad corporations[48] or accusing President McKinley of appointing "Deutschen-Hasser" (German haters) to his cabinet.[49] When McKinley ran for re-election in 1900, the paper ran a lengthy opinion piece titled "Do Germans have reason to vote for McKinley?"[50] It addressed specifically the interests of the German American population which, according to the author, were threatened by the president. The article accused politicians, especially presidents, of habitually taking off their "Nativist mask" leading up to an election to cater to German Americans in an expertly well-rehearsed but insincere performance wearing the "'German-brother' mask."[51] Further, it described the government's immigration policy as "America for Americans only" and, among other policies and matters of foreign affairs, criticized the appointment of nativist Terence V. Powderly as Commissioner-General of Immigration in 1898.[52] Hence, political opinions and ideology were not missing from the pages of the newspaper, but the publishers merely refused to align their newspaper with one political party and rather utilized a shared German ideological identity in conveying information. Looking at the references to the Republican and Democratic parties long-term, both parties enjoyed similar coverage in the publication, increasing every four years corresponding with presidential elections, with the winning party usually receiving slightly more coverage.[53]

The *Nachrichten und Herold* was renamed *Nachrichten-Herold* in 1901 and finally published under the title *Deutscher Herold* from 1907 until 1918. It continued to be listed as politically independent as Sallet took on editorship and the publication became a mouthpiece for the feud between Sallet and Ellermann, discussing the ethics and implications of a politically biased press. In 1907, its masthead called the *Herold* the "Leading German Newspaper in the State."[54] Although its circulation had grown to over 2,500 subscribers, this claim was likely false.[55] The *Freie Presse* had a much larger readership, but since it was also widely distributed outside of the state, exact comparable numbers are hard to estimate.[56]

While many German-language newspapers appeared on the scene as an outlet published by and for German-speaking immigrants, the industrialization of the press turned printing foreign-language publications into a lucrative business opportunity. Previously, newspaper printing offices had to hire typesetters who arranged the movable type, letter by letter, and meticulously assembled a page to be printed. By the 1890s, however, new technology arrived. The linotype machine could cast complete lines of text in metal and saved publishers time and money by replacing the work of five average typesetters.[57] In 1909, the *Deutscher Herold* provided its readership a look into its editorial and printing offices with photographs and descriptions of the printing process with the linotype machine.[58] It did so not without congratulating the Morgenthaler Linotype Company on the brilliance of their business model of inventing a machine every publisher longed for but simultaneously ensuring that constant maintenance and repair bound them to the company for all eternity. Nevertheless, publishing offices like the *Herold* were now able to mass produce their newspapers and print publications in multiple languages. In addition to German, the *Herold* began offering printing services in Norwegian, Swedish, and English. The industrialization of the press and the technological improvement of the printing process caused a shift from newspapers functioning as an intrinsic medium of political and cultural identity fostering solidarity of an immigrant community to an opportunity in the pursuit of economic profit. Not only German publishing companies saw an opportunity in expanding to readers of other languages. In 1889, the printing office of Flinn & Lutgen, which had been publishing the English-language *Eureka Independent*, decided to venture out. Taking advantage of the lack of German-language news publications in the local German immigrant community, they were able to grow their audience by printing in German.

Michael Lutgen, who was originally from Luxembourg, served as editor of the newly established weekly *Eureka Post*.[59] When he acquired the entire publishing company later that year, Lutgen turned to his apprentice for help. Theodore Giedt took over the editorship of both the English and German-language newspapers and started managing the printing process. Giedt was born in Danzig, part of the German Empire at the time, and had ancestors in the German colonies in Russia. His parents had relocated the family to Dakota Territory in 1886.[60] Not only did his personal background qualify him to relate to and address a readership of Germans and Russian Germans, Giedt had also received his education in both German and English in Germany and Minnesota. Later, he entered a business partnership with

Irishman M. O. Ronayne to purchase both newspapers from Lutgen. The *Independent* was soon merged with the *McPherson County Herald* and a much shorter English-language version of the *Post* entered the scene in 1896. The publishing business was not Giedt's sole ambition, however, and the ownership shifted out of German-speaking hands completely two years later. Giedt, who had been elected to public office sold the *Eureka Post* to Orvin Jarper Roe, a Vermont Yankee who neither spoke nor wrote in German.[61]

Out of necessity, the publisher continued to hire German-speaking editors to continue the German-language publication. Among them was Francois Martin who, like Lutgen, was from Luxembourg and had learned the printing trade in Europe before arriving in Eureka.[62] Although not all editors were from Germany or from the colonies in Russia, their fluency in the language preserved a certain quality of the German-language product they were sending to their subscribers. However, the frequent change in leadership indicated a lack of consistency and true dedication to the preservation of cultural and ideological cohesiveness seen in other German-language newspapers. Between 1904 and 1912, for example, the word "Heimat" in proximity to "Deutsch" can only be found on ten pages of the *Post;* the term "Vaterland" in proximity to "Deutsch" was used on merely five pages.[63] This suggests a stark difference in attitude towards the readership's cultural heritage than displayed in the *Herold*.

That is not say that the *Post* was not successful or influential. The *Post* expanded from a four-page spread to eight pages in 1891, showing that there was a demand in the community for more news delivered in German.[64] The English version focused mostly on public notices, as well as local and state news, while the German *Post* provided national and international news with an emphasis on current events in Russia, and stories of interest to Russian Germans in particular.[65] Despite its relatively small reach, other publications occasionally reprinted parts of the *Post*, thereby acknowledging its reputation. Although initially listed as independent, by 1899, the newspaper had begun to identify as Republican, showing a similar political assimilation to that seen in other Russian German immigrant communities.[66]

While in 1906, a midterm election year, both political parties were covered nearly equally, the newspaper's political leaning began to come to the forefront in 1908. The Democratic Party was mentioned on at least twenty-eight pages, whereas the, for the most part, outright support for the Republican Party can be seen on at least forty-one pages.[67] In May, the *Post* recommended a list of Republican candidates running on the state and county level and guaranteed its readers that none of the candidates listed had ever been affiliated with the Populist or Democratic Parties.[68] Moreover, it ran statements by Republicans announcing their candidacies and was not shy about speaking out against the Democratic Party: "If the Democrats do not receive support from Republicans, they will be buried under an avalanche of votes in South Dakota November 3rd. The Democrats have only built on sand because Republicans will not turn Democratic this year. Why would they since after experiencing great times under the Republican government!"[69] Following the 1908 election, the *Post's* mentions of the Democratic Party dropped significantly, while mentions of the Republican Party spiked again in 1910 and 1912.

Although the political views expressed in the *Eureka Post* were similar to those published in the *Herold*, there were clear differences in the editorial strategy of each. In 1908, an appeal to the "German vote" in the *Post* can be found only in a reprinted article originally published in the *Herold*.[70] Overt political opinions and voting suggestions based on a shared German identity are mostly voiced in letters sent to the editor and printed in the weekly "Korrespondenzen" (correspondence) section. In a 1912 letter, for example, Karl Ritter from Mound City encouraged readers to vote for John H. Fischer, a German candidate for state senator.[71] Fischer's German background and social standing in the immigrant community played a much larger role in the endorsement than any policies he supported. The correspondence section became the stage for lively exchange of political opinions not only from the readers within the Eureka area, but also from German immigrant communities out of state. A 1908 letter from North Dakota, for example, described the local discussions around temperance, suggesting that it would be best if Prohibition was handled as in most other states, where one could decide to drink alcohol on one's own accord. He argued that Prohibition did not stop the consumption of liquor: "denn wer saufen will der sauft doch" (because who wants to guzzle alcohol, will guzzle nevertheless).[72]

Political campaign advertisements could also be found on the pages of the *Post*, but they seldom directly addressed the readers as Germans

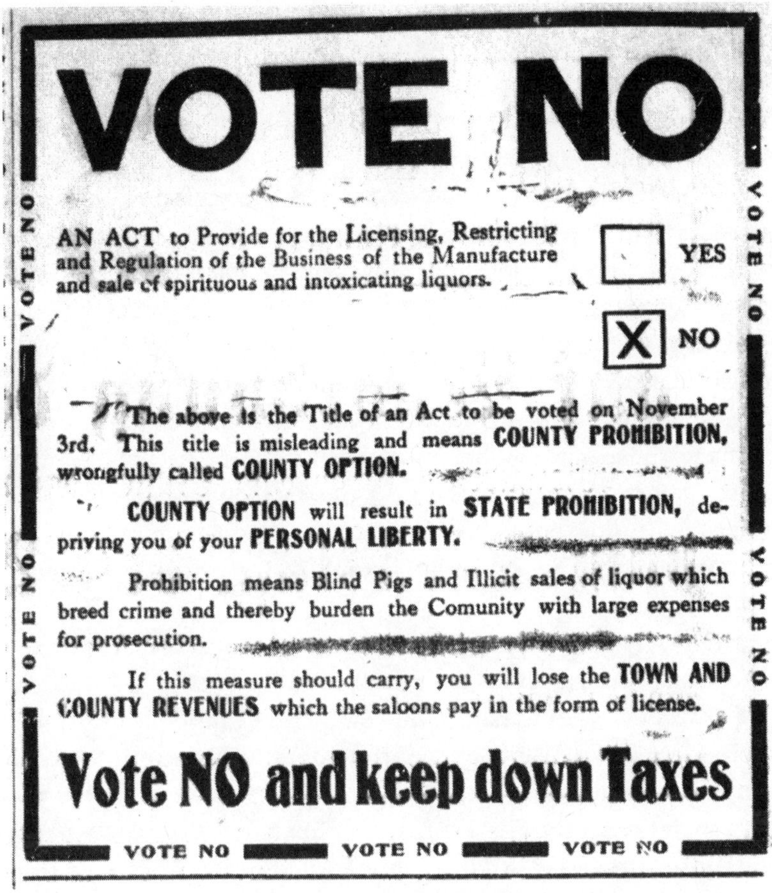

Like many German-language newspapers, the Eureka Post *featured anti-Prohibition ads, including this one from 29 October 1908. Chronicling America*

or catered to a German political identity. Anti-prohibition ads in 1908 asked readers to “Vote No and keep down Taxes” in English.[73] A detailed explanation of why it was in the interests of the readers to oppose the so-called “County Option Law” was also published in English.[74] It is not clear who placed the ad, but it was likely part of a larger anti-prohibition campaign, as the same ad was also printed in English-language newspapers such as the Webster *Reporter and Farmer* and the Gann Valley *Dakota Chief*.[75] It likely made economic sense for the campaign to place the same advertisement in as many newspapers as possible. It also shows, however, that the overt support for the anti-prohibition movement came from outside the editorial office and was linked to economic advertising revenue rather than an internal ideological conviction based on German values and interests.

Initially, Flinn & Lutgen's economic ambitions proved to be fruitful. The German-language *Post* registered a circulation of fourteen hundred subscribers in 1903, surpassing its English-language counterpart by one thousand.[76] By 1908, however, the subscription count had dropped to one thousand, likely a result of a number of factors, including shifts in the newspaper industry and generational development and assimilation in the German community.[77] However, the history of the *Post* speaks to the influence of the local German-speaking community. The purpose of the publication may have been external economic interests, but its long-lasting success proves the significant economic role German immigrants played in the area. Their settlement in South Dakota influenced the way existing publishing offices operated and expanded.

Russian Germans from the Black Sea continued to arrive in South Dakota well into the early twentieth century, settling in the counties of Edmunds, McPherson, Walworth and Campbell.[78] As a result, German-language newspapers continued to flourish until World War I. Although overall more Germans from Germany now called South Dakota their home, they had spread out further in the state and failed to constitute a majority in any county. In contrast, it was the former colonists from Russia who were able to create linguistic and cultural islands, established and then reinforced with the help of their local newspapers.[79] Their majority in a handful of counties not only allowed them to preserve a sense of the isolated colonies they had come from, but also endowed them with the potential of political leverage in elections.

Over time, the German-language newspaper industry experienced different influences and changes which ultimately led to its decline. Americanization in many forms was unstoppable; surges of assimilation and desires for integration were inevitable. The more generations were born into the New World, the more the demand for foreign-language newspapers ebbed. Some newspapers were merged in economically driven attempts at consolidation. In June 1912, for example, the German version of the *Eureka Post* merged with the *Da-*

kota Freie Presse.[80] Another factor was the anti-German sentiment fueled by the advent of World War I. Starting in 1917, federal law required foreign-language publications to file translations of articles concerning the war or parties involved in the war. Publishers and editors who failed to comply with this time consuming and laborious requirement were arrested. In January 1918, Sallet was accused of having filed false translations and was taken into custody by federal law enforcement.[81] The new owner of the *Deutscher Harold* was likewise arrested under the Espionage Act. The pressure to remain relevant by printing up-to-date information while also meeting the federal government's requirements complicated the work of German-language publishers. In addition, they struggled to juggle between the preservation of the linguistic, cultural, and ideological concept of Germanity and a push for American patriotism at a time of war. In many cases, the continuation of the German-language press was conceived as a threat to American solidarity.

Ultimately, World War I was not the end of the German-language press in the state or the country. Its decline, however, further demonstrates the importance of the early publications as vital parts of the immigrant experience and an attestation of the German immigrant communities' entry point into the political arena of the United States.

NOTES

1. Herbert T. Hoover, et al., *A New South Dakota History* (Sioux Falls, S.Dak.: Center for Western Studies, 2005), p. 133.

2. Herbert S. Schell, *History of South Dakota,* 4th Edition (Pierre: South Dakota Historical Society Press, 2004), p. 116.

3. Ibid., pp.116–17.

4. Ibid., p. 117.

5. La Vern J. Rippley, "Two German-American Papers as 'Communications Satellites': Die Dakota Freie Presse and Die Welt-Post Preserved the Identities of the Germans from Russia," In *The German-American Press*, ed. Henry Geitz (Madison: Max Kade Institute for German-American Studies, 1992), p. 169.

6. Ibid., p. 170.

7. Ibid., p. 171.

8. *Daily Press and Dakotaian* (Yankton), 25 May 1878.

9. *Der Nordstern* (St. Cloud, Minn.), 1 July 1880.

10. Hoover, *A New South Dakota History*, p. 133; Schell, *History of South Dakota*, p.169.

11. Rippley, "Two German-American Papers as 'Communications Satellites,'" p. 172.

12. Ibid., p. 175.

13. George W. Kingsbury and George Martin Smith, *History of Dakota Territory,* Vol. 5 (Chicago: S. J. Clarke Publishing Company, 1915), p. 976; Rippley, "Two German-American Papers as 'Communications Satellites,'" p. 174.

14. Rippley, "Two German-American Papers," p. 172.

15. Hoover, *A New South Dakota History*, p. 134.

16. Frank Van Nuys, "Immigrants and Politics in South Dakota, 1861–1930," in *The Plains Political Tradition: Essays on South Dakota Political Culture*, ed. Jon K. Lauck, John E. Miller, and Donald C. Simmons (Pierre: South Dakota Historical Society Press, 2011.), p. 47.

17. Kingsbury and Smith, *History of Dakota Territory*, p. 976.

18. Ibid.

19. Ibid., p. 977.

20. "Presse," *Süd Dakota Nachrichten* (Sioux Falls), 29 June 1899.

21. Van Nuys, "Immigrants and Politics," p. 48.

22. Hoover, *A New South Dakota History*, p. 198.

23. "Ellerman vs. Kittredge," *Dakota Farmers' Leader* (Canton, S.Dak.), 27 Sep. 1907.

24. Rippley, "Two German-American Papers as 'Communications Satellites,'" p. 175.

25. Ibid., p. 177.

26. F. W. Sallet, "Ankündigung," *Nachrichten Herold* (Sioux Falls), 28 Mar. 1907. All translations by author.

27. "Aufklärendes zur Controverse der Dakota Freien Presse gegen F. W. Sallet," *Deutscher Herold* (Sioux Falls), 5 Sep. 1907.

28. Rippley, "Two German-American Papers as 'Communications Satellites,'" p. 175.

29. Dana Reed Bailey, *History of Minnehaha County, South Dakota* (Sioux Falls: Brown & Saenger, 1899), p. 481.

30. *Süd Dakota Nachrichten*, 30 July 1891.

31. "Große Demonstration seitens der Deutsch-Amerikaner von Süd-Dakota," *Süd Dakota Nachrichten*, 27 Apr. 1899.

32. *Süd Dakota Nachrichten*, 9 Feb. 1893.

33. Hans Demuth, *Süd Dakota Nachrichten*, 12 Apr. 1900.

34. Anton H. Richter, "'Gebt Ihr Den Vorzug': The German-Language Press of North and South Dakota," *South Dakota History* 10 (Fall 1980): 200.

35. Philipp Th. Bertheau, "Introduction" in *Blackletter: Type and National Identity* (New York: Princeton Architectural Press, 1998), p. 10.

36. Ibid., p. 14.

37. Philipp Luidl, "A Comparison of Fraktur and Roman Type: A German Study," in *Blackletter: Type and National Identity* (New York : Princeton Architectural Press, 1998), p. 18.

38. Yvonne Schwemer-Scheddin, "Broken Images: Blackletter between Faith and Mysticism," in *Blackletter: Type and National Identity* (New York: Princeton Architectural Press, 1998), p. 50.

39. Hans Peter Willberg, "Fraktur and Nationalism," in *Blackletter: Type and National Identity* (New York: Princeton Architectural Press, 1998), pp. 40–41.

40. A proximity search of the keywords "Heimat" and "Deutsch", as well as "Vaterland" and "Deutsch" within 10 words of each other in the *Süd Dakota Nachrichten* (1891–1900), the *Süd-Dakota Nachrichten und Herold* (1900–1901), the *Nachrichten-Herold* (1901–1907), and the *Deutscher Herold* (1907–1918) was conducted by the author using the Chronicling America database (5 July 2021). The search for the keyword "Deutsch" allows for results to also include the articles referring to "Deutschland" (Germany), "Deutsche," "Deutscher" (person(s) of German heritage), as well as the adjective "deutsch" (German). Because Optical Character Recognition (OCR) software is not 100 percent accurate, the actual counts of keyword incidences may be higher.

41. "Aus welchem Grunde man den 'Deutscher Herold' halten sollte," *Deutscher H*erold, 9 Feb. 1911.

42. Demuth, Hans. "Ankündigung," *Süd-Dakota Nachrichten und Herold* (Sioux Falls), May 03, 1900. https://chroniclingamerica.loc.gov/lccn/sn98069095/1900-05-03/ed-1/seq-4/.

43. Demuth,"Ankündigung."

44. "Tea," *Süd Dakota Nachrichten*, 14 May 1896.

45. *Süd Dakota Nachrichten*, 27 Oct. 1898.

46. "Frauenstimmrecht," *Süd Dakota Nachrichten*, 10 Mar. 1898.

47. *Deutscher Herold*, 8 May 1913.

48. "Lincoln County," *Süd Dakota Nachrichten*, 29 Oct. 1896.

49. *Süd Dakota Nachrichten*, 19 Aug. 1897. 1

50. "Zur Wahlcampagne. Haben die Deutsch-Amerikaner Ursache für McKinley zu stimmen?," *Süd Dakota Nachrichten und Herold,* 11 Oct. 1900.

51. Ibid.

52. Ibid.

53. The analysis of the coverage of the political parties is based on the occurrences of the terms "Republikanisch" (republican as adjective) or "Republikaner" (person affiliated with the Republican Party) with the term "Partei" (party), and the occurrences of the terms "Demokratisch" (Democratic) or "Demokrat" (a person affiliated with the Democratic Party) with the word "Partei" in the *Süd*

Dakota Nachrichten, the *Süd-Dakota Nachrichten und Herold*, the *Nachrichten-Herold*, and the *Deutscher Herold*. The keyword search was conducted in Chronicling America (5 July 2021).

54. *Deutscher Herold*, 5 Sept. 1907.

55. *N. W. Ayer & Son's American Newspaper Annual: Containing a Catalogue of American Newspapers, a List of All Newspapers of the United States and Canada*, Volume 2 (Philadelphia: N. W. Ayer & Son's, 1907), p. 822.

56. Ibid., 823.

57. "Ein Rundgang," *Deutscher Herold*, 4 Nov. 1909.

58. Ibid.

59. Kingsbury and Smith, *History of Dakota Territory*, p. 564.

60. Ibid.

61. Richter, "'Gebt Ihr Den Vorzug'" p. 203.

62. Francois Martin, "Die deutschen Ansiedlungen in den Dakotas," *Die Eureka Post*, 21 Mar. 1906.

63. A proximity search of the keywords "Heimat" and "Deutsch", as well as "Vaterland" and "Deutsch" within 10 words of each other in the *Eureka Post* (1904–1912) was conducted by the author using the Chronicling America database (24 July 2021).

64. *Süd Dakota Nachrichten*, 31 Dec. 1891.

65. Richter, "'Gebt Ihr Den Vorzug,'" p. 203.

66. *Süd Dakota Nachrichten*, 31 Dec. 1891; *N.W. Ayer & Son's American Newspaper Annual,* p. 925.

67. The analysis of the coverage of the political parties is based on the occurrences of the terms "Republikanisch" (republican as adjective) or "Republikaner" (person affiliated with the Republican Party) with the term "Partei" (party), and the occurrences of the terms "Demokratisch" (Democratic) or "Demokrat" (a person affiliated with the Democratic Party) with the word "Partei" in the *Eureka Post* (1904–1912). The keyword search was conducted in Chronicling America (24 July 2021).

68. *Eureka Post,* 14 May 1908.

69. Ibid., 29 Oct. 1908.

70. C. H Unruh, "Crawford und Reformer," Ibid., 21 May 1908.

71. Karl Ritter, "Mound, City, Süd Dakota," Ibid., 16 May 1912.

72. Jakob Schmitt, "Alden, Hettinger Co., N.D.," Ibid., 2 July 1908.

73. Ibid., 29 Oct. 1908.

74. "The County Option Law. Reasons for voting against it," Ibid., 15 Oct. 1908.

75. *Reporter and Farmer* (Webster, S.Dak.), 8 Oct. 1908; *Dakota Chief* (Gann Valley, S.Dak.), 22 Oct. 1908. 7

76. *N.W. Ayer & Son's American Newspaper Annual,* p. 941.

77. Ibid., p. 1132.

78. Hoover, *A New South Dakota History*, p. 133.

79. Richter, "'Gebt Ihr Den Vorzug,'" p. 195.

80. Ibid., p. 203.

81. "Redakteur eingesperrt," *Der Tägliche Demokrat* (Davenport, Iowa), 23 Jan. 1918.

JUSTIN BLESSINGER

3 | GENERAL WILLIAM H. H. BEADLE: ABOLITIONIST, SOLDIER, STATESMAN, EDUCATOR

• • •

General William H. H. Beadle is known for his contributions in several states to constitutional provisions for the use of public lands to fund and support education. He is especially celebrated in South Dakota for the outsized role he played in the final years of the territorial period and early years of statehood. He was surveyor general from 1869 to 1873. In 1876, he served as secretary of a special commission on laws for the new state, writing "nearly all the codes in Dakota." He was a member of the territorial legislature in 1877, superintendent of public instruction from 1879 to 1885, and president of the first teachers' college.[1] His statue stands as South Dakota's selection for the National Statuary Hall in the U.S. Capitol, with copies in the state capitol in Pierre and on the campus of Dakota State University (which grew from the teachers' college he led).

Beadle seemed to have had something of a gift for friendship while a young man, if we are to trust the testimony of his friends in the Alpha Nu literary society while he was an undergraduate in civil engineering at the University of Michigan. But in later life, he developed a reputation (often deserved) as a cantankerous and difficult man. The cause of this changed temperament may have been his combat experiences in the Civil War, or it may have been the residual effects of the wartime illnesses that confined him to a hospital bed, but nearly all biographical accounts tiptoe around the sense of his Dakota contemporaries that he could be touchy and disagreeable. One story—recounted by a former student—relates Beadle's berating a worker at the college for attempting to stop him from planting a tree. The senior class had asked Beadle to speak at the occasion, the tree being a way to commemorate their graduating class. The worker took his complaint to the college president, returning with a note directing Beadle to stop digging—prompting Beadle to threaten to thrash the employee on the spot and have him dismissed for his impudence.[2]

This disagreeable disposition had consequences in the early years of South Dakota's history. It made, for example, local politicians unwilling to nominate or support him as a candidate for elected office, despite his acknowledged intellectual gifts. Beadle nonetheless managed to become one of the most influential figures in South Dakota, with a profound effect on the state that lasts to the present day, by holding various non-elected offices—a role that was only possible in those first moments of statehood.

A sign of his importance are the acknowledgements in South Dakota. Beadle is particularly celebrated in the east-central region of the state: Beadle County bears his name, and, in Lake County, Dakota State University features not only his statue but several busts of the university's third president. The oldest surviving building on campus is named Beadle Hall, and the university itself was known as General Beadle State Teachers College (from 1947 to 1964) and General Beadle State College (from 1964 to 1969). In recent years, the university named its honors program in memory of Beadle, and created a digital institutional research platform known as "Beadle Scholar" in 2018.[3]

Born in a cabin built by his father, James Ward Beadle, in Liberty Township, Parke County, Indiana, on 1 January 1838, Beadle spent his first years on the family farm, learning of bigger cities far downriver where his father made flatboat trips to sell his crops. After his service in the Civil War, Beadle apparently served in the short-lived Freedmen's Bureau, which, in the aftermath of the Civil War, provided supplies, clothing, and fuel to freed slaves and their families.[4] It also sought to reunite black families and oversaw contract negotiations between (often illiterate) blacks and whites. The bureau generally monitored state and local treatment of former slaves.[5]

After a short stint in the legal profession from 1867 to 1869 in both Indiana and Wisconsin, Beadle accepted an appointment in late 1869 as surveyor general in Dakota Territory.[6] He seems to have been in familiar company. In a survey of the 1885 Dakota Territory Census, Kurt Hackemer notes that veterans who settled in Dakota Territory had, like Beadle, seen unusually high levels of combat. Using William F. Fox's identified "Three Hundred Fighting Regiments," Hackemer records that fully 21.4 percent of veterans in Dakota Territory had served in one of these high-combat, high-casualty regiments. Unsurprisingly, they also were significantly more likely to have been wounded than the national average for Union soldiers.[7] And as further evidence of Beadle's succinct manner, where most veterans on the census had indicated a specific number of battles in which they had been engaged, Beadle had only replied, "Several."

Beadle, with his small surveying team, documented the enormous span of Dakota Territory, and it was during this time that Beadle seems to have begun considering how unscrupulous investors had, in other territories and new states, purchased enormous swaths of land that had been identified for public use, especially to support schools. As first practiced in the Northwest Ordinance, it was common practice to designate a certain acreage for school use—often a 640-acre section—in every six-mile by six-mile township, essentially 1/36 of new land opened for settlement. While this was a way to plan for future funding of schools, there were few constitutional provisions in those days governing the sale of these public lands—and thus regions settled earlier than the Dakotas had seen school lands sold for a pittance to generate needed revenue. Perhaps Beadle's greatest contribution was in the state constitutional provision regarding the sale of school lands, which insists on an appraised value as the absolute minimum price.

Beadle's biographers largely lack details about Beadle's life prior to his arrival in Dakota Territory after the Civil War. Whatever reason he had to begin his own autobiography with his April 1869 arrival in Yankton, the capital of the territory, the decision left his past more obscure than it should be. From other biographers' notes, we have basic facts about Beadle's birth in Indiana, a few details of his early education in a rural schoolhouse, his departure from home to attend the University of Michigan, and the essentials of his military service.[8] Finally, in 1937, at the time of the South Dakota's celebration of the centennial of Beadle's birth, Barrett Lowe was able to fill in much of what had remained only a rough outline.

Lowe notes that while Beadle kept very few personal records, Beadle's brother John had been more attentive to recording his experiences in the war, and, as was common at the time, John had served in the 31st Indiana Volunteers with his brother and other young men from their area of Parke County, Indiana. Their "Company A" was known as the Wabash Riflemen, and it was at the siege of Corinth, Mississippi, that young William Beadle first distinguished himself. He had only just recovered from an illness so severe that he had resigned his commission over it, only to find his service desperately needed when senior officers were unavailable. Indeed, John Beadle's account notes that a form of "camp fever"—a term used to describe a number of maladies, but often a form of typhoid—had fairly decimated the Hoosiers. In addition to the many ill in Company A, he recounts that "Company B had almost disappeared" and "of Company K, only two non-commissioned officers were on duty. . . In fact, no one was really well."[9] He adds the haunting anecdote that death had become so familiar that the nearby mockingbirds had learned to whistle the death march. Nevertheless, the young Captain W.H.H. Beadle determined he was well enough to return to the fray, and in many ways, that resolve and commitment to duty would characterize Beadle's entire life, one of selfless service to his nation and state. Indeed, his tenacity and resolve were apparent even earlier in a number of events from his early college years.[10]

Meanwhile, in his autobiography, William Beadle proves painfully laconic and short on anecdotes. His military training, in this regard, seems to conflict with his training as a historian: his accounts read like a morning debriefing, more a cataloguing of events than a curator's tour. One wonders, in reading Beadle, if he is modest to a fault. He tells us what happened, but little about what he thought about it, what other options he entertained, or whether there were repercussions beyond the immediate event.

It was a surprise, then, to have come across a short article written by General Beadle for *The Michigan Alumnus,* an alumni publication of the University of Michigan, which possesses an altogether different voice, one belonging to a storyteller. His primary purpose in the article is to recount the experiences of the "Boys of '61"—the young men whose graduation was imminent when war broke out. Yet, Beadle identifies himself as much more radical in his anti-slavery beliefs than many of his fellow students, who were typically opposed to the expansion of slavery into the western territories while not holding to full-blown abolitionism. He recalls only one student whose opinion differed sharply enough that he left to join the Confederacy when war broke out. The student body "differed," he admitted, "somewhat in politics and holding at first all shades of opinion, from conservative to radical [abolitionist]." But "its members" mostly "shared the general trend of opinion in their sections" of the country. Only "a few, like the writer, though coming from below the 40th parallel, sprang from southern ultra anti-slavery ancestry."[11]

By this, Beadle means his own ancestry, of course, and his family home along the Wabash River in Indiana. The few existing biographies of Beadle make little mention of the religious or political habits of his family, although Beadle's primary biographer, O. W. Coursey, notes that Beadle's father, James Ward Beadle, was born in Kentucky "of ancestry that had landed very early at Salem," and that young William had walked "two or three miles to a half-Quaker Sunday School."[12] The Quakers were well known as abolitionists and supporters of the Underground Railroad.

A few paragraphs later in his alumni piece, Beadle displays a telling familiarity with the habits of the Michigan abolitionists, their meeting places, and speakers they invited (despite the secrecy surrounding these matters). Masking himself in a third-person description as "a young speaker" at the Alpha Nu literary society (perhaps out of modesty, perhaps because he is describing what technically had been a crime forty years before), Beadle tells of serving as a messenger delivering letters for the Underground Railroad:

> There was a group of abolitionists in Ann Arbor and vicinity that would harbor every fugitive slave that came that way. It was a fraternity; its doors were sealed with secrecy. The law and its agents were against it, backed by an almost brutal conservatism whose method sometimes was the mob. It happened that a member of the Alpha Nu literary society in the early autumn of '58 denounced the Mexican war as begun and waged for the extension of slavery, which he severely attacked. The quality of that speech was quickly known by these abolitionists, and one of them casually asked this young speaker if he would not enjoy a long ride upon a good horse. He was a true horseman, and was happy in the opportunity. He received President Tappan's permission to be out of town, and started Friday afternoon to carry a sealed mes-

> sage southward. On and on he rode into the lonely autumn night, down by the rural home of a leading and eccentric abolitionist, past Saline, across Lodi plains and into the forest-bordered roads beyond. Halting in the woods awhile to rest and moving forward at daylight, at breakfast time he delivered his message to a sturdy farmer among the Quakers of Lenawee County. Before noon on Monday a fugitive slave in that house was transferred to Canada at a point below Port Huron. The warning that led to this had come from the deputy United States marshal who held the warrant. That young man had half unconsciously taken his novitiate in abolitionism. Others did likewise. Individual opinion was forming. Such things were not then news items in the papers.[13]

Beadle himself notes that abolitionists were often on the receiving end of mob justice, which makes it telling that Beadle knew so much about the locations, speakers, and discussion topics of these abolitionist meetings. Author James Tobin remarks that "a small, secret circle of Ann Arborites were helping fugitive slaves get to Canada. But many U-M students saw abolitionists as dangerous radicals—'roving, crazy fanatics,' as the *Argus* put it. When the abolitionists Josephine Griffing and Parker Pillsbury came to town on their circuit of the western states, a mob stormed the church where they were speaking and chased them out."[14]

At another speech, this time by abolitionist and women's rights activist Wendell Phillips, Beadle and a number of others took up arms to defend the speaker against the mob. Beadle describes the event in another article written for the *Michigan Alumnus*, "The Days of Auld Lang Syne":

> An awakening force in those days was the addresses and lectures by the great men of the times. For a boy from the forest it was no small thing to hear Wendell Phillips, Nathaniel P. Banks, Edward Everett, Horace Greely, Bayard Taylor, George William Curtiss, and as many more equally strong, in the first year. And the stress of the times appeared in the fact that some sixty or seventy-five of us went armed with heavy clubs under our overcoats to defend Phillips from a threatened attack. Part of the mob actually began a disturbance, but found it dangerous. The meeting was held

in the old congregational church. We were not all abolitionists then; we were defending free speech.[15]

Equally telling is that Quakers, whose co-religionists Beadle had worshipped with in his youth, were active members of the Underground Railroad nationwide, but especially so in Lenawee County, Michigan.

Finally, the Alpha Nu literary society to which Beadle's unnamed third-person identity belonged was a significant part of Beadle's experience at the University of Michigan. A history of the class of 1861 written by Beadle's classmates H.M. Utley and Gen. B.M. Cutcheon remarked that "'Beadle was an active member of the Alpha Nu [Literary Society], and during his senior year was its president.'"[16]

So why the secrecy about the incident, four decades later? Why does Beadle feel the compulsion to adopt this convention of Victorian modesty, telling a story clearly about himself yet in the anonymous third person? Is he still evasive, given his participation would have been illegal at the time? Is he aware of the growing hostility to Republicans and allies to black Americans in places like his childhood home in Indiana? By the mid-1920s, according to scholar Leonard J. Moore, some communities in Indiana saw fully one-third of white men enrolled as members of the Ku Klux Klan (KKK). Terre Haute, a mere twenty-five miles south of Beadle's childhood home, was a hotbed of Klan activity. It's likely Beadle would have been aware of emerging hatred of that sort. Beadle would also have known that white supporters of black rights and black Republican candidates had been targeted in the decades prior to Beadle's article by such organizations as the White League and the Red Shirts.

Beadle would have been no stranger to such hate groups. According to Maurice Murphy in a 1913 article appearing in the *Indiana Magazine of History*, the Knights of the Golden Circle were very active in Parke County, Indiana, during Beadle's youth. Murphy notes that from 1843 on, Parke County elections were acrimonious affairs. The county leaned Whig, but nevertheless had a strong Democrat presence, and the latter engendered the formation of the Knights of the Golden Circle, which, according to Gerard W. Gawalt in his 2015 article "Clashing Dynasties," was a pro-slavery society that promoted fever dreams of creating a new nation whose northern border roughly matched the

Mason-Dixon line and ran in a long arc south to include Mexico, Central America, and Cuba.[17] The organization plotted to kidnap Lincoln and install Buchanan's former Vice President John Breckinridge.[18] Murphy states that in later years, they reformed as the Sons of Liberty and continued to operate in Parke County.[19]

Ultimately, it seems unlikely that a veteran of such battles as Spotsylvania and the siege of Carthage—a man who had risen from his sick bed to fight alongside his men—would feel compelled to silence by an emerging racist fraternity. Likely the best explanation is the most direct. He wished to not seem prideful, and his method of telling the story retains the anonymity of all the specific people involved: recruiters, conductors, freed slaves, and marshals. Clearly, he wished his audience to understand he had been the rider. Beadle's 1937 biographer Lowe is equally confident that Beadle is simply writing under the guise of modesty. Lowe writes that, in this article, Beadle clearly "wrote . . . in the third person" of his lived experiences in the underground railroad.[20]

As Beadle's work with and support for the Underground Railroad while a college student becomes more apparent, one cannot help but wonder whether his encounter after the speech he gave to the Alpha Nu literary society was even his first acquaintance with assisting abolitionists. The particular route, for example, Beadle rode was one of two major "lines" of the Underground Railroad that passed through Ann Arbor. Researcher Grace Shackman described these routes in her 1998 article, "The Underground Railroad in Ann Arbor,"

> Fugitives usually came north from Quaker settlements in Indiana to Cassopolis, near Niles, where there was another Quaker settlement. They then traveled east through Battle Creek, Jackson, and Ann Arbor. A north-south route came from Toledo (where James Ashley, founder of the Ann Arbor Railroad, was an active member) to Adrian [Lenawee County], an important hub where Haviland and a group of fellow Quakers ran a school, the Raisin Institute [along the River Raisin], for students of all colors.[21]

Perhaps not coincidentally, Beadle's childhood home was along the southern Indiana underground railroad. Given his religious instruction by Quakers, and given his elementary education under his be-

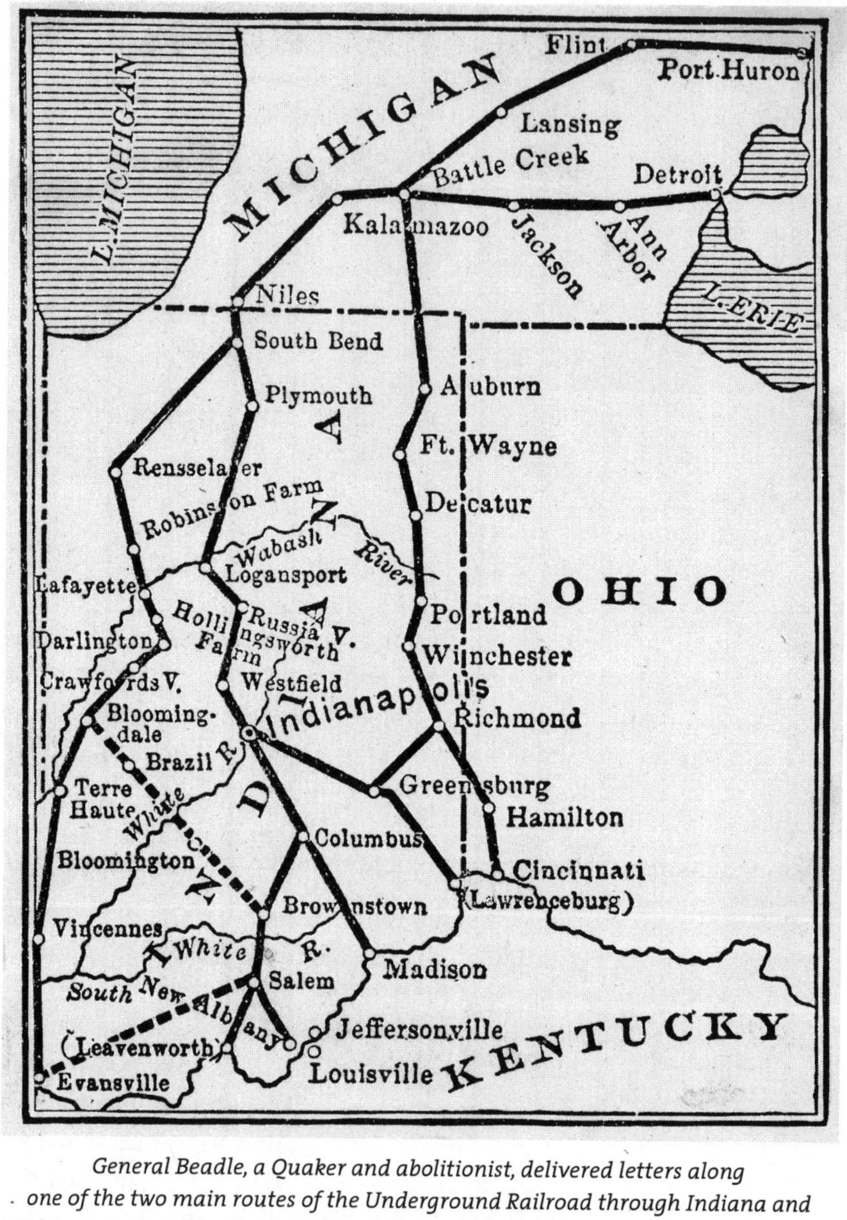

General Beadle, a Quaker and abolitionist, delivered letters along one of the two main routes of the Underground Railroad through Indiana and Michigan, as traced by Lewis Falley on this map from page 138 of Wilbur H. Siebert's book, The Underground Railroad from Slavery to Freedom *(1898).*
Ohio History Connection

loved teacher, Miss Lavinia Tucker, who, Lowe recounts, was raised as a Quaker herself, it is entirely possible that Beadle's family had been involved with the Underground Railroad even before his involvement in Michigan.[22] Wilbur H. Siebert, author of one of the earliest efforts to document the Underground Railroad, the 1898 *The Underground Railroad from Slavery to Freedom*, writes:

> From the two crossing-places on the Michigan border the northern extensions of the Indiana routes found their way to Battle Creek, from which station one trail led directly east to Detroit, and the other, by a more northerly course, to Port Huron. In southern Indiana the eastern route was connected with the middle route by a branch between Greensburg and Indianapolis, and the middle with the western by two branches, one between Salem and Evansville, and the other between Brownstown and Bloomingdale.[23]

Bloomingdale, Indiana, is the site of a Quaker-run school that educated Lavinia Tucker, who in turn educated Beadle. George Kingsbury suggests in his 1915 *History of Dakota Territory* that James Beadle, William's father, may have helped Tucker afford her lessons in Bloomingdale. He also adds that, even years later, brothers John and William still visited the grave of their beloved teacher in "affectionate and tender remembrance."[24] We may never know if Tucker took the Quaker's abolitionist views to heart while under their tutelage, but we can say with confidence that the Quaker community that educated her was part of the Underground Railroad of Bloomingdale described by Siebert.

Another of Siebert's maps, one hand drawn, shows an additional stop at Annapolis, a smaller town less than one mile north of Bloomingdale.[25] John Beadle's birthplace (and likely his brother William's) is named as a cabin two miles east of Lodi, Indiana, in the extreme northeastern corner of Parke County, but we know that in 1849, when William would have been eleven, the boys' father James was elected sheriff and the family moved to "the farm near Rockville", a town a mere six miles south of Bloomingdale.[26] By 1874, we can find that James W. Beadle was living in section two of Adams township, roughly four miles east of Rockville, perhaps a mile southeast of Nyesville.[27] Interestingly, this places the Beadle farm on the diagonal Underground Railroad line between Green Castle and Bloomingdale, just south of

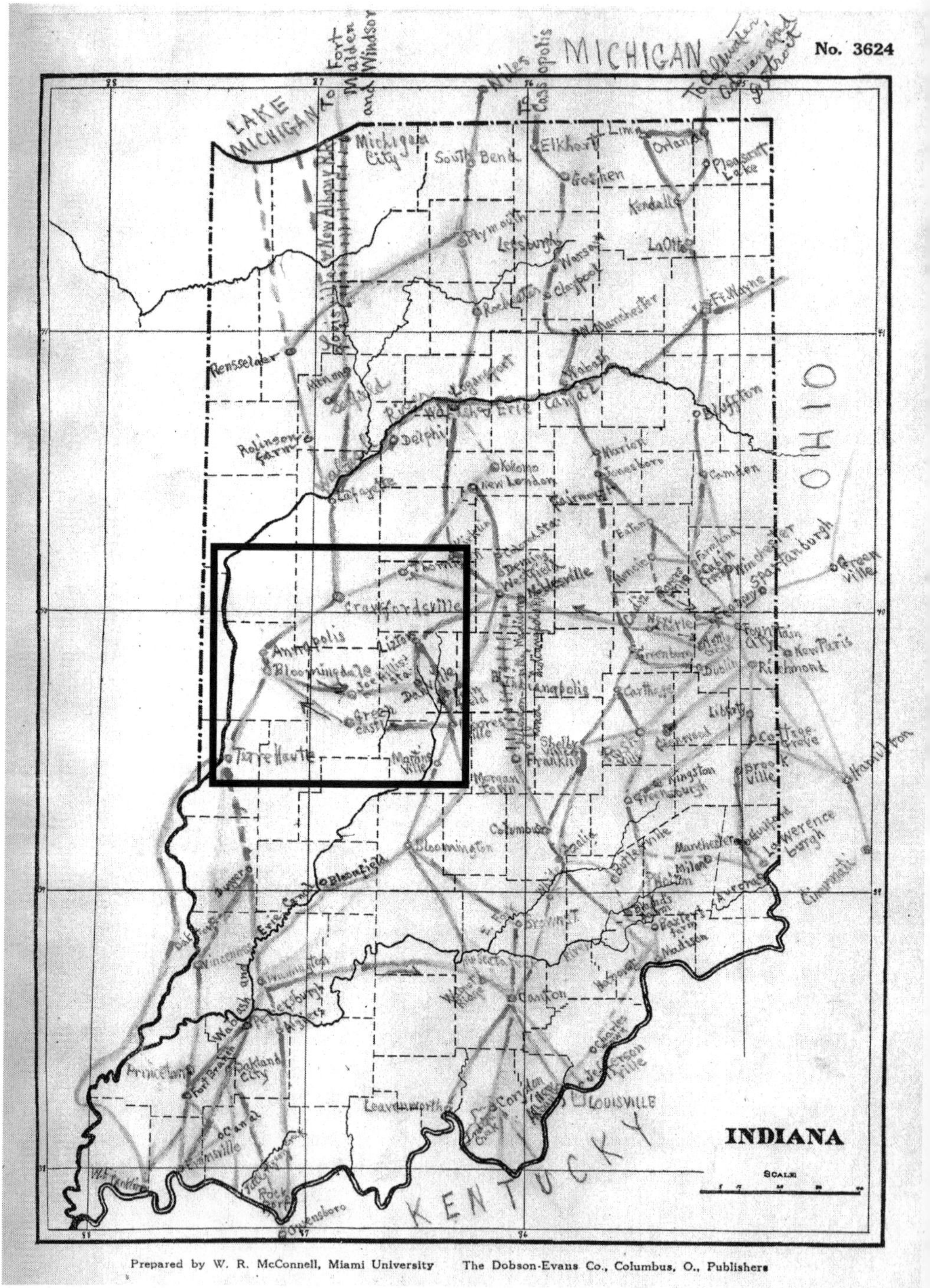

Prepared by W. R. McConnell, Miami University The Dobson-Evans Co., Columbus, O., Publishers

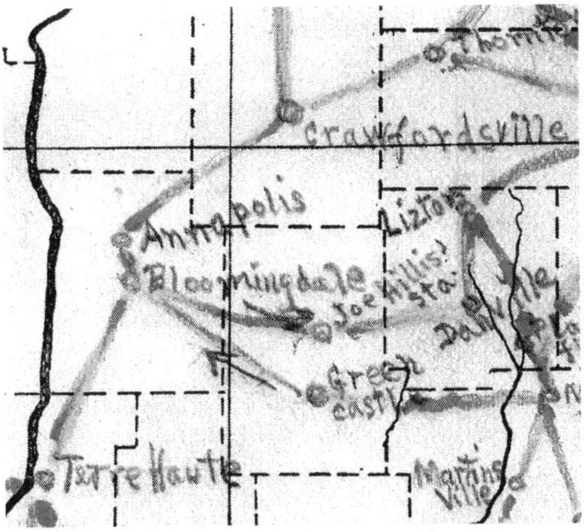

This hand-drawn map out of Siebert's The Underground Railroad from Slavery to Freedom *shows the location of the Beadle farm in section 2 of Adams township near Rockville, on the west side of the map in the third grid row, just southeast of Bloomingdale, along the Underground Railroad. Ohio History Connection*

the "L" in Bloomingdale on Seibert's hand drawn map. Obviously, this may be mere coincidence, but it places the Beadle family in precisely the right geographic location to assist on the railroad, had they the inclination, and given William Beadle's description of his family as "ultra anti-slavery" and his documented involvement with the Underground Railroad by 1857, an older Beadle family involvement with the railroad is both plausible and geographically feasible.

In a letter to Wilbur Siebert dated 4 March 1944, Frank H. Hadley recounts several stories of the Underground Railroad near Bloomingdale, as told to him by his grandfather Alfred Hadley, a Quaker farmer. One anecdote offers a tenuous connection to Beadle: Alfred's son Newton (Frank's father) attended the Bloomingdale Quaker School, the same school where Beadle's teacher Lavinia Tucker had been educated. Newton was approached by a runaway slave, who pleaded with Newton for help escaping, as his former owner was hot on his heels in pursuit. Young Newton cast about for help and spied the principal's horse and buggy tied up nearby. Without permission, he took the buggy, and he and the runaway slave made their getaway to the next station, with Newton not returning until dawn. As it turns out, the principal, Harvey Thomas, was also Newton's uncle, and Thomas had not only misdirected the pursuing slave hunters, but had concocted a story as to why his carriage and nephew had disappeared all night.[28] So here we see the active participation in Underground Railroad activities by the principal of the Bloomingdale Quaker school.

Without further evidence, we cannot identify the source, if indeed there was a main source, of William Henry Harrison Beadle's profound sense of fairness and equality for all. We know that he refers to his ancestors as "ultra anti-slavery", that he had meaningful and frequent association with Quaker abolitionists, that influential people in his education were similarly shaped by the Quakers of Parke County, and that he was personally anti-slavery to the point that he was giving speeches to that effect in his first weeks of arriving at university: speeches rousing enough that he attracted the attention of the Michigan Quakers and other Abolitionists, who then recruited him.

Beadle's commitment to fairness and equality informed the rest of his life and service to his nation and the new home he made for himself in Dakota Territory and, for many years, in Madison, South Dakota, where he served as both president and faculty member of the Normal School, now Dakota State University. He came by the position partly from his five years of experience as Superintendent of Public Instruction, his political connectedness from his years of service in various capacities, and the luck of his timing: the position of president of the Normal School had just opened as he took his leave from a brief—and apparently unhappy—stint in charge of Chemawa Indian school (Salem Indian Training School, at the time) in Salem, Oregon. Beadle noted in his resignation letter that there had been substantial tension between his predecessor, John Lee, and the faculty. Although Beadle claimed that things had much improved, nevertheless he left after only four months and fourteen days.[29] He wrote just before leaving there that he was ready to "return to the suffering, fire-swept, but beloved Dakota."[30]

Nevertheless, Beadle's disposition must certainly have been a complicating factor. In a piece that otherwise praises Beadle extensively, his former student from his earliest time at Madison Normal School, Joseph Schafer, admits some imperfections: "He was impatient, easily flustered, had an exceedingly short but tempestuous temper, and was always worrying about something."[31] Later in the same piece, Schafer remembers: "Though his faculty aides. . . might smile at his unconscious manifestation of egoism, as well as at his almost childish helplessness in the presence of the everyday problems and distractions of school management, none failed in the respect and admiration which the General's exceptional qualities of mind and heart inspired."[32]

A final anecdote serves to show how Beadle's character revealed itself early in his time in Dakota Territory while serving as Surveyor General but before the bulk of his career of service. In one of the extremely rare anecdotes recounted by Beadle in his autobiography, he offers a characteristically breviloquent account of what many writers might have developed into a grand event of tension and derring-do. Beadle remembers facing a group of armed American Indians who demanded Beadle and his small crew of surveyors hand over their equipment:

> Going up the west side of the Dakota river[33] in June, 1873, with, I believe, the first party to traverse its nearly entire length, we were surprised, some thirty miles above where Huron is, to find a considerable river flowing from the west and apparently a small one coming beyond it from the north, and we had to travel west some ten miles or more to the abrupt land where Redfield lies. That and similar features in many parts were lacking upon our previous maps. And it seemed double trouble the next morning, when midway between the mouths of Turtle and Snake creeks, that a band of Yanktonais Indians under Drifting Goose crossed the Dakota from their summer tepees on the east side, halted us, demanded that we leave with them all we had and return whence we came. There were 130 or 140 of them, men and women, in blankets, no weapons visible. The women began to sing a weird cry, men caught our front horses by their bridles and another began to unhitch the tugs. We were all armed, seven of us. I had a double-barrelled shot gun and a pocket full of buckshot shells. Pointing my gun a moment at others to drive them back, I handed my gun to the driver, caught the Indian by the arm and shoulder, and with a tremendous effort whirled him around and away, quickly rehitching the tug I took my gun, pulled back both hammers and held it to my shoulder pointing it at the nearest; then laying one hand upon the hook of the tug I warned them back and held up my gun again. The men, other than the drivers, stood along before the wagons, and all had guns or revolvers in hand. My men perfectly understood that under no provocation were they to fire until after I did. The declaration of hostilities was in my hands. Fortunately, the Indians gave way somewhat and did not disclose their weapons that were under their blan-

> kets, though they were probably not numerous. Speaking to the teams to start, we formed behind them and walked backwards some distance, holding our guns at "a ready." There had been a little conference at first and small presents of food and tobacco offered and dropped on the ground for the Indians. We could not afford to fight; one wounded man would disable us. We had no desire to harm the Indians, and had not been sent as missionaries to them.[34]

Beadle recounts the bare facts of the confrontation. The breveted general who had seen plenty of combat just a few short years before was in no rush to engage in further combat, yet neither has he become conflict-averse. He understands the motivations of Drifting Goose's band, makes apparent his commitment to fairness—some "small presents" from the surveyors were indeed appropriate to demonstrate their good faith—but they would not lie down and allow themselves to be robbed, either. Beadle did not record his thoughts in his writings, and we have no record of his thinking about policy regarding the creation of the reservations and the breaking of treaties. Similarly, we have no record of his thinking about the slaves he encountered both in his youth in Indiana and his college years in Michigan. But we have an excellent record of his *actions* with regard to the runaway slaves, and in this one instance, a band of Yanktonai facing the inexorable encroachment of white settlers. With no desire to harm nor to change those he encountered, Beadle carefully withdraws to a safe distance, and offers a small gesture of respect. And just as in his modest recounting of his brave involvement with the Underground Railroad back in Michigan, what Beadle does *not* say speaks loudest about that which he is proudest: he does not resort to unnecessary violence yet was able to treat his fellow humans with a modicum of respect. Beadle the educator and statesman was refined in these crucibles.

NOTES

1. Doane Robinson, ed., "Memoirs of William H. H. Beadle," in *History of South Dakota*, Vol. III (Pierre: South Dakota State Historical Society, 1906), pp. 716–19.

2. Joseph Schafer. Unpublished single chapter from a lost memoir. "Chapter IV: The General; personal reminiscences of Joseph Schafe [sic]." RG I; DSU 1: Oversize; S2: Individual Files; SS3; William Henry Harrison Beadle, folder 9, box

5, Miscellaneous papers relating to the life and career of W. H. H. Beadle, Dakota State University Archives, Karl Mundt Library.

3. "Dakota State University." Wikipedia, 12 Aug. 2021. https://en.wikipedia.org/wiki/Dakota_State_University.

4. Joseph Schafer. "Chapter IV: The General," p. 18. Details of this period are few, but one document posted to familysearch.org names Beadle as a Superintendent of the Southern District in Wilmington, North Carolina, from February to March of 1866. https://www.familysearch.org/wiki/en/Freedmen%27s_Bureau_North_Carolina_Field_Office_Coverage_Table

5. Mary Farmer-Kaiser, "Freedmen's Bureau," in *Encyclopedia of Race and Racism*, ed. Patrick L. Mason (Detroit: Macmillan, 2013).

6. Doane Robinson, "Memoirs," p. 717.

7. Kurt Hackemer, "Wartime Trauma and the Lure of the Frontier: Civil War Veterans in Dakota Territory, " in *The War Went On: Reconsidering the Lives of Civil War Veterans*, ed. Brian Jordan (Baton Rouge: Louisiana State University Press, 2020), p. 83.

8. O. W. Coursey, *A Complete Biographical Sketch of General William Henry Harrison Beadle* (Mitchell, S.Dak.: Educator Supply Company, 1913).

9. Barrett Lowe, *Twenty Million Acres : The Story of America's First Conservationist, William Henry Harrison Beadle* (Mitchell, S.Dak.: Educator Supply Company, 1937), p. 21.

10. Ibid, pp. 18–25.

11. William H. H. Beadle, "Ascendat!" *Michigan Alumnus,* Vol. 9 (Ann Arbor: Alumni Association of the University of Michigan, 1903), pp. 242–46.

12. Coursey. *A Complete Biographical Sketch,* p. 20.

13. William H. H. Beadle, "Ascendat!" p. 242.

14. James Tobin, "The Boys of '61," *Michigan Today*, 11 Jan. 2017, https://michigantoday.umich.edu/2017/01/11/the-boys-of-61/.

15. William H. H. Beadle. "The Days of Auld Lang Syne—Recollections of Michigan Alumni: Pedagogic Reminiscences," *Michigan Alumnus*, Vol. 9, pp. 9–12.

16. Coursey. *A Complete Biographical Sketch,* p. 24.

17. Maurice Murphy, "Some Features of the History of Parke County," *Indiana Magazine of History*, Vol. XII (Mar. 1913).

18. Gerard W. Gawalt, *Clashing Dynasties : Charles Francis Adams and James Murray Mason in the Fiery Cauldron of Civil War* (North Charleston, S.C.: Createspace Independent Publishing Platform, 2015).

19. Murphy, "Some Features."

20. Lowe, *Twenty Million Acres*, p. 67.

21. Grace Shackman, "The Underground Railroad in Ann Arbor: Ann Arbor District Library," *Ann Arbor Observer*, Dec. 1998, https://aadl.org/aaobserver/15566.

22. Lowe notes that Lavinia Tucker was probably not a Quaker in adulthood but was raised and educated by them.

23. Wilbur H. B. Siebert, *The Underground Railroad from Slavery to Freedom* (New York: Macmillan, 1898).

24. George Kingsbury, *History of Dakota Territory,* Vol. 4 (Chicago: S. J. Clarke Publishing Company, 1915).

25. "Map of Indiana Underground Railroad Routes," Wilbur H. Siebert Underground Railroad Collection, Ohio History Connection, 2020, https://ohiomemory.org/digital/collection/siebert/id/14680.

26. "History of Parke County—Adams Twp. Biographies: 1880," www.usgenealogyexpress.com. Transcribed from *History of Vigo & Parke County, Indiana* (Chicago: H. H. Hill & N. Iddings, 1880), http://www.usgenealogyexpress.com/~in/parke/parkeco_hist_1880/parkeco_hist_1880_adams_bios.htm#beadleJasW.

27. Karen Zach, ed., "Parke County, Indiana Atlas—1874 Adams Township," http://ingenweb.org/inparke/1874AtlasSubscribersAdamsTownship.htm.

28. Frank Hadley to Wilbur H. Siebert, 25 Apr. 1944, Wilbur H. Sierbert Underground Railroad Collection, Ohio History Connection, https://ohiomemory.org/digital/collection/siebert/id/11665.

29. Burton Carlyle Lemmon, "The Historical Development of the Chemawa Indian School" (master's thesis, Oregon State College, 1940), p. 35.

30. Schaffer, "Chapter IV: The General," p. 6.

31. Ibid., p. 5.

32. Ibid., p. 7.

33. Here, when the author says, "Dakota River," he is referring to the James River.

34. W. H. H. Beadle, *Autobiography of William Henry Harrison Beadle*. (Pierre: Hipple Printing Co., 1938).

DARYL WEBB

4 | SAFEGUARDING THE INTERESTS OF THE PEOPLE: GOVERNOR PETER NORBECK AND CONSERVATIVE REFORM

• • •

On 2 January 1917, newly elected Republican governor Peter Norbeck addressed the South Dakota legislature. "The people of the state have much for which to be thankful. We live in era of wonderful development. The natural resources of the state excel . . . [and] our people are prosperous," he told lawmakers. Norbeck went on to explain that South Dakotans were fortunate for two reasons. They lived "in the right age" and they lived in the right place—South Dakota. For the state "is not only the land of opportunity, but it is home of honest, intelligent, progressive, hard working, God fearing people."[1] While Norbeck spoke glowingly of the state and its citizens, he and many others believed that rural America was in decline and threatened by radical change. Farmers were deprived of an open and free market as monopolies destroyed competition. Socialism was on the rise, threatening the long-established capitalist economic system. Nature itself was threatened by mass extinctions and the depletion of natural resources. However, Norbeck believed that it was not too late to reverse this decline and devoted his four years as governor to a bold program of reform designed to preserve the existing order and save rural America. To conserve South Dakota's wildlife and natural resources, Norbeck created Custer State Park. To keep young people on the farm, he reformed country schools and improved rural education. Norbeck acted most boldly on economic policy. He saw capitalism as threatened by monopolies that were destroying competition on one side and Socialism that would prohibit competition on the other. Norbeck worked to find a middle ground between these two extremes. He instituted a series of economic reforms, including government ownership of a coal mine, a cement plant, and the creation of a rural credit program to help restore competition to South Dakota. He also believed that these state-run enterprises would hold off the more extreme proposals advocated by Socialists. This effort to stop radicalism and preserve the existing order places Norbeck in the conservative tradition of South Dakota politics.

Norbeck's conservative reform program arose in response to the dramatic changes taking place in the United States. Since the beginning of the republic, agriculture had dominated the nation's economy and yeoman farmers were seen as the ideal citizens. Thomas Jefferson asserted that "those who labor in the earth are the chosen people of God" who possessed "substantial and genuine virtue."[2] However, after the Civil War, a drastic transformation of the economy took place that displaced agriculture as the nation's leading economic sector. In the last decades of nineteenth century, Andrew Carnegie, John D. Rockefeller, and other talented entrepreneurs industrialized the nation's economy. These entrepreneurs exploited the nation's natural resources to help fuel this industrial revolution. This led to the devastation of the country's landscape and the first surge of extinctions of animal species. By 1890, however, the United States was the world's leading industrial power and for the first time ever the total value of manufactured goods exceeded the value of agricultural products.[3] As new industrial cities boomed and became the center of America's economic life, more and more rural Americans, particularly young people, abandoned country living and headed to towns and cities. In 1880, farmers made up almost 44 percent of the nation's population but by 1920, barely one-third of Americans lived on farms.[4] "To live in the countryside in 1900 was to have the sense that the nation was passing you by [and] leaving you behind," observed historian David Danbom.[5]

Not only was agriculture falling behind industry, but competition in the marketplace was significantly diminished. The same entrepreneurs who industrialized the economy used innovation, mergers, and ruthless tactics to drive much of the competition out of business and established large scale monopolies or trusts, as they were commonly known in the era. By 1900, these trusts dominated almost every sector of the economy. Typically, at least 40 percent of the market in each economic sector was controlled by one of these corporations and in about one-third of these sectors a single company controlled 70 percent of the market.[6] Farmers complained that these new trusts controlled their fates. The railroad trusts charged farmers high prices for freight, big banks placed exorbitant interest rates on loans, and monopolies that controlled elevators, stock yards, flour mills, and packing houses took large cuts of farmers' profits. In the late nineteenth century, farmers tried to retain their power by organizing collectively. In the 1880s, agriculturalists formed the Farmers Alliance and, in what became the South Dakota Alliance, men organized a collective purchasing program, established a crop insurance plan, and operated an elevator. However, all of these ventures were short lived due to poor management and the ruthless tactics of trusts. In the 1890s, farmers organized the Populist Party and demanded public ownership of warehouses, railroads, and postal savings banks. In 1892, the South Dakota Populists won the governor's office, numerous state legislative seats, and sent James Kyle to the U.S. Senate. The Populist governor and legislators created a railroad rate commission and regulated railroad rates. However, the party faded away by the end of the decade, leaving farmers falling further behind as they tried to compete in an economy dominated by trusts.

The dominance of monopolies caused some Americans to embrace radicalism. By the early twentieth century, Socialism was beginning to take root in pockets of the nation. In 1910, the Socialists won control of the city government in Milwaukee, Wisconsin, capturing the mayor's offices and the majority on the city's Common Council. In the following year Socialists won majority control of twenty-three other city governments including Butte, Montana; Flint, Michigan; and Schenectady, New York. And in 1912, Socialist presidential candidate Eugene Debs ran a vigorous campaign and captured over nine hundred thousand votes. The Socialist movement also began to emerge in South Dakota, targeting two distinct groups—itinerant agricultural workers and farmers. The Socialist labor union, the Industrial Workers of the World (IWW), actively recruited itinerant farm workers. The Wobblies, as they were known, became active in South Dakota by 1909 and used aggressive and sometimes confrontational tactics to organize temporary farm hands during harvest season. In 1915, the IWW members led a parade of over one hundred farm workers through the streets of Mellette, Spink County, demanding shorter hours. Near Hoven the Wobblies organized a sit-down strike for higher wages, and outside Aberdeen IWW leaders put railroad spikes in threshing machines to protest low wages and poor working conditions. These tactics were not just disruptive, but they sometimes turned violent. In 1915, a confrontation caused an IWW organizer to shoot and kill a Northwestern Railroad brakeman. The following year, IWW organizers were accused of beating a man in Emery, causing riots in Mitchell and in Redfield, and murdering a man in Aberdeen. The Wobblies' violence and confrontational tactics generated significant fear and deep concern in the state. A former U.S. attorney for South Dakota argued that state officials were "seriously at fault for the way they are tolerating the lawlessness of the I.W.W. members in this state."[7] The *Mitchell Capital* called the Wobblies' activity a "reign of terror" and pleaded, "[i]s it not time that something were being done . . . to impress upon these deliberately lawless characters some respect for the authority of the laws of South Dakota and for the peace of communities all over the state?"[8]

While the Wobblies were organizing itinerant agricultural workers, the Nonpartisan League (NPL) emerged and targeted farmers. The NPL was founded in 1915 and grew out of the small Socialist Party in North Dakota. It combined Socialist ideology with ideas from the agricultural cooperative movement and called for state-owned terminal elevators, flour mills, packing houses, and cold storage plants. It also called for a government-run hail insurance program and a state-operated rural credit program to lend farmers money at low interest rates. The NPL took over the North Dakota Republican Party and won the governor's office and control of the state legislature in the 1916 election. The league-dominated legislature passed railroad regulations and created a state-controlled grain grading system. With its success in North Dakota, the NPL quickly began to expand, recruiting members in surrounding states, including South Dakota. Initially, only South Dakota's Socialists embraced the NPL, but in 1916, the league won the endorsement of the South Dakota Farmers Union and membership ballooned to almost twenty thousand members.[9]

As the nation faced the growing threat of radicalism, domination of trusts, and the decline of rural America, a new group of reformers known as the progressives emerged to address these challenges. Led by Republican president Teddy Roosevelt, Democrat and Populist champion William Jennings Bryan, and future Democratic president Woodrow Wilson, the progressives initiated a wide range of reforms. One of their prime targets was trusts. Some, like Bryan, called for state ownership of monopolies, but most rejected public ownership and successfully championed legislation that broke up trusts and regulated big business. Progressives also reformed the education system, established conservation programs, and enacted a host of other political, social, and economic reforms. In South Dakota, progressives became a driving force in state politics in 1906 when Republican Coe Crawford won the race for governor. Crawford and the Progressives in the legislature worked to regulate railroads and improve education. In 1908, Peter Norbeck stepped away from his very successful artesian well-drilling business and ran for state senate. When Norbeck announced his candidacy, he aligned himself with progressives, proclaiming, "I am anxious to do all I can to promote the cause for which Progressive Republicans stand."[10] He ran an energetic campaign that emphasized his Progressive ideas. "I assure you it is not my own success that I have at heart," Norbeck explained, "but it is the success of the principles for which Mr. Crawford and the Progressive Republicans stand."[11] These progressive principles carried the day and he easily won the fall election. In the state senate, Norbeck advocated for legislation regulating railroad passenger rates, improving safety on trains, and creating a rural credit program.

By 1914, Norbeck was one of the state's leading progressives and was selected as the nominee for lieutenant governor with Frank Byrne at the top of the ticket. Byrne and Norbeck promised to enact progressive policies and easily won. The Byrne Administration created a tax commission, passed a bank deposit guarantee law, and got the legislature to place a rural credit program on the 1916 ballot. In 1916, Byrne stepped aside and Norbeck sought the Republican nomination for governor. In the campaign Norbeck called for "practical progressive legislation" and advocated for the rural credit program, improved roads, tax reform and laws that would "materially aid in the up-building of the state's greatest resource—our agricultural interests."[12] In the primary, he ran against George Egan, a disbarred lawyer and crank who falsely believed political corruption was everywhere. Egan took Norbeck to task for a state contract his drilling company received while he served as lieutenant governor. Egan called the contract illegal and accused Norbeck of an ethical lapse. Despite the criticism, Norbeck easily defeated Egan, winning the Republican primary. In the fall, the Democrats criticized Norbeck for being the boss of the Republican machine, but this had little effect and Norbeck won the general election by over twenty thousand votes.[13]

As governor, Norbeck championed a bold reform program that reflected his conservatism. As a conservative, Norbeck believed that long-standing institutions and the existing order need to be maintained. Competitive capitalism, rural America, and the abundance of natural resources and wildlife had brought stability and prosperity to the nation for generations. But in the early twentieth century, this existing order was threatened by monopolies, socialism, urbanization, and environmental degradation. To stop these radical forces and to save the established order, Norbeck believed government intervention was necessary. In fact, Norbeck argued that it was the responsibility of government to act. He asserted that government had a duty to protect these long-established systems and institutions, like capitalism and rural communities, that had developed over many generations. The government's "first duty is to safeguard all the interests, educational, moral and economic, of the people of this state," Norbeck asserted.[14] "The state must protect its people" from the forces of radical change, he argued.[15]

Norbeck believed the most serious problems the state and its farmers faced were the dramatic changes to the economy. The power of trusts and loss of competition in the marketplace threatened the fundamentals of capitalism and caused people to turn to Socialism, Norbeck argued. These trusts were so large that they easily and unfairly destroyed the competition. When farmers co-ops and other businesses tried to compete with one of these monopolies, the co-ops "soon found their businesses destroyed by unfair competition of the large corporation," Norbeck asserted. "A farmers lumber yard, or creamery or an elevator or similar enterprise would be put out of business because of the price fixing activities of the large corporation," he concluded.[16] Once a trust dominated the market, it faced little to no competition and Norbeck argued that the law of supply and demand no longer functioned. He believed this unfair competition took "profits away from the producer" and Norbeck argued that farmers were "entitled to their full share" of the profits.[17]

To restore competition and ensure farmers received their fair share of profits, Norbeck believed a multipronged approach was needed. "There is no one remedy, no sure cure, but relief lies in effort in several directions," Norbeck explained. He urged farmers to act as individual producers and make adjustments to their operations. He also endorsed farmers cooperatives and pointed to South Dakota's Farmers Union and its cooperative grain elevators as a means to help restore competition. Norbeck also championed state intervention in the economy. He implemented new business regulations and strengthened old ones. His administration aggressively carried out laws preventing rate and price discrimination by railroads. He rigorously enforced regulations on mines, food processing companies, and railroads and significantly expanded state regulatory agencies' budgets. Between 1916 and 1920, the Railroad Commission's budget increased by 34 percent, the Food and Drug Commission saw a 36 percent increase, and the Office of Mine Inspectors' budget almost doubled.[18] Additionally, Norbeck passed a workmen's compensation law that provided $3,000 to the widow of a man killed on the job and $12 of weekly pay to persons injured at work.

Norbeck believed that sometimes regulation was not enough to counter the effects of trusts and state-ownership was necessary. "Where men attempt to extort an unreasonable profit," Norbeck asserted, "it is the business of the government to step in and regulate it and where the regulation can best be had by government ownership and operation this plan should be adopted."[19] Norbeck did not see state-owned enterprises as radical. "I do not consider that government ownership or control of monopolies is Socialism," Norbeck explained.[20] He saw state ownership as "protection against monopolies"[21] and as a means of restoring competition to the marketplace. He pointed to the privately owned cement company at Yankton as an example. "It [the Yankton cement plant] has passed into the control of the cement trust. Private capital will not engage in the business; the risk of unfair competition from without the state is too great. The state [government] can well afford to operate such a plant at cost in order to re-establish competition and reduce the price to the consumer."[22] While Norbeck did embrace public ownership to restore competition, he did not advocate for state ownership of all businesses and saw state ownership only as a last resort. "In my mind we cannot remedy all our ills by the state or federal government owning every industry," Norbeck said. "There are many things which an individual can do better than state," he argued. However, Norbeck asserted that if a company "control[ed] the market and extort[ed] unreasonable profits," then "public necessity requires" the government to step in and establish state ownership to provide competition.[23]

The first place Norbeck believed that the state must provide competition was with banks that charged high interest rates. He argued this was not only hurting individual farmers, but South Dakota as a whole. "Our state development has, in the past, been greatly retarded by the inability of the farmer to secure long term real estate loans at low rates of interest," observed Norbeck.[24] He believed that farmers needed an alternative to these private banks. In 1916, Norbeck campaigned for the rural credit program, explaining that the plan would help farmers be more productive. He additionally reassured voters that "the state system [of rural credit] proposed is not radical, it is based on the experience of other countries."[25] So when South Dakota voters authorized the state-run rural credit plan in 1916, Norbeck made the program his top priority as governor. One of the first bills introduced in the 1917 legislative session made the rural credit program operational and Norbeck shepherded the plan through the legislature. The bill allowed the state to sell bonds to raise capital and then to lend the money to farmers at low interest rates. The bill passed overwhelmingly and the program was quickly up and running, providing competition in the rural credit market. By 1921, when Norbeck left the governor's office, the rural credit program had loaned almost $30 million to the state's farmers. Norbeck boasted that "[t]housands of young men have been assisted. The state has helped them to become home-owners and has placed them in a fair way to become prosperous and successful."[26]

After creating an alternative in the credit market, Norbeck and the legislature began to work to restore competition to other sectors of the economy through state-owned enterprises. In 1917, the legislature sent five government-ownership proposals, including a government-operated cement plant, coal mine, and terminal elevator, to voters for their approval in the 1918 election. During Norbeck's successful 1918 reelection campaign, he urged voters to support these state-ownership constitutional amendments. Government ownership will allow the people "to co-ordinate their forces and co-operate in bringing about certain necessary reforms," Norbeck argued.[27] In the fall, Norbeck won reelection by over 33,000 votes and the public-ownership amendments passed overwhelmingly, each winning 60 percent or more of the vote.[28] In the 1919 legislative session, Norbeck asked lawmakers to study the feasibility of state ownership of a terminal elevator, flour mill, packing house and a hydroelectric plant. He further pressed the body to quickly establish a government owned and operated hail insurance program, cement plant, and coal mine. The legislature responded by passing all three bills and Norbeck worked quickly to get the state-run enterprises up and running. The state hail insurance program began operations in 1919 and after two years the program fund contained $900,000. The following year Norbeck closed a deal to buy land in Haines, North Dakota, for the state coal mine and by 1926, the enterprise produced two hundred thousand tons of coal. In 1920, the state purchased land in Rapid City for its cement plant, which opened in 1924 and provided cement mainly for public buildings and highways. "We have established in South Dakota a good record for progressive, sane legislative enactments," Norbeck proclaimed as he left the governor's office in 1921, "and our state stands today in the front rank of progressive commonwealths."[29]

The restoration of competition through state ownership was also a fundamental part of Norbeck's effort to stop the advance of Socialism in South Dakota. Norbeck saw Socialism as great a threat to the existing order as trusts. Socialism would entirely upend the established capitalist system. It would prohibit competition, fail to reward initiative and hard work, and implement collective ownership of all private property, Norbeck believed. Under socialism "[e]ven the farms will be owned by all the people in common," Norbeck asserted. "I am not in favor of compelling the farmer to divide his land or his property with the I.W.W. or even the harmless sloven loafer."[30] Norbeck believed government ownership was a means to restore competition, not a way to abolish it. So Norbeck saw the IWW and NPL activities in South Dakota as significant threats that needed to be aggressively countered. "There is no immediate threat from external enemies, but there are very evident signs of internal dangers [from socialism]," he warned. "What we need now in our country is a real first class housecleaning."[31] To stop the NPL, Norbeck adopted aspects of its platform, while condemning its leaders as free spending Socialists.[32] The rural credit program, state hail insurance, government-owned elevators, stockyards, and flour mill were all part of the Nonpartisan League platform. When Norbeck embraced and began to implement these ideas, he made the

NPL irrelevant in South Dakota politics. While Norbeck supported key pieces of the NPL's agenda, he condemned NPL programs. He argued that League programs were expensive and would create a huge debt for the state. The NPL proposes "using the credit of the state without limit," Norbeck observed. "They try to conceal the fact that the state's credit is just another name for another man's money." Additionally, he told South Dakotans that the "Non-Partisan League is only another name for 'Socialism,'" and warned that if they took control of the state all farms would be placed under collective ownership.[33]

Norbeck took an even more aggressive approach to the Industrial Workers of the World. Since the IWW had little support in the state, Norbeck was open in his disdain for the Wobblies. He called them "undesirables" who caused serious troubles for the state. [34] He then shepherded two bills through the legislature to address the threat the Wobblies posed. Most IWW organizers, who sometimes carried weapons, entered the state by stealing rides on trains so Norbeck urged the legislature to outlaw this practice. The legislature quickly acted and passed a bill that required anyone riding on a freight train to obtain the permission from the conductor before boarding. The legislation also made it a crime to carry concealed weapons on trains. Once Norbeck signed the bills, trainmen were urged to evict violators from the cars and turn them over to local authorities. To help local authorities deal with the protests and unrest caused by the IWW, Norbeck won the passage of a bill creating a state police force. The legislation also gave the governor the power to mobilize local police to help address any threat the state faced, particularly from the Wobblies.

When the nation was thrust into World War I in 1917, Norbeck used the crisis to further delegitimize and isolate the IWW and the NPL. During the war, Norbeck heightened his rhetoric branding the groups as un-American. He proclaimed that "the N.P. League . . . organizers who have come to this state are not loyal" and charged that the IWW was a "threatening menace" because it used a "reign of terror" to undermine the war effort.[35] He also privately urged the state's Republican newspapers to condemn the IWW and NPL and many papers eagerly complied. The *Sioux Falls Daily Argus-Leader* branded the NPL leaders as Bolsheviks who opposed the war.[36] The *Rapid City Journal* condemned the IWW for trying to sow anarchy and demanded that Wobblies either be forced to work for the war effort or be put in jail.[37] And the *Pierre Weekly Free Press* accused the IWW of being "pro-German."[38] These charges and Norbeck's long campaign against these groups helped make the NPL and IWW targets of vigilantes, police, and the state's Home Guard, a private paramilitary organization designed to protect the state and enforce loyalty. During the eighteen months of the war, the Home Guard broke up numerous IWW encampments and arrested several Wobblies, including four for sending explosive materials through the mail. Police arrested twenty-nine Hutchinson County Socialists for interfering with the draft and arrested a Nonpartisan League leader in Lyman County for attempting to organize farmers in the area. Additionally, vigilantes broke up NPL meetings in Britton, Madison, and Watertown. Norbeck did make a half-hearted attempt to stop these activities. He made statements about the need to protect free speech and civil liberties, but at the same time continued to vigorously condemn both groups. He even accused the NPL of stirring up trouble for their own benefit. "The [NPL] leaders do not want protection," Norbeck asserted. "They live and grow on trouble. When trouble is not real they manufacture it."[39] These efforts successfully undermined these groups; local officials reported significantly less IWW activity during the war and the NPL was so isolated that it struggled to organize.

While Norbeck was trying to stop Socialism from taking root in the state, he worked to revive rural South Dakota. Norbeck argued that agriculturists built the state. "Thru the persistent and earnest effort of the farmers, land came into value, cities sprung up, State institutions were established . . . and while we are truly a young state, our progress compares favorably with any state in America."[40] However, during the first part of the twentieth century, South Dakota's town and city population increased three times faster than its rural areas.[41] Norbeck worried that as the farm population declined, South Dakota's great progress would stall. So he developed policies to renew rural South Dakota. In developing these plans, Norbeck drew on a group of reformers in the Country Life Movement. Organized by educators, ministers, social scientists, and other reformers, the Country Life Movement grew out of the progressive reform effort. Country Life reformers were deeply concerned about loss of population in rural areas and called for a rejuvenation of rural America to keep people on the farm. Norbeck fully embraced two key elements of the Country Life agenda. First, he enacted a program of road building in the state. Country Life leaders believed that a network of paved roads would allow rural Americans to have access to the conveniences of town and cities, while still remaining on the farm. So, in 1917, Norbeck convinced the legislature to create the South Dakota Highway Department with a $130,000 budget. By 1920, the new department had developed a $10 million road building plan.[42]

The other Country Life reform Norbeck championed was improving rural education. He believed that education was the best way to rescue the rural way of life. The country school was the anchor of most rural communities, but it was falling behind schools in towns and cities. "Education conditions in South Dakota are not what they ought to be," Norbeck warned at the opening of the 1919 legislative session. "The city schools of our State will compare favorably with any in the land, but we cannot point with pride to the country schools."[43] Norbeck believed education was fundamental because it would "properly prepare them [children] for the duties of citizenship and to better equip them for the struggle incident to human life."[44] However, many country schools did not go beyond the primary grades and this caused boys and girls who wanted to continue on to high school to go to surrounding towns and cities to continue their education. This forced many of the smartest young people off the farm, never to return. To keep young people in rural America and provide them with the education and skills necessary to succeed in agriculture, Norbeck believed the state's country schools had to evolve.

Norbeck championed a multipronged strategy to reform rural education. The first step was to encourage school consolidation. Norbeck believed the merging of schools allowed the pooling of limited resources, "equalizing the educational advantages between the children growing up in the country and those in the town."[45] Further, these new consolidated schools could expand beyond the primary grades and open a high school. This would prevent the out migration of older students. To encourage school mergers, in 1919 Norbeck won the passage of legislation providing additional state aid to consolidated schools that met certain benchmarks. By 1920, thirty-one schools had consolidated and most were receiving additional state support. Additionally, Norbeck argued that "[o]ne of the principal reasons for the low standard in the rural schools, is the difficulty that is experienced in obtaining a sufficient supply of trained teachers."[46] So Norbeck found new ways to improve teacher training and attract educators to country schools. Norbeck believed that the state normal schools, located in Aberdeen, Madison, Springfield, and Spearfish, were too far away from most rural students and this prevented them from going into education. Country schools were then forced to hire people with only an eighth-grade education or to accept city educators, who were not interested in rural living and quickly left their posts. To address this rural teacher shortage, Norbeck shepherded a bill through the legislature that allowed high schools to open normal training programs. Within a year there were over 215 students enrolled in teacher training programs in twenty-six high schools.[47] Norbeck also successfully rose teachers' certification standards and by 1920 over 90 percent of teachers had a high school education and one in four had graduated from a college normal school or four-year college.[48] To help country schools retain their faculty, Norbeck created a program to assist with housing for rural instructors. Often times country teachers had a tough time finding housing near their schools, making it difficult for districts to recruit and retain teachers. So Norbeck won legislative approval of state aid to assist rural districts to construct teacher housing on school grounds. Within a year, nine of the state's country school districts had received the state housing aid.[49]

While Norbeck was enhancing teacher training and encouraging school consolidation, he took steps to ensure country schools kept pace with city schools, but still remained uniquely rural. Urban education officials were strengthening mandatory attendance laws, expanding resources, and enhancing curriculum. To ensure that rural South Dakota children kept up with city boys and girls, Norbeck advanced legislation that followed suit. First, to help ensure that country school students were getting the education they needed, he convinced the legislature to pass a bill that strengthened the mandatory attendance law. To help small schools improve instruction, the governor gained approval of state funding to buy textbooks for country schools. Additionally, he won passage of legislation requiring each school to spend at least one quarter of its instruction time on history, civics, and hygiene. However, Norbeck did not want rural education to replicate urban schools' curriculum. He believed that country schools should be unique and prepare students for rural life. So Norbeck called for courses in agricultural and domestic science in an effort to train rural youth for farm work. In 1917, the U.S. Congress passed the Smith-Hughes Act, which provided federal matching money to states that provided education in farming and homemaking. Norbeck quickly won legislative appropriation for matching monies and by 1920, twenty South Dakota schools received over $18,000 to provide agricultural and domestic education to rural youth.[50] While Norbeck argued that these programs "changed the entire educational outlook of the state," they did little to counteract the shift in the balance of power from rural to urban.[51]

Norbeck's most notable and longest lasting legacy in his effort to preserve rural America was in conservation. By the early twentieth century, virgin land and wildlife were vanishing away. In South Dakota, the state's forests and minerals in the Black Hills were aggressively harvested. The state's bison population was almost wiped out, Norbeck observed. He told the governor of Wyoming that the "the number [of big horned sheep] has been reduced to almost extinction," and Norbeck warned the legislature that the "birds, such as [the] grouse and prairie chicken are in danger of extermination."[52] He feared this extinction trend would continue and the natural world that had inspired people since the dawn of time would be destroyed. The wildlife and natural beauty of the state had to be conserved, Norbeck asserted. "The value of wildlife and especially bird life to the agricultural and horticultural interests of the state is not realized and therefore not appreciated. If the game department could do nothing more than prevent the brutal slaughter of innocent birds, it would be of wonderful service to the people of this state," Norbeck explained.[53] Initially, the governor required that the game department improve the state's wildlife management. South Dakota had a strong fishing and hunting culture that wildlife experts recognized needed to be maintained through conservation. During Norbeck's administration, the money spent on wildlife management almost doubled and millions of fish and thousands of pheasants and other birds were introduced into the state. This helped sustain South Dakota's hunting and fishing tradition. In fact, it was during Norbeck's governorship that the state authorized the first pheasant hunting season that lasted only a single day.

However, Norbeck believed more needed to be done to conserve wildlife and natural resources. When Norbeck took office, Custer Park in the Black Hills was not officially a state park, but simply state-owned land and thus subject to sale. Norbeck called the area a "place of beauty," saying, "it is an inspiring sight to see our native wild game gazing quietly along the wayside."[54] He feared the area might fall into private ownership and be exploited or even be destroyed for profit. In 1919, Norbeck urged the legislature to "create a permanent State Park, a place of scenic grandeur, an ideal recreation spot, and a home for the preservation of the fast-disappearing wild animal life of the state."[55] Norbeck won passage of the legislation and then spent the next two years expanding the park's holdings, including adding Black Elk Peak and Sylvan Lake to the park. He convinced the legislature to appropriate money to purchase private land adjacent to Custer to further expand the park. Norbeck also successfully lobbied congressmen and senators to support legislation that granted the state twenty-five thousand acres of federal land to add to Custer State Park. He told South Dakota congressman Harry Gandy that by supporting the bill, Gandy would be "doing a great service to the people of South Dakota."[56]

Then Norbeck oversaw almost every aspect of the park's development. He was involved with the placement of roads and bridges and the running of telephone lines through the park. He also reached out to the War Department seeking barbed wire left over from the war to use for fencing. Additionally, he worked hard to secure animals for the park. He sought the Department of the Interior's help in securing beavers from Yellowstone National Park and wrote to the governor of Wyoming seeking mountain sheep and moose to add to Custer's herd. While Norbeck believed it was vital to "preserve this place of natural beauty" before it disappeared, he still believed that the state's natural resources could be utilized for profit and should advance South Dakota's economic growth.[57] He believed that South Dakota's rivers should be developed to provide hydroelectric power and asserted that if Custer State Park's forests were managed properly, the sale of timber could bring the state millions of dollars in revenue. Additionally, Norbeck quickly came to see the state's natural resources could bring tourists to South Dakota. In the early twentieth century, Custer State Park and the Black Hills began to draw out of state visitors and became a thriving tourist hub after President Calvin Coolidge's visit to the Black Hills in 1927—a visit Norbeck was pivotal in arranging.

After two successful terms as governor, Norbeck was elected to the United States Senate in 1920. While in Congress, he continued to advance conservation and the development of the Black Hills. He was instrumental in the creation of Mount Rushmore. He also continued to champion rural education and road development. However, the program of restoring competition through state ownership was quickly abandoned by Norbeck and the rest of the state. While the program was endorsed by 60 percent of voters in 1918, within a year strong opposition began to appear. An editorial in the *Sioux Falls Daily Argus-Leader* called the state-run enterprises "a doubtful experiment" and "socialistic" and worried about the "many millions of dollars [that] would be required" to pay for state-owned ventures.[58] In the 1920s, most South Dakotans came to agree with the *Argus-Leader* and reversed course. In 1922, when the construction of a state-owned hydroelectric plant was placed before voters, it lost by a four-to-one margin and was never built. In the same election, a proposed state-run bank was rejected by 64 percent of voters. While voters rejected additional state ownership, the government-operated enterprises that were already up and running continued, but suffered under poor management. Mismanagement and the agricultural crisis of the 1920s caused the rural credit program to be discontinued. It took another thirty years to fully liquidate the remaining $57 million still owed to the state.[59] The coal mine and hail insurance programs did not survive the Great Depression and closed in the early 1930s. Both enterprises lost money. When the hail insurance program disbanded, it was $263,000 in debt and the coal mine lost $174,000.[60] The cement plant was the only profitable venture. According to historian Larry Remele, it was managed effectively and turned a small profit, but it had little effect on the cement market in South Dakota.[61]

Most scholars who examine Norbeck see him as liberal because he used government activism and state-ownership.[62] However, as this study demonstrates, these were just a means to conservative ends. Norbeck implemented his agenda because he believed the existing order needed to be preserved from radical change. Competition needed to be restored, the state's natural resources and physical beauty needed to be conserved before they disappeared, and the country school needed to be preserved to save rural America. He was not trying to create a new society, but rather to conserve and to restore the existing rural way of life. Like all good conservatives, he did not oppose change. He believed in evolutionary change, but opposed revolutionary change.

So when regulation did not effectively rein in trusts, Norbeck turned to public ownership as the next step to prevent big business's domination of the economy. When country schools were unable to provide the education rural boys and girls needed to run farms, Norbeck championed the reform of schools to fully prepare rural youth for life in the twentieth century.

Understanding Norbeck as a conservative reformer also requires a new perspective on South Dakota politics. The standard interpretation of the state is that South Dakota is generally politically conservative, with a liberal streak. Seeing Norbeck and the progressives of the early twentieth century as conservative reformers trying to save rural life places them not in the liberal camp, but within the conservative tradition of South Dakota politics. They are not a liberal aberration, but a continuation of the state's conservatism. It is certainly a different type of conservatism than the small and limited government approach, but it is conservatism nonetheless. It is a conservatism that used government to protect and preserve the existing order from radical and fundamental change.[63] Norbeck also points to the flexibility of South Dakota conservatism. It is both small government with an emphasis on individual freedom and it is government activism and government ownership. Both protect the traditional rural way of life and preserve individual opportunity. This also suggests that scholars should reexamine other South Dakota leaders such as George McGovern and Tom Daschle. Were these Democratic lions successful because they aided farmers, worked to keep them independent producers, and tried to preserve the rural way of life? While both men embraced liberalism, perhaps they were seen by South Dakota voters as helping them to save the existing order and preserve their farms. Certainly, for Norbeck, public ownership, the creation of Custer State Park, and education reform were conservative and all in an effort to safeguard the interests of the people.

NOTES

1. Peter Norbeck, *Governor's Message, Inaugural: State of the State Address, 1917* (Pierre: South Dakota Legislature, 1916), p. 4.

2. David Danbom, *Born in the Country: A History of Rural America*, 2nd ed. (Baltimore: Johns Hopkins Press, 2006), p. 67

3. Ibid, p. 133.

4. *Historical Statistics of the United States: Colonial times to 1970* (Washington D.C.: United States Census Bureau, 1975), p. 457.

5. Danbom, *Born in the Country*, p. 134.

6. Michael McGerr, *A Fierce Discontent: The Rise and Fall of the Progressive Movement in America, 1870–1920* (New York: The Free Press, 2003), p. 151.

7. "South Dakota Laws Flouted," *Mitchell Capital,* 3 Aug. 1916.

8. Ibid.

9. Michael J. Lansing, *Insurgent Democracy: The Nonpartisan League in North American Politics* (Chicago: University of Chicago Press, 2015), p. 59.

10. Gilbert Courtland Fite, *Peter Norbeck: Prairie Statesman* (Pierre: South Dakota Historical Society Press, 2005), p. 33.

11. Peter Norbeck to Reverend J. Arneson, 4 June 1908, File 4, Box 55, MSS 116: The Peter Norbeck Papers, University of South Dakota Archives and Special Collections, Vermillion.

12. Peter Norbeck, "Announcement," *Daily Deadwood Pioneer-Times,* 24 Feb. 1916.

13. *South Dakota Legislative Manual—1919* (Pierre: State Publishing Company, 1919), p. 374.

14. Norbeck, *Inaugural Address*, p. 39.

15. Peter Norbeck, *Governor's Message: State of the State Address, 1918* (Pierre: South Dakota Legislature, 1918), p. 4.

16. Ibid., p. 29

17. Ibid., p. 3.

18. *South Dakota Legislative Manual—1921* (Pierre: South Dakota Printing Office, 1921), pp. 223–25.

19. Norbeck, *Governor's Message, 1918*, p. 44.

20. Ibid.

21. Ibid.

22. Ibid., p. 10.

23. Ibid., p. 44.

24. Ibid., p. 16.

25. "Norbeck Discusses Political Issues," *Sioux Falls Daily Argus-Leader*, 15 Oct. 1916.

26. Peter Norbeck, *Governor's Message: State of the State Address, 1921* (Pierre: South Dakota Legislature, 1921), p. 5.

27. Norbeck, *Governor's Message, 1918*, p. 4.

28. *South Dakota Legislative Manual—1917*, (Pierre: South Dakota Printing Office, 1917), p. 119; Alan Clem, *South Dakota Political Almanac* (Vermillion: Dakota Press, 1969), pp. 35–36.

29. Norbeck, *Governor's Message, 1921*, p. 14.

30. Ibid., pp. 43–44

31. Peter Norbeck to Reverend O.H. Olson, n.d., file 2, box 84, Norbeck Papers.

32. Gilbert Fite in *Peter Norbeck* makes a similar argument. He asserts that Norbeck appropriates some of the NPL's policies to reduce the organization's support in the state.

33. *Sioux Falls Argus-Leader*, 1 Nov. 1918.

34. Norbeck, *Governor's Message, 1917*, pp. 31–32.

35. Norbeck to Olaf Eiden, 8 May 1918, file 9, box 52, Norbeck Papers; Norbeck, *Governor's Message, 1918*, pp. 17, 28

36. "N.P. Leader for Bolsheviks," *Sioux Falls Daily Argus-Leader*, 25 Sept. 1918.

37. "Handling the I. W. W.," *Deadwood Daily Call*, 16 July 1917.

38. "Pro-German Activity Seen in Many Fires," *Pierre Weekly Free Press*, 29 Nov. 1917

39. "Norbeck Replies to League Whine," *Sioux Falls Daily Argus-Leader*, 9 Oct. 1918.

40. Norbeck, *Governor's Address, 1918*, p. 3.

41. "Perisho Solves Problem," *Lead Daily Call*, 21 Feb. 1916.

42. *South Dakota Legislative Manual*—1921, p. 238; Larry Remele, "An Experiment in State Sponsored Economy: Peter Norbeck and William Henry McMaster," in *South Dakota Leaders: From Pierre Chouteau, Jr. to Oscar Howe*, ed. Herbert T. Hoover and Larry J. Zimmerman (Vermillion: USD Press, 1989), p. 212.

43. Peter Norbeck, *Governor's Message: State of the State Address, 1919* (Pierre: South Dakota Legislature, 1919), p. 5.

44. Ibid., p. 8.

45. Ibid., p. 5.

46. Ibid.

47. *Fifteenth Biennial Report of the Superintendent of Public Instruction of the State of South Dakota, 1918* (Pierre: South Dakota Department of Education, 1920), p. 25; Norbeck, *Governor's Message, 1921*, p. 3.

48. *Fifteenth Biennial Report*, p. 7.

49. Ibid., p. 30.

50. Ibid., p. 5.

51. Norbeck, *Governor's Message, 1921*, p. 3.

52. Peter Norbeck to Robert Carey, 18 Feb. 1920, file 2, box 95, Norbeck Papers; Norbeck, *Governor's Message, 1917*, p. 22.

53. Ibid., pp. 21–22.

54. Ibid., p. 21.

55. Norbeck, *Governor's Message, 1919*, p. 22.

56. Peter Norbeck to Harry Gandy, 20 Sept. 1919, file 1, box 95, Norbeck Papers.

57. Norbeck, *Governor's Message, 1919*, p. 22.

58. "Practical Considerations," *Sioux Falls Daily Argus-Leader*, 28 Jan. 1919.

59. Larry Remele, "An Experiment in State Sponsored Economy," p. 217

60. Ibid., p. 214; Fite, *Peter Norbeck*, p. 89.

61. Remele, p. 214.

62. Fite, p. ix; Remele, pp. 207–8.

63. Jon Lauck, John Miller, and Edward Hogan made a similar argument in their 2004 article that appeared in *South Dakota History*. They argued that South Dakota is politically conservative, but in hard times reformers can win if they are seen as preserving the state's faming economy. (Lauck, Miller, Hogan, "Historical Musings: The Contours of South Dakota Political Culture," *South Dakota History* 36 [Fall 2006]: 157–78.)

TONNIS H. VENHUIZEN

5 | WILLIAM J. BULOW: THE CONSERVATIVE DEMOCRAT WHO TIME PASSED BY

• • •

The year 1924 was a watershed moment for South Dakota's progressive Republicans. William H. McMaster, a Yankton banker, was completing his final year as the state's tenth governor, and was the fifth in a row to belong to the state's the progressive Republican faction. That year, McMaster was easily elected to the U.S. Senate, where he joined South Dakota's greatest progressive, former governor Peter Norbeck, and other notable progressives such as Wisconsin's Robert La Follette and Nebraska's George W. Norris. McMaster had carried out Norbeck's plans for a state cement plant and had administered the state rural credits program, which made direct state loans to farmers. He had also made his own mark by taking on "unconscionable" gasoline prices, competing head on with wholesalers by selling gasoline directly to consumers from state highway shops.[1]

In fact, 1924 would mark the beginning of the end of the progressive movement in South Dakota. That fall, the governor's office was won by Carl Gunderson, a conservative or "stalwart" Republican who would commit his tenure to investigating and dismantling the progressive agenda. The farm crisis of the late 1920s brought about the collapse of the rural credits program, as farmers defaulted and turned over land that had been bought at inflated prices.[2]

The next two decades—from the 1924 election until the 1942 election—brought about an unsettled era in South Dakota politics. For the first time, the Democratic Party became competitive with Republicans, even as the Democrats vacillated between the party's agrarian, Jeffersonian roots and the new, liberal direction set by President Franklin D. Roosevelt, who sought to expand the power of the central state. Looming large over this era were the first two Democrats to be elected governor of South Dakota: William J. "Bill" Bulow and Thomas M. "Tom" Berry.

When South Dakota achieved statehood in 1889, the Democratic Party was a weak force in the state's politics. The first state legislature included 143 Republican legislators, and only 20 Democrats.[3] The state's first governor, Republican Arthur C. Mellette, prevailed over his Democratic opponent, P. F. McClure, by nearly 40 percent.[4] The Democratic Party's fortunes didn't improve markedly over the next two decades; ten of the state's first eleven governors were Republicans, and the Democratic Party didn't elect any candidate to statewide or federal office, without relying on a coalition with other parties for support, until 1914.[5]

The only success the Democrats achieved during this period was in fusion with other parties or factions. The 1890s had brought the Populist movement to South Dakota. In 1896, Nebraskan William Jennings Bryan, a Democrat, carried South Dakota in the presidential election, running on a joint Democratic-Populist ticket.[6] That same year, a Populist-Democratic "fusion" ticket in South Dakota won both U.S. House seats and the governor's race as Andrew E. Lee, a Populist who also enjoyed the support of "Free Silver Republican" U.S. senator Richard F. Pettigrew, was elected governor.[7]

The Democratic-Populist fusion, although it narrowly elected Lee as governor in 1896 and 1898, collapsed after it lost the election for governor in 1900.[8] The demise of the fusion with the Populists in South Dakota coincided nationally with Theodore Roosevelt's succession to the presidency in 1901. Roosevelt brought "progressivism" into the mainstream of the Republican Party, sapping the reformist energy from the Populist movement and leaving the South Dakota Democrats, once again, a spent force.[9] The party's nominees for governor failed to win even 30 percent of the vote in 1902, 1904, or 1906.[10]

The election of 1906 was significant for the emergence of Coe I. Crawford, a former railroad executive and attorney general, as the state's first progressive Republican to be elected statewide. Crawford won the governor's race in 1906, after grabbing the Republican nomination from incumbent Samuel H. Elrod, a conservative. Two years later, in 1908, he mounted a successful primary challenge against the conservative Republican "boss," U.S. senator Alfred B. Kittridge. Crawford also orchestrated the nomination of fellow progressive Robert S. Vessey to succeed him as governor, and over the next fifteen years, the governor's chair remained in progressive hands.[11]

During this time, the only Democrat who achieved any electoral victories was Edwin S. Johnson. Johnson's electoral success was due, though, to his ability to capitalize on fissures within the Republican coalition. In 1912, Republicans were split by the competing presidential candidacies of incumbent William Howard Taft and of Theodore Roosevelt, running his famous "Bull Moose" progressive campaign. Johnson ran for governor that year, losing to Republican Frank M. Byrne by less than 3 percent. In 1914, the first year of direct election of U.S. senators, Senator Crawford was defeated in the Republican primary by conservative Charles H. Burke. Johnson took advantage of the split to win a seat in the U.S. Senate, the first Democrat to win statewide office in South Dakota's history.[12]

Notwithstanding Johnson's success, though, the 1910s were an era of domination by South Dakota's progressive Republicans, and the era reached its apogee in 1916 with the election of Peter Norbeck as governor. Norbeck overcame divisions within the party to win broad support from conservatives as well as progressives.[13] At its core, Norbeck progressivism was conservative, in that he sought to conserve and protect South Dakota's agrarian way of life: small farms and ranches, traditional values, and the outdoors. Even when Norbeck's programs were activist and reformist, such as the creation of Custer State Park or the establishment of a state-owned cement plant, a flour mill, and a coal mine, his motives were ultimately conservative in their nature. He did not seek to remake South Dakota but rather to protect it from outside interference.[14] Likewise, his successor, William H. McMaster, continued Norbeck's programs and took on big business interests when he sold gasoline from state highway shops at two cents above wholesale to hold down retail costs. McMaster won election to the U.S. Senate in 1924, joining Norbeck.[15]

By that year, though, Norbeck progressivism was beginning to fray. Norbeck himself remained personally popular, as he would for the rest of his life, having won election to the U.S. Senate in 1920.[16] Nationally, though, the progressive movement had lost steam with the passing in 1919 of Theodore Roosevelt, the departure from office in 1921 of President Woodrow Wilson (a progressive Democrat), and the election in 1920 of President Warren G. Harding. Harding promised "a return to normalcy" to a nation fatigued by reform and war. After Harding's death in 1923, his successor, Calvin Coolidge, took a lasseiz-faire approach, famously declaring that "the chief business of the American people is business."[17]

The Republican nominee for governor in 1924 was Lieutenant Governor Carl Gunderson. A longtime legislator, Gunderson was a Clay County native who had relocated to Mitchell; he had farming interests in both areas. Like President Coolidge, Gunderson was known to be "exceptionally closed-mouthed," and he also touted fiscal conservatism. Gunderson was acceptable to progressive Republicans too, however, and he won the Republican nomination without opposition.[18]

Gunderson's Democratic opponent was Andrew S. Anderson, a farmer and state legislator from Beresford. Anderson had easily won the Democratic nomination with 73 percent in the primary.[19] He did not live to compete in the general election, however. As the 12 August 1924 *Sioux Falls Daily Argus-Leader* explained it:

> Mr. Anderson went to the pasture to drive in the milk cows early in the morning. When he did not return to the barn yard as quickly as it was thought he should, Elmer Westling, 20 years old, who had been working on the Anderson place, went to the pasture to investigate. He found a drove of cattle surrounding a spot and acting in an excited manner. Fearing that Mr. Anderson had been killed or injured, the young man summoned members of a threshing crew who hurried to the scene, drove the cattle away and found Mr. Anderson dead.
>
> It is believed Mr. Anderson was attacked by the animal from the side or rear and that he did not notice it until he had been knocked down. His chest was badly crushed and it is believed death was practically instantaneous. His body was not badly mangled as the bull which made the attack has no horns. The animal is 18 months old and was not known to be vicious.[20]

Three months before election day and suddenly lacking a candidate, the Democratic Party turned to Beresford attorney William Bulow, a fellow Beresford native and a friend of Anderson. Writing his own memoirs years later, Bulow would describe the death of Anderson as follows:

> Andrew S. Anderson was the Democratic nominee for governor. A few weeks before the election he walked out into the pasture.

William J. Bulow listens to a presentation in Washington, D.C., on 5 July 1939.
Library of Congress

> The pasture was the domain filled by the bull. The bull would not stand for any intrusion on his domain and hocked, and bunted, and trampled Mr. Anderson to death. This created a vacancy of the ticket and the Democratic State Central Committee filled that vacancy by having my name printed on the ticket.[21]

Bulow would go on to recall of his abbreviated 1924 candidacy:

> I was not acquainted over much of the state, and was only known over a little corner in the southeastern part of the state where I had practiced law, bought and sold real estate, and had done quite a bit of farming. South Dakota is a mighty big state and the few days that I had before election did not give sufficient time to get acquainted. I did the best I could and got gloriously beaten. I wasn't much disappointed, as I had expected to be beaten. I enjoyed the campaign very much and had a lot of fun, and discovered that South Dakota had a wonderful lot of mighty good people, and I enjoyed very much getting acquainted with them.[22]

Gunderson defeated Bulow in 1924, winning 53.9 percent of the vote, with Bulow at 22.9 percent and two other candidates combined for 23.3 percent. It was a result typical of the era. South Dakotans in 1924 supported Coolidge's reelection bid over that of progressive U.S. senator Robert La Follette of Wisconsin, who ran on a third-party ticket. Outgoing governor McMaster was elected to the U.S. Senate, Republican incumbents held all three U.S. House seats, and the Republicans won every statewide election.[23]

Once in office, Gunderson displayed his conservative philosophy, as he forced state agencies to accept an 8 percent budget cut, created a state budgeting process, attempted to close several normal schools, and tried to reorganize state government into just two departments. He signed progressive legislation to create commodity marketing associations.[24]

Gunderson broke with Norbeck, though, by opposing state funding of the construction of Mount Rushmore, and he even proposed that Custer State Park, Norbeck's signature gubernatorial achievement, be turned over to the federal government as a cost-saving measure.[25] In 1925, the South Dakota Supreme Court struck down the state's direct involvement in the retail gasoline market, requiring Gunderson to end McMaster's outstanding achievement as governor.[26]

Gunderson also presided over the demise of the rural credits program. As the farm economy collapsed, the state rural credits program became insolvent. The program had made loans to farmers against land based on inflated land prices. Falling commodity prices led farmers to default on payments, and plummeting land prices meant that even the value of the land couldn't cover the cost of the loan. The end result was a $57 million deficit in the rural credits program.[27]

Gunderson launched an investigation into the rural credits program, ultimately discovering embezzlement and comingling of funds by the treasurer of the rural credits board. This malfeasance hadn't caused the demise of the program—the farm economy was to blame for that—but it did allow Gunderson to point the finger back at the Norbeck and McMaster administrations for mismanagement. In doing so, Gunderson spared himself from blame, but he also earned the enmity of the remaining progressive Norbeck loyalists.[28]

Following his 1924 loss, Bulow returned to his Beresford law office. The governorship had never been Bulow's ambition. Bulow had been born in an Ohio log cabin on 13 January 1869. His parents were German immigrants, and he grew up speaking their native tongue. Schooling was intermittent as he worked on his father's farms, but as he reached his late teens, Bulow became more committed to his education.[29] Eventually, he was mentored by A. G. Turnipseed, who encouraged him to go to law school at the University of Michigan. As Bulow wrote in his memoirs, Turnipseed, who was also enrolling at the school, went to great lengths to help Bulow achieve admission:

> When I first went to Ann Arbor with Prof. Turnipseed, we were not at all sure that I could get in. The entry requirement then was either a diploma from high school, or to pass an entrance examination on American and English history. I felt fairly sure that I could make the grade on American history, but I had serious doubts about English history.
>
> Prof. Turnipseed and I registered together and paid our matriculation fee together. He submitted his credentials and was okay. I had no credentials to submit and had to take my place on

> the mourners bench for a period of probation. The dean gave me a certificate telling me when and where the examination would be given. When that time came there were more than a dozen other boys to write that examination. They all were strangers and we knew none of them and none of them knew us. We were reasonably sure that none of the examining board knew Turnipseed from Bulow, nor Bulow from Turnipseed. I was afraid of the examination. So I appointed the Professor, as my attorney-in-fact, to write that examination for me. I passed. I passed with flying colors and entered upon the study of law in the great University of Michigan and my real hard work as a student began.[30]

It was on this basis that Bulow would attend and graduate from the University of Michigan. He found his way to Sioux Falls, where he was hired by Joe Kirby, one of the state's early leaders and the forefather of a prominent Sioux Falls family:

> When I arrived in Sioux Falls I looked up my classmate George Jeffries and he took me up to Joe Kirby's law office and introduced me. C. A. Christopherson had been working for Mr. Kirby, but he had just opened up a law office of his own. I hired out to Joe Kirby for one year—twenty dollars per month for the first six months and forty dollars per months for the last six months—but Kirby fired me before I got into the higher pay brackets. When I hired out to Kirby, his office was in the Edmison-Jameson building; C.A. Christopherson officed in the same building. Kirby took me to Christopherson's office and introduced me, saying, "Charley, this is Billy. I have just hired him. Get him a place to sleep and eat at your boarding house." So saying, Kirby left and put it up to Charley and I to talk things over.[31]

Bulow's lifelong friend "Charley" Christopherson was a Republican. He would later serve South Dakota's First District, which included Sioux Falls, in the U.S. House from 1919 to 1933.[32]

Kirby helped Bulow travel to Beresford and establish himself in the young and growing city. In Beresford, Bulow established a prosperous practice and invested in farmland. He served one term in the State Senate from 1899 to 1901, but lost reelection and gave up on state politics. Instead, he focused on local affairs, serving as city attorney from

1902 until 1927, with a two-year gap during which he served as mayor. The 1920s farm crisis affected Bulow's practice since many of his clients were farmers; it also affected him personally as his investments in farmland turned upside down.[33]

Bulow had enjoyed his abbreviated 1924 campaign for governor and when the Democrats asked him to run again in 1926, challenging Governor Gunderson's reelection, he happily accepted:

> At the end of that campaign I went back to the practice of law and my farming activities with enthusiasm, deciding that this was my last fling in politics, that my political sun had set for good; in fact it had never risen. But when the next Democratic convention met, I was not hard to persuade to make another campaign because I had enjoyed the first one so very much. I started in immediately after the convention, and during the summer and fall I visited about every nook and corner of the state. I made use of every mode of conveyance there was except flying. I did not use the airplane but did use the railroads, automobiles, horse and buggy, and horseback riding; where a horse could not go, I walked and had a lot of fun and a real good time.
>
> At the close of the campaign, I was hopeful that I would do considerably better than I had done two years before, but I did not expect to be elected. My friend Mr. Gunderson did not expect to be defeated. When they got through counting the vote, there were two of us very much surprised.[34]

Bulow had achieved an improbable victory, winning 47.4 percent to Gunderson's 40.3 percent and 12.3 percent for two other candidates.[35] Gunderson's loss to Bulow in 1926 was a surprise. In the fourteen previous elections for governor, South Dakotans had elected Republicans twelve times, usually by large margins, and had twice elected the Populist Andrew E. Lee, who won with Democratic support. Bulow was the first Democrat to be elected governor of South Dakota.[36]

As for Gunderson, he earned the ignominious distinction of being the first South Dakota governor to lose reelection in a general election. Although Democrats tend to perform well in South Dakota during bad times for farmers, Gunderson's loss was a personal blow. He was the only Republican to lose statewide in 1926. South Dakota voters reelected Senator Norbeck, reelected all three Republican congressmen, and elected Republicans to every other statewide office. Gunderson stood alone in his defeat.[37]

Gunderson's antagonism toward Norbeck-era progressivism likely led some Norbeck loyalists to consider defecting from Gunderson in 1926. Bulow recorded his impressions from the 1926 campaign:

> I knew that my friend Carl Gunderson had made a good governor, but in running the office of governor he had made most everybody mad. He had a peculiar way about him, and even if he gave people everything and all that they asked for and wanted, he would make them mad by the way he gave it to them. He had a peculiar way of doing a thing right and making the people believe he was doing wrong. The few that Carl did not make mad himself, his wife had by her activities as the First Lady of the state. I took advantage of everything I heard, as best I could, without spending too much time to make things easy for my friend Carl. I had not been so much concerned about how much people loved me, but I was concerned to learn that they loved Carl less. I never knew before that a person could make so many people mad when he gave them what they asked for.[38]

Writing in 2012, historian John E. Miller offered a similar justification for Bulow's win:

> Bulow's win came about not primarily because of his own endowments or because of the splendid organizing and campaigning abilities of the Democratic party. Rather, he happened to be in the right place at the right time. Although a number of clues point to consideration disgruntlement and ferment within the Republican party, little has been written about this aspect. It is truer to say that the Republicans lost the 1926 election than that the Democrats won it, although the latter certainly benefited from the situation.[39]

Bulow, a likeable, plain-spoken, and conservative Democrat, profited from Gunderson's "peculiar way," and found himself as the state's first Democratic governor.

Bulow was sworn in as governor in January 1927. As he took office, he knew that he faced an uphill battle, since the State Legislature re-

Bulow and his wife, Sarah, attend the Black Hills Roundup in Belle Fourche while he served as governor.
South Dakota State Archives

mained overwhelmingly Republican, and there was no precedent for a Democrat in the governor's office. As he recalled:

> The senate had a membership of forty-five. Sixteen were Democrats—just enough to sustain a veto if all of them stayed put. I based a lot of hope upon those sixteen Democratic members to keep the Republicans from passing any law over my veto, and that loyal bunch stayed by me in good shape. Before going to Pierre, I was not sure that these Republican statesmen would have anything to do with me—I was not sure that they would even speak to me, in as much as I had called them many different kinds of names during the campaign. But after I had made my inauguration speech and been sworn in twice, and everybody knew that I was governor, that Republican bunch gave me a reception in the rotunda of the capitol building. They stood me up and all the Republicans came marching by and shook hands with me. They all looked very pleasant and happy and none of them seemed to be mad. I felt a good deal better after the reception.[40]

The good feelings wouldn't last, though. The day after the inauguration, the Republican-controlled Senate convened and confirmed all the appointments that Governor Gunderson had made during the nearly two years since the previous legislative session. When Governor Bulow attempted to fill these offices himself, the Senate refused to consider his appointments, informing him that there were no vacancies to be filled.[41]

Bulow soon got the better of the Republican legislature, however, and in doing so he demonstrated his credentials as a fiscal conservative. He would later explain the hard line he had drawn during his 1926 campaign:

> I had made my campaign stressing a balanced budget. That state expenses must be kept within revenue income. I said that if we continued to expand each year in excess of revenue income, and without giving any attention to revenue income. We were headed for bankruptcy. The Republican stewardship had been wrong and there needed to be a change. I told people that when I came to the state as a young man, the state then had no bonded indebtedness. It was then the boast of the people of South Dakota that the state had the highest per capita income, and the lowest per capita tax, of any state in the union, but under the Republican stewardship over the years, we now had a bonded debt of over sixty-five million dollars, and we were fast approaching the record of becoming the highest per capita debt of any state in the union.[42] I said that this thing had to stop – this reckless spending without regard to revenue income had to be halted. I put great stress on this in my message to the legislature and gave the members of that body to understand that I would not approve appropriations in excess of revenue income.[43]

But despite that, the 1927 legislature passed a state budget in which expenditures exceeded projected revenues by more than a million dollars. Bulow vetoed the general appropriations act, reminding legislators of his hard line, and asked them to either cut spending or raise taxes. The House of Representatives, which Republicans controlled by a margin of eighty-one to twenty-one, easily overrode Bulow's veto, but in the Senate, Bulow's sixteen Democratic colleagues supported him, upholding his veto.[44]

It became a political standoff, and Bulow made it clear that he wouldn't budge:

> [The overriding of the veto] made the Republican legislative members awfully mad, and they decided not to pass any other appropriation bill. They had ample time in which to do so before the sixty-day limitation of the session expired, but they decided not to do so. They sent word to me and wanted to know how I was going to collect my salary and how I was going to run the governor's office after the first day of July when all appropriations expired and there would be no money to pay me. I sent word back that I did not need any money to run the governor's office; that all I needed to run that office was plenty of chewing tobacco, and a few good Democrats had agreed to supply that. I was going to get along all right, but I was wondering what all the Republican officeholders were going to do after July 1st.[45]

Republican legislators filed a lawsuit, contending that Bulow's gubernatorial veto authority did not extend to a general appropriations bill. This argument was rejected unanimously by the State Supreme Court, which upheld Bulow's veto.[46] Bulow called a special session for June, shortly before the end of the state's fiscal year:

> When the legislature reassembled, everyone was in better humor. The legislative members had visited with "the boys back home" and had discovered that the "boys back home" were not particularly mad at the governor and were in favor of cutting down state expenses. We had no difficulty in getting together on a new appropriation bill and fixed it so that all the boys on state payroll had a little money to spend in celebrating the 4th of July.[47]

Bulow had prevailed over the Republican legislature, and in doing so had cemented his image with the public as a sensible administrator, a fiscal conservative, and a good-humored everyman who was liked by Republicans and Democrats alike. Bulow's image was further enhanced in 1927 when he helped Senator Norbeck host President Coolidge at the State Game Lodge in Custer State Park, and supported Norbeck's effort to create Mount Rushmore.[48] On the strength of this record, Bulow was reelected in 1928 with 52.5 percent to 46.9 percent for Attorney General Buell F. Jones, the Republican nominee.[49]

The Great Depression began in October 1929 with the stock market crash. Although South Dakota had been suffering under the farm crisis for years, the depression began a new chapter in the economic struggle. Even in South Dakota, voters turned against President Herbert Hoover and the Republicans in Washington who failed to effectively respond to the depression.[50] Bulow, ending his second term as governor in 1930, capitalized with a bid for U.S. Senate, challenging McMaster, the progressive Republican and former governor, in McMaster's bid for a second term. Bulow won a narrow victory with 51.6 percent to 48.4 percent for McMaster, and he joined the U.S. Senate in 1931.[51]

The Election of 1932 was a Democratic landslide of historic proportions. Franklin D. Roosevelt was elected President of the United States, defeating President Hoover and winning the electoral votes of many Republican strongholds, including South Dakota.[52] At the state level, South Dakota voters also dramatically turned to the Democrats. Both incumbent Republican congressmen, including Bulow's old friend C. A. Christopherson, were defeated, and Democrats swept every statewide office and won control of the State Legislature. Warren Green, the obscure farmer and former legislator whom Republicans had nominated for governor as a compromise in 1930, lost reelection to another charismatic Democrat, Tom Berry.[53]

On first impression, Tom Berry could have been a West River version of Bulow. Berry biographer Paul Higbee wrote of the pair: "[T]he two Democrats resembled each other in manner – both were business-savvy, wry, unafraid of conflict and fond of tobacco and wisecracks . . . To Berry's delight, Bulow became the state's first Democratic governor."[54] Berry was a native Nebraskan who had come to South Dakota to ranch, eventually settling in Mellette County. After President Theodore Roosevelt ordered sixteen open range cattle operations to clear fifty thousand head of cattle from the Pine Ridge and Rosebud reservations, Berry joined 450 others as the "Cowboys of 1902" in what was remembered as "the last great cattle roundup on the open range." Berry spent six years in the State House, serving in the minority while Bulow was governor.[55] Bulow would write of Berry:

> Tom Berry and I had been good friends for many years. I always liked Tom. I liked his wit and humor. I liked his showmanship. Tom Berry was a great showman. He liked the limelight. He al-

ways wanted to be in the center of the stage where the lights were the brightest.[56]

In 1932, Berry threw his cowboy hat in the gubernatorial ring against Warren Green. Berry traveled the state with a hatchet and ran on the slogan "Tom Berry will use the axe" as he pledged to cut state spending by 25 percent amidst the Great Depression.[57]

Once in office, Berry was true to his word and achieved the promised 25 percent cut. He cut higher education by 40 percent, reduced the state payroll by 10 percent, and ended progressive programs such as the state coal mine, state hail insurance, and the state bonding department. Berry eliminated the state property tax levy, replacing it in part with a protectionist tax on "chain stores" (as opposed to those that were locally owned).[58]

Berry diverted half of the state gasoline tax from highway maintenance to retirement of the rural credits debt. He established an "ore tax" to capitalize on the Homestake Gold Mine in Lead. After the prohibition of alcohol was repealed, Berry pushed to legalize and tax alcohol, making it an important state revenue source.[59]

Amidst all the budget cutting and tax raising, Berry found himself in a disagreement within his own party over the creation of an income tax. Berry himself favored a 1 percent *gross* income tax—that is, a tax on income that didn't allow any deductions for expenses. He saw this as a tax that was fair and easy to administer. Farm organizations, however, strongly objected, as in some years a farmer's expenses could overtake his gross income. They advocated instead for a *net* income tax, which would address this concern but bring in considerably less revenue.[60]

Berry ultimately folded to pressure from the farm organizations, agreeing to a net income tax and a two-cent state sales tax. The breach led, though, to a primary challenge in 1934 from the lieutenant governor, Hans Ustrud, who criticized Berry's budget cuts and advocated for the big spending approach taken by President Roosevelt's New Deal.[61]

Berry easily repelled Ustrud's challenge, winning the primary with 79.3 percent of the vote, but he ultimately followed the path that Ustrud advocated.[62] Berry made himself the state relief director, the only governor in the country to personally take on administration of the

New Deal's "alphabet soup" of relief programs.[63] He created a State Planning Commission to institute "scientific central planning" in the state's economy.[64] His enthusiasm for Roosevelt grew to such an extent that at the 1936 Democratic National Convention, it was Berry who moved to dispense with a roll call vote and renominate FDR by acclamation.[65]

Bulow entered the U.S. Senate in 1931. He carried to Washington his agrarian roots and the same fiscal conservatism that he had applied as governor. In later years, he would hearken back to Thomas Jefferson as the ideal of these principles and the founder of the Democratic Republicans.

Two years later, in 1933, Bulow did not join Berry, and most other Democrats, in becoming a disciple of the newly inaugurated President Roosevelt. Rather, Bulow quickly became a critic of Roosevelt and the New Deal, finding it to be anathema to the Jeffersonian values that Bulow himself espoused:

> Unfortunately, at a time when the lean years had brought on drastic economic readjustments, and the nation and its people were passing through a crucial test the administration of government came into control of men who undertook to plan the future without any regard for the experiences of the past. The New Deal was created. The policies and politics of the New Deal were substituted for the time-tried and tested rules set forth in the Constitution as guides . . . The Democratic theory of government, that the people are best governed when least government, cannot be reconciled with the theory of the New Deal, "leave everything to the planning of the Great White Father who will take care of all of the people's needs." The transition from our Democratic form of government to that of the New Deal was remarkable and swift. It was no gradual economic or political evolution, brought about gradually, over the ages but it came all of a sudden like the crash of a thunderbolt. People went to bed the evening a new President was inaugurated, a new pilot was guiding the Ship of State. They woke up the next morning and could not find any place where their check could be cashed no matter how much money they had in the bank. All banks were closed. The New Deal had ordered all banks closed; had ordered all money to be locked up in

the banks and to be kept locked up until further orders. In due course of time the New Deal would decide what to do.[66]

Despite Bulow's opposition, Roosevelt's leadership during the Great Depression made him a heavy favorite when he sought a second term in 1936. South Dakota joined all but two states in casting its electoral votes for Roosevelt against the Republican challenger, Governor Alfred M. Landon of Kansas.[67] Bulow was also reelected in 1936, winning a second term in the U.S. Senate against Chan Gurney, a conservative Republican. Gurney was a Sioux Falls businessman and a member of the family that owned Gurney's Seed and WNAX radio in Yankton.[68]

South Dakota Democrats were already descending from the peak of 1932, however. Republicans in 1936 dashed Berry's reelection hopes, denying him a place in history as the first South Dakota governor to win a third consecutive term.[69] Berry was defeated by Leslie Jensen, a Hot Springs businessman who owned the local telephone company. Jensen's victory was narrow, as he won 51.6 percent to 48.4 percent for Berry.[70] Although Democrats won most statewide offices, Republicans retook control of the State House of Representatives and came within one seat of retaking the State Senate.[71]

Jensen, a political newcomer, considered himself a Norbeck loyalist. His campaign platform, however, with its commitment to sound financial management and non-political operation of state government, was reminiscent of Bulow's.[72]

In December 1936, Norbeck died in Redfield. His death created a potential opening for Berry, now a lame duck governor. Berry had run for reelection in 1936, in part, to set himself up to run for the U.S. Senate in 1938 and, despite his reelection loss, he still hoped to seek the Senate seat. Following Norbeck's death, the most straightforward way for Berry to enter the Senate would have been to resign as governor, so that Lieutenant Governor Robert Peterson could succeed Berry as governor and then appoint Berry to succeed Norbeck. Although there was much speculation that Berry would do exactly that, Peterson was under investigation for embezzlement from his Centerville bank. Berry did not feel that he could turn the governor's office over to a man in such a situation. Rather, Berry appointed as a caretaker Herbert Hitchcock, an aging Democratic official from Mitchell.[73]

Bulow would write that Berry erred in seeking a third term, and believed that it prevented Berry from entering the U.S. Senate:

> The people of South Dakota were not for a third term for anyone. Senator Norbeck died when Tom Berry's second term as governor was ending. Had Tom Berry not run for a third term, the Democrats would have elected any other candidate with the ticket. The new governor-elect could have, and no doubt would have, appointed Tom Berry to the United States Senate to fill the unexpired term of Senator Norbeck. Tom still blames everyone else, except himself, for his failure to get a seat in the United States Senate.[74]

In February 1937, President Roosevelt, frustrated by rulings of the United States Supreme Court that stifled his attempts to increase federal control of the economy, unveiled the Judicial Procedures Reform Bill of 1937, commonly known as the "court-packing plan." As Bulow would write:

> The Supreme Court was a stumbling block in his road to success. When he found that the members of that court were independent and that he could not impose his will upon them, he undertook to change the personal of that court and substitute judges of his own selection. . . . It did not take me long to make up my mind as to how I would vote, when that time came, but I said nothing about it.[75]

As a Jeffersonian Democrat, Bulow's commitment to small government once again placed him in opposition to Roosevelt. He joined a group of Democratic senators who decided to unite in opposition to the court-packing plan; they asked Vice President John Nance Garner to deliver the message to the President that the bill would be defeated. Their action handed Roosevelt, who was just beginning his second term, the first major legislative defeat of his presidency. Bulow suffered the consequences:

> The President did not take his defeat gracefully. He was not a good loser. He became embittered at those who had disobeyed his orders, at least embittered at some of them. I never was again invited to the White House. I had had many pleasant visits with the

President and had enjoyed those visits very much. The end of the court fight was the end of those visits. It also was the end of the administration pressure to shape legislation so far as I was concerned. I was charged off of the President's book as a total loss.[76]

Berry made his first bid for U.S. Senate in 1938. Perhaps to his surprise, Berry's "caretaker" senator, Herbert Hitchcock, grew comfortable in the U.S. Senate and sought election to a full term. Berry found himself in the unusual position of challenging his own appointee, but overcame the oddity to handily win the Democratic primary. Berry won nearly two-thirds of the vote in a primary field that also included Congressman Fred H. Hildebrandt, who represented the state's East River First U.S. House district.[77]

Berry's Republican opponent was Chan Gurney, the conservative businessman whom Bulow had defeated two years prior. Gurney had won the nomination against Governor Jensen, who forewent a second term as governor to run for U.S. Senate.[78]

In addition to Gurney, the Republican ticket in 1938 featured two newcomers from the conservative wing of the party. Running to succeed Jensen as governor was Harlan J. Bushfield, a Miller attorney who, like Bulow, espoused Jefferson as his political model.[79] The nominee for First District U.S. House, taking the place of Hildebrandt, was Karl E. Mundt, a Madison professor known for his isolationist views.[80] Bushfield and Mundt were opposed, respectively, by Oscar Fosheim and Emil Loriks, two New Deal Democratic state legislators who were known as the "Gold Dust twins" for their efforts to tax gold extracted from the Homestake Mine.[81]

The 1938 election was a triumph for the Republicans, as Gurney, Bushfield, and Mundt were elected. It was a setback for Berry and his fellow New Dealers, Fosheim and Loriks, and signaled that the Democrat ascendancy of 1932 had come to an end. Republican Francis Case, the incumbent congressman for the Second District, was reelected, and Republicans swept statewide offices and won control of the State Legislature.[82]

The election also signaled the end of progressivism in the Republican Party. The progressive faction had emerged in 1904, been a dominant force throughout the 1910s and early 1920s, and remained relevant as long as Norbeck served in the U.S. Senate. With Norbeck's death, and the defeat of his loyalist Leslie Jensen in the Senate race to take Norbeck's place, the South Dakota Republican Party returned to its roots as a conservative party.

The Japanese attacked Pearl Harbor, an American naval base in its Hawaiian territory, on 7 December 1941. Throughout the 1930s, as Nazi Germany marched throughout Europe and the Japanese Empire asserted itself in the Pacific, Americans had resisted involvement in another foreign war. The attack on Pearl Harbor brought the war to America, though, and isolationists including Bulow and Mundt rallied behind President Roosevelt's call for a declaration of war against Japan on 8 December 1941.[83]

Bulow's career had been built upon his commitment to Jeffersonian Democracy. He had seen his domestic policies of limited government and fiscal conservatism fall prey to FDR's New Deal amidst the Great Depression. Now, nearly ten years later, Bulow's commitment to isolationism had likewise been overtaken by events. Although Bulow backed the declaration of war after Pearl Harbor, he continued to blame Roosevelt's interventionism for drawing the United States into the war:

> Up to Pearl Harbor, in the votes I cast, I reflected the wish of the overwhelming majority of the people I represented in my attempt to keep them out of war. After Pearl Harbor most of these people seemed to feel that I made a mistake and that I should have joined with the administration and put them into war. . . . Had the isolationists had their way, Pearl Harbor never would have happened. Had they have had their way, we never would have gotten into this war, but that is now a thing of the past. Isolationists and interventionists met and merged at Pearl Harbor, and from there, marched together in an effort to win the war, and while the war was on, they were in step to win the war as quickly as possible.[84]

By 1942, Bulow found that as a Jeffersonian Democrat, he was increasingly out of place in the modern Democratic Party of Franklin Roosevelt. Berry, still ambitious to enter to U.S. Senate, recognized Bulow's vulnerability and mounted a challenge. Emphasizing his support of Roosevelt, Berry prevailed handily in the primary, winning 64.6 percent to 27.8 percent for Bulow and 7.6 percent for Edward Prchal.[85]

Berry, though, found himself on the wrong side in the general election. Berry's New Deal Democratic platform was no longer competitive against the conservativism of the South Dakota Republicans, who nominated outgoing governor Harlan Bushfield. Bushfield won 58.7 percent to 41.3 percent for Berry, who retired from politics after the loss.[86]

Bulow was bitter about his 1942 loss, but remarkably clear eyed about what had happened:

> The man who beat me [Berry] says that he never would have tried it had I obeyed the orders of the President. I, myself, am to blame for that disobedience. Had I obeyed the orders of Mr. Roosevelt and been a rubber stamp senator, I could have had the nomination, but I would have lost, and ought to have lost, the election in the fall.[87] The Democratic state organization does not seem to realize that it takes more than Democratic votes for a Democrat to win an election in South Dakota, especially at a time when the Democratic organization was at a low ebb.[88]

Bushfield served in the U.S. Senate for nearly six years, dying near the end of his single term.[89] His seat in 1948 was won by Karl Mundt, who would hold it for the next twenty-four years.[90] The Republican Party from 1938 to 1954 would win 101 straight victories in federal and statewide contests, still the longest such streak in state history.[91]

William J. Bulow entered statewide politics taking on Peter Norbeck's Republican Party and left his seat to the Republican Party of Karl Mundt. As a charismatic Jeffersonian Democrat, Bulow represented a clear alternative to the Norbeck progressives, with a commitment to balanced budgets, small government, an isolationist foreign policy, and an agrarian sensibility. It was a winning formula in South Dakota, as Bulow was undefeated in the four general elections he contested—not including his 1924 campaign—making him the state's first Democratic governor and the first Democrat to serve the state for two terms in the U.S. Senate.

South Dakota Democrats could perhaps have remained competitive had they maintained Bulow's Jeffersonian track. The rise of Tom Berry, in the Roosevelt wave of 1932, took the Democratic Party in an entirely different direction, in support of government intervention in the economy, the New Deal's panoply of new programs, and an interventionist foreign policy. It was a formula for success in the short term, but once Roosevelt's popularity faded in the state, Democrats were uncompetitive once again. Bulow's time had passed.

Following Bulow's defeat, Karl Mundt paid tribute to him on the floor of the U.S. House of Representatives:

> A Democrat of the school of Thomas Jefferson, Senator Bulow was never blinded by the seductive theories of the New Dealism and resisted all trends towards collectivism in America with as much vigor as the most ardent of Republicans. Having come up the hard way, Mr. Bulow knows the value of a dollar and refused to accept the theory that a nation can spend itself rich or borrow itself prosperous.[92]

As for Bulow, in the end he gave credit to where it all started:

> Had that bull not created that vacancy I never would have run for governor. If I had not run, I never would have been elected. Had I not been elected governor I never would have run for, nor been elected to the senate. Had I never been elected to the senate the Democrats would never have had a chance to put me out of a job in 1942 and fixed it so that I would have nothing to do but write a book. That roan bull was to blame for the whole thing; yet, it was no premeditated aforethought on the part of the bull. He acted on the spur of the moment. He did not intend the consequences of his act. He apparently did not know what he was doing.[93]

William J. Bulow's political career was launched by happenstance—as he would say, by the bull. Over sixteen years, he served South Dakota as a Jeffersonian Democrat, committed to small government, fiscal conservatism, and isolationism. That philosophy led him to four election wins, but time placed him in opposition to Franklin D. Roosevelt and ultimately ended his political career at the hands of Tom Berry. It was only fitting that the final tribute to Bulow came from Karl Mundt, the dominant figure of the conservative Republican era that followed that of Bulow.

NOTES

1. Larry Pressler, *U.S. Senators from the Prairie* (Vermillion: Dakota Press, 1982), p. 91; Tonnis H. Venhuizen, "Leaders in the Land of Infinite Variety: A Collective Portrait of South Dakota Governors," *The Plains Political Tradition: Essays on South Dakota Political Culture,* Vol. 2, ed. Jon K. Lauck, John E. Miller, and Donald C. Simmons, Jr. (Pierre: South Dakota Historical Society Press, 2014), pp. 242–86, 252.

2. Herbert S. Schell and John E. Miller, *History of South Dakota,* revised edition (Pierre: South Dakota State Historical Society Press, 2004), pp. 277–78; Alan L. Clem, *Prairie State Politics: Popular Democracy in South Dakota*, (Washington, D.C.: Public Affairs Press, 1967), p. 7.

3. "Historical Listing," South Dakota State Legislature, Legislative Research Council, https://sdlegislature.gov/Legislators/Historical.

4. South Dakota Secretary of State, *South Dakota Election History 1889–2014*, vol. 1 (Pierre: Curt Merriman Printing, 2014), p. 4. Mellette had been the last Dakota territorial governor and was a leading statehood advocate. William O. Farber, "From Territorial Status to Statehood: Arthur Calvin Mellette," in *South Dakota Leaders: From Pierre Chouteau, Jr. to Oscar Howe*, ed. Herbert T. Hoover and Larry J. Zimmerman (Vermillion: University of South Dakota Press, 1989), pp.173–75.

5. See South Dakota Secretary of State, *South Dakota Legislative Manual* (Pierre: Merriman Printing, 2019), pp. 96–97, 150–51, 157–61, 165.

6. R. Alton Lee, *Principle over Party: The Farmers' Alliance and Populism in South Dakota, 1880–1900* (Pierre: South Dakota Historical Society Press, 2011), pp. 132–39.

7. Ibid., pp. 138–39; Herbert S. Schell, "Andrew E. Lee," in *Over a Century of Leadership: South Dakota Territorial and State Governors*, ed. Lynwood E. Oyos (Sioux Falls: Center for Western Studies, 1987), p. 67; Kenneth E. Hendrickson Jr., "The Populist-Progressive Era: Richard Franklin Pettigrew, Andrew E. Lee, and Coe I. Crawford," in *South Dakota Leaders: From Pierre Chouteau, Jr., to Oscar Howe*, ed. Herbert T. Hoover and Larry J. Zimmerman (Vermillion: University of South Dakota Press, 1989), pp. 194–98.

8. Lee, *Principle over Party,* pp. 166–72.

9. Ibid., pp. 173–86. Lee quotes newspaper publisher William Allen White, who said that the Progressives "caught the Populists in swimming and stole all of their clothing except the frayed underdrawers of free silver," pp. 180–81.

10. *South Dakota Election History,* pp. 82, 98, 114.

11. C. Perry Armin, "Coe I. Crawford and the Progressive Movement in South Dakota," *South Dakota Department of History Report and Historical Collections*, Vol. XXXII (Pierre: South Dakota State Historical Society, 1964), pp. 23–231, 107–

16, 132–40; Schell and Miller, *History of South Dakota,* pp. 261–65; Venhuizen, "Leaders in the Land of Infinite Variety," pp. 248–49.

12. Pressler, *U.S. Senators from the Prairie*, pp. 70–72.

13. Armin, "Coe I. Crawford," p. 212 Armin wrote: "Yet, from the fall of these two political titans [Congressman Charles H.] Burke and [U.S. senator Coe I.] Crawford, arose a new and stronger Progressive leader. This was Peter Norbeck, perhaps the greatest and undoubtedly the most liberal governor and senator of the state of South Dakota. His election to the former post in 1916 marked the first time unity existed within the Republican Party of South Dakota in twelve years and this harmony was not attained at the sacrifice of Progressive principles. The defeat of Charles Burke in November, 1914, coupled with the refusal of his colleague, [Congressman] Eben Martin, to seek re-election, both disheartened the Stalwarts and showed them that continual strife with the ever-stronger Progressives was useless." See also Venhuizen, "Leaders in the Land of Infinite Variety," pp. 251–52.

14. See Daryl Webb's chapter in this collection.

15. Pressler, *U.S. Senators from the Prairie*, p. 91.

16. *South Dakota Election History,* p. 388. Senator Johnson chose not to seek a second term, rather than face Norbeck.

17. See Edmund Morris, *Colonel Roosevelt* (New York: Random House, 2010), pp. 562–64; John Milton Cooper Jr., *Woodrow Wilson: A Biography* (New York: Random House, 2009), pp. 570–73; Francis Russell, *The Shadow of Blooming Grove: Warren G. Harding in his Times* (New York: McGraw-Hill, 1968), pp. 397–416; Amity Shlaes, *Coolidge* (New York: HarperCollins, 2013), pp. 323–24. Shlaes writes that Coolidge's famous quote had been taken out of context, as it was one line a speech arguing for idealism and public service by all Americans. Despite that, the line became emblematic of the Coolidge era, sandwiched between 1910s progressivism and 1930s New Dealism. Coolidge struggled to maintain support in farm states, particularly after he vetoed the McNary-Haugen bill, an attempt by western and midwestern members of Congress to raise commodity prices through government intervention. Norbeck was a fervent supporter of the bill. Seth Tupper, *Calvin Coolidge in the Black Hills* (Charleston, S.C.: History Press, 2017), pp. 21, 27.

18. Venhuizen, "Leaders in the Land of Infinite Variety," pp. 252–53.

19. *South Dakota Election History*, p. 437.

20. "Anderson Rites Held Tomorrow," *Sioux Falls Daily Argus-Leader*, 12 Aug. 1924. Peter Norbeck was one of Anderson's honorary pallbearers.

21. William J. Bulow, "Forward," *Three Score and Ten: The Autobiography of William J. Bulow*, unpublished. After Bulow's time in public office ended, he bought a typewriter and wrote his autobiography. The manuscript was never published

but remained in the Bulow family. The present author obtained a copy of the manuscript from Bulow's granddaughter, Barbara Bulow Dwyer, and deposited it at the South Dakota State Archives. Bulow's intelligence, charisma, and humor all come through in his writing; however, it also demonstrates the erratic nature of his education. The present author edited Bulow's manuscript for spelling, punctuation, and clarity, and the excerpts from Bulow's manuscript included in this article incorporate those edits. A longer selection of excerpts from Bulow's manuscript, edited by this author, was published by the South Dakota Historical Society Press in 2021. *See* William J. Bulow "Three Score Years and Ten: Selections from the Autobiography of William J. Bulow Sr.," ed. Tonnis H. Venhuizen *South Dakota History* 51 (Spring 2021): 2–72. As the edited manuscript does not have fixed page numbers, citations are made to the manuscript's chapter titles.

22. Bulow, "The Governor's Office," *Three Score and Ten: The Autobiography of William J. Bulow.*

23. *South Dakota Election History*, p. 480.

24. George S. McGovern, "Carl Gunderson," in *Over a Century of Leadership: South Dakota Territorial and State Governors*, ed. Lynwood E. Oyos (Sioux Falls: Center for Western Studies, 1987), pp. 112–13; Venhuizen, "Leaders in the Land of Infinite Variety," p. 252.

25. John E. Miller, "Defining Moments in Twentieth-Century South Dakota Political History," *South Dakota History* 42 (Summer 2012): 178–79.

26. *White Eagle Oil & Refining Co. v. Gunderson*, 48 S.D. 608 (1925).

27. Gilbert C. Fite, *Peter Norbeck: Prairie Statesman* (Pierre: South Dakota Historical Society Press, 2005), pp. 80–87. See also R. Alton Lee, *A New Deal for South Dakota* (Pierre: South Dakota Historical Society Press, 2016), pp. 3–6.

28. Miller, "Defining Moments in Twentieth-Century South Dakota Political History," pp. 178–79.

29. William J. Bulow, "William John Bulow," *Over a Century of Leadership: South Dakota Territorial and State Governors,* ed. Lynwood E. Oyos (Sioux Falls: Center for Western Studies, 1987), p. 115

30. Bulow, "School Days," *Three Score and Ten: The Autobiography of William J. Bulow.*

31. Bulow, "Growing Up with the Country," *Three Score and Ten: The Autobiography of William J. Bulow.* Bulow states that when he arrived in Sioux Falls, he looked up George Jeffries, a law school classmate who introduced him to Kirby, but he does not otherwise explain why he came to Sioux Falls.

32. "Christopherson, Charles Andrew," *Biographical Dictionary of the United States Congress*, https://bioguide.congress.gov/search/bio/C000384.

33. Bulow, "William John Bulow," p. 115; Bulow, "Buying and Selling Farmland," *Three Score and Ten: The Autobiography of William J. Bulow.*

34. Bulow, "The Governor's Office," *Three Score and Ten: The Autobiography of William J. Bulow.*

35. *South Dakota Election History*, p. 500.

36. Alan L. Clem, *South Dakota Political Almanac* (Vermillion: Dakota Press, 1969), pp. 43–46

37. George S. McGovern, "Carl Gunderson," pp. 112–13; "The 1926 election would seem to have been a personal defeat for Gunderson because his party captured virtually all of the other state and national offices."

38. Bulow, "Growing Up with the Country," *Three Score and Ten: The Autobiography of William J. Bulow.*

39. Miller, "Defining Moments in Twentieth-Century South Dakota Political History," pp. 178.

40. Bulow, "The Governor's Office," *Three Score and Ten: The Autobiography of William J. Bulow.*

41. Ibid.

42. Bulow's superlative statements are likely exaggerated for effect.

43. Ibid.

44. Ibid.

45. Ibid.

46. *Erskine v. Pyle*, 51 S.D. 262 (1927).

47. Ibid.

48. See Tupper, *Calvin Coolidge*, pp. 33–34, 39–40; Bulow, "A Visit from the President," *Three Score and Ten: The Autobiography of William J. Bulow*; Bulow, "Rushmore," *Three Score and Ten: The Autobiography of William J. Bulow.*

49. *South Dakota Election History*, p. 543.

50. Lee, *A New Deal for South Dakota*, pp. 21–22; Paul Higbee, *South Dakota's Cowboy Governor: Tom Berry* (Charleston, S.Car.: The History Press, 2017), pp. 35–40.

51. *South Dakota Election History*, p. 557.

52. Higbee, *South Dakota's Cowboy Governor*, pp. 35–40.

53. *South Dakota Election History*, pp. 597–610

54. Higbee, *South Dakota's Cowboy Governor*, p. 30.

55. Ibid., pp. 9–32.

56. Bulow, "The Philosophy of Defeat," *Three Score and Ten: The Autobiography of William J. Bulow.*

57. Higbee, *South Dakota's Cowboy Governor*, pp. 36–40.

58. Joseph V. Ryan, "Tom Berry," in *Over a Century of Leadership: South Dakota Territorial and State Governors*, ed. Lynwood E. Oyos (Sioux Falls: Center for Western Studies, 1987), p. 128–29.

59. Ibid.

60. Matthew Cecil, "Democratic Party Politics and the South Dakota Income

Tax, 1933–42," *South Dakota History*, Vol. 26 (Summer/Fall 1996): 144–45; Lee, *A New Deal for South Dakota*, pp. 36–40.

61. Cecil, "Democratic Party Politics," pp. 144–45, 158, 161–62.

62. *South Dakota Election History,* p. 618.

63. Lee, *A New Deal for South Dakota*, pp. 40–44.

64. See Thomas Biolsi, "New Deal Visions v. Local Political Culture: The Agony of the South Dakota State Planning Board," in *The Plains Political Tradition: Essays on South Dakota Political Culture, Volume 2*, ed. Jon K. Lauck, John E. Miller, and Donald C. Simmons, Jr. (Pierre: South Dakota Historical Society Press, 2014) pp. 77–102.

65. Higbee, *South Dakota's Cowboy Governor,* p. 82.

66. Bulow, "The New Deal," *Three Score and Ten: The Autobiography of William J. Bulow.*

67. Conrad Black, *Franklin Delano Roosevelt: Champion of Freedom* (New York: Public Affairs, 2003), pp. 390–92. Senator Norbeck, although a Republican, supported Roosevelt's reelection in 1936. Fite, *Peter Norbeck,* pp. 202–4.

68. *South Dakota Election History,* p. 655; "Gurney, John Chandler (Chan)," *Biographical Dictionary of the United States Congress*, https://bioguide.congress.gov/search/bio/G000532.

69. Although as of 1936 no previous South Dakota governor had run for a third term, the law did not prohibit a third term until the 1940s. *See Kneip v. Herseth, as Secretary of State et al.*, 214 N.W.2d 93 (1974). M. Q. Sharpe also sought, unsuccessfully, a third term as governor in 1946. *South Dakota Election History,* p. 744.

70. *South Dakota Election History*, p. 659.

71. "Historical Listing," https://sdlegislature.gov/Legislators/Historical.

72. Will G. Robinson, "Leslie Jensen," in *Over a Century of Leadership: South Dakota Territorial and State Governors*, ed. Lynwood E. Oyos (Sioux Falls: Center for Western Studies, 1987), p. 133–36.

73. *Associated Press*, "Norbeck Death Overshadows Opening of Special Session: Governor Berry Mentioned as Successor to Senator: Arrest of Lt. Governor Peterson for Embezzlement Complicates Situation," *Huron Daily Plainsman*, 21 Dec. 1936; "Hitchcock, Herbert Emery," *Biographical Dictionary of the United States Congress*, https://bioguide.congress.gov/search/bio/H000646.

74. Bulow, "The Philosophy of Defeat," *Three Score and Ten: The Autobiography of William J. Bulow.* Writing in the 1940s, Bulow was likely influenced by Franklin Roosevelt's later bids for a third and fourth presidential term, as well as Berry's decision to challenge Bulow in 1942.

75. Bulow, "Senate Reflections," *Three Score and Ten: The Autobiography of William J. Bulow.*

76. Ibid. See also Jean Edward Smith, *FDR* (New York: Random House, 2007), pp. 477–89.

77. "Hildebrandt, Fred Herman," *Biographical Dictionary of the United States Congress*, https://bioguide.congress.gov/search/bio/H000584; Berry won 63.3% to 23.5% for Hildebrandt and 13.2% for Hitchcock (*South Dakota Election History,* p. 677).

78. *South Dakota Election History,* p. 677. Gurney won 46.8 percent to 38.7 percent for Jensen; two other candidates won the balance.

79. Venhuizen, "Leaders in the Land of Infinite Variety," p. 256.

80. Scott N. Heidepriem, *A Fair Chance for a Free People: A Biography of Karl E. Mundt* (Madison, S.Dak.: Leader Printing Company, 1988), pp. 21–8. Mundt had run for the U.S. House seat in 1936, losing narrowly to the Democratic incumbent, Fred H. Hildebrandt, by less than 3,000 votes.

81. Elizabeth E. Williams, *Emil Loriks: Builder of a New Economic Order*, (Sioux Falls: Center for Western Studies, 1987), pp. 29, 33–4. Williams writes that "attempts would be made to smear [Loriks and Fosheim] as Communists" during the 1938 campaign, but that the two had steered clear of Communist elements. It was a common attack against ardent New Dealers.

82. *South Dakota Election History,* pp. 679–99. On a separate ballot, Republican Gladys Pyle was elected to serve the final few months of Norbeck's term in the U.S. Senate, making her the first women to represent South Dakota in Congress. See also Jeannette Kinyon and Jean Walz, *The Incredible Gladys Pyle* (Vermillion: Dakota Press, 1985), p. 35.

83. Germany quickly declared war on the United States as well, drawing Americans into both theaters of the World War.

84. Bulow, "The Philosophy of Defeat," *Three Score and Ten: The Autobiography of William J. Bulow.*

85. *South Dakota Election History.* p. 725.

86. Ibid., p. 726.

87. Although Bulow doesn't mention it explicitly, Bulow is likely referencing here Roosevelt's ill-fated attempt in 1938 to purge dissident Democrats from Congress in 1938, following the defeat of his court-packing plan in 1937. Bulow had not been up for reelection in 1938; had he been, he likely would have been among those targeted that year. See Jean Edward Smith, *FDR*, pp. 409–15.

88. Bulow, "The Philosophy of Defeat," *Three Score and Ten: The Autobiography of William J. Bulow.*

89. Pressler, *U.S. Senators from the Prairie*, pp. 124–26.

90. Robert L. McCaughey, "Forward: The End of a Distinguished Career," in *A Fair Chance for a Free People: A Biography of Karl E. Mundt* by Scott N. Heidepriem (Madison, S.Dak.: Leader Printing Company, 1988), p. ix.

91. Tonnis H. Venhuizen, "2018 SD GOP looks to extend its winning streak," *SoDak Governors*, https://sodakgovs.wordpress.com/2018/06/23/2018-sd-gop-looks-to-extend-its-winning-streak/.

92. Bulow, “Senate Reflections,” *Three Score and Ten: The Autobiography of William J. Bulow.*

93. Bulow, “Forward,” *Three Score and Ten: The Autobiography of William J. Bulow.*

SEAN J. FLYNN

6 | THE EASTERN ESTABLISHMENT ON TRIAL: CONGRESSMAN KARL MUNDT, 'INLAND' REPUBLICANISM, AND THE HISS CASE

• • •

No politician is more closely associated with the Hiss Case, the investigation and trial that linked former State Department official Alger Hiss to espionage, than Richard Nixon. Few historians would dispute biographer Roger Morris's assertion that Nixon's performance on the House Committee on Un-American Affairs (HUAC)—the investigatory body that spearheaded the case—was "the fount of his remarkable rise."[1] The California congressman rose to prominence in 1948, his pursuit of Hiss catapulting him into the Senate and earning him the admiration of Dwight Eisenhower, who selected Nixon as his running mate in 1952.

Conversely, too many writers credit Nixon with playing a singular role in the Hiss Case, an assessment that derives in part from Nixon's account of the investigation in his 1962 bestseller *Six Crises*. HUAC assistant Robert Stripling made important contributions, as did Representative Karl E. Mundt of South Dakota, who engaged Hiss in some of the most dramatic and damning exchanges in one of America's most consequential congressional hearings. Undeterred by Hiss's evasiveness about his Communist ties, Mundt probed Hiss's past and delivered stinging summations that dissolved the aura surrounding the aristocratic New Dealer, who counted cabinet secretaries, federal judges, and senators among his defenders.

Yet Mundt's role in the Hiss Case was not limited to his skill as a cross-examiner. Whereas Nixon represented burgeoning Southern California, Mundt embodied "inland America," the trans-Allegheny heartland that, in the minds of the "eastern establishment," was peopled by unimaginative farmers and Rotarians who profited from the progressive ideals of the New Deal brain trust. The Midwest in particular, observes Jon K. Lauck, was derided by the eastern intelligentsia for being "backward and regressive and a stronghold of political reaction," if not out-and-out Fascism.[2] Having embraced his role as spokesman for the "midwestern viewpoint," Mundt articulated inland Republican suspicions about the loyalties of the Ivy League elites and New Deal technocrats who Alger Hiss personified. From his seat on HUAC, the congressman defended investigations of domestic Communism as critical to national security. When he helped to expose Hiss's treasonous activities, Mundt embarrassed northeastern liberals, vindicated critics of President Franklin Delano Roosevelt's administration's screening procedures, and legitimized rural attitudes toward Communism ridiculed by the political elite.

Mundt launched his crusade against Communism while he was coaching his speech and debate teams at Eastern State Normal College in Madison, South Dakota, to national prominence. Professor Mundt became a popular speaker with civic groups that heard him highlight the dangers of Communism and Fascism.[3] He felt especially strong about the "Trojan Horse policy of Communism," which, by fulminating class hatreds, posed a unique threat to American democracy.[4]

In 1938, Mundt, having suffered defeat in the 1936 congressional elections, won the First District House seat as a member of a transformed South Dakota GOP that exchanged progressivism for conservativism. Depicting his opponent, Emil Loriks, as a slavish devotee of Franklin Roosevelt, Mundt aired the frustrations of tradition-bound voters who associated New Deal rhetoric with labor organizers and Marxist intellectuals. The urban liberals implementing Roosevelt's agenda appeared to intrude on local control, undercut rural conventions, and threaten capitalism. The New Deal smacked of bohemian radicalism, if not bolshevism.[5]

Conservative commentators perpetuated stereotypes about the New Deal, which contributed to an underappreciation of the relief that federal programs brought to South Dakota. Yet Mundt registered reasonable complaints about propagandistic New Deal promotions like the film *The Plow That Broke the Plains* or Dorothea Lange's staged photographs of Great Plains rural life.[6] His constituents, furthermore, harbored valid concerns about the expansion of a federal bureaucracy that grew 50 percent from 1933 to 1938. South Dakotans raised legitimate questions about applicants to federal jobs, many of whom were from Northeastern universities and committed to social revolution.[7]

In the words of historian Earl Latham, "the bright young person with a social conscience" drawn to the New Deal made government service his or her career. Some were members of the Communist Party of the United States (CPUSA). "It is in this milieu," Latham writes, "that the 'penetration' of the agencies of the Federal government and the 'infiltration' of its offices by the Communists must be seen."[8]

Mundt harbored well-founded concerns about the vetting of federal employees. But in the years preceding World War II, it was his isolationism that captured headlines. Mundt embraced the vision of "America Firsters" who hoped to "create a fortress America immune from foreign attack and insulated from the perils of international intrigue."[9] Though not a rigid non-interventionist—he advocated limited aid to Moscow following the Nazi invasion of the USSR in June 1941, for instance—Mundt's isolationism was consistent with conservative notions that world wars abetted Communism.[10] Remote from the nation's financial and cultural hubs, midwesterners distrusted the internationalism of eastern liberals.[11] Deducing that FDR's preoccupation with Europe diverted attention from the shortcomings of the New Deal, they also feared the impact that military involvement would have on free enterprise. With his power left unchecked, Roosevelt would encourage Socialism and steer the nation into a war that would cripple capitalism.[12]

This outlook helps explain Mundt's desire to secure a seat on HUAC, then referred to as the Dies Committee after Martin Dies of Texas, chairman of the committee from its inception in 1938 until 1944.[13] Historian Ted Morgan writes that in combining his hatred for Marxism with his skepticism toward FDR, Dies "pioneered the issue of Communists in the government, using it to undermine the New Deal." While Mundt was campaigning in 1938, the Dies Committee investigated the Federal Theater and Writers Project and targeted labor organizers who were allegedly plotting to "push President Roosevelt and his administration more to the left."[14]

During a floor speech in June 1940, Representative Mundt alerted Americans to the threats posed by "European and Asiatic ideals and 'isms.'"[15] The address fixed his reputation as an anti-Communist, and when in 1943 he won a seat on HUAC, he joined a culture war of sorts.[16] Liberals perceived HUAC as reactionary and representative of small business Babbitts, simple farmers, and southern bigots whose ham-fisted campaign against Communism masked their detestation of the New Deal. HUAC's defenders extolled the committee as the voice of steadfast, God-fearing men who endured liberal smears in their crusade against Communism and its corrupting influence on American democracy.[17] "What Dies represented," observes an historian, was "the small town populated by a few hundred neighborly descendants of early settlers and against the big cities with their polyglot masses." Dies saw threats emanating from Manhattan "as much as from Moscow" and endeavored to insulate inland America from "eastern cosmopolitanism."[18]

Mundt distanced himself from the racism exhibited by Dies and John Rankin of Mississippi, a vocal segregationist whose malicious comments about African Americans and Jews sullied HUAC's reputation.[19] Instead Mundt focused on expanding HUAC's jurisdiction over foreign policy. His appointment to the Committee on Foreign Affairs in January 1941 had provided Mundt a perch to attack the controversial Lend-Lease program within the context of "the men and the methods of the New Deal," the programs of which represented "a distrust in the average citizen" and a "deification" of government.[20]

Japan's attack on Pearl Harbor, however, showed midwesterners that they could not isolate themselves from world affairs. Mundt threw his unqualified support behind the Allied war effort, the success of which hinged on U.S.-Soviet cooperation.[21] He retained his prejudices toward Communism, however, and his seat on HUAC afforded him the opportunity to combine his foreign policy interests with his eagerness to investigate Soviet espionage.[22]

Biographer Scott Heidepriem writes that after the war, Mundt "saw the United States locked in a struggle with the Soviet Union. The hearts and minds of the citizens in all the other nations of the world were the prize to be sought."[23] To win those hearts and minds, Mundt coauthored the United States Information and Education Exchange Act of 1948, designed to counter Soviet propaganda by expanding Voice of America broadcasts in Europe.[24] As valuable as the law was, South Dakotans judged suppressing domestic Communism an equally important objective of Cold War strategy. In his constituent newsletters, Mundt updated voters on HUAC activities, which were supported by Governor Merrell Q. Sharpe and the state's American Legion commander, who praised Mundt for his work on the committee.[25]

Mundt's presence on HUAC boosted the credibility of a committee ridiculed for its "primitive methods." The editors of *Life* commended Mundt for the "serious and public-spirited manner" in which he performed his duties.[26] Though he did not hesitate to share his unfavorable opinion of the film industry, Mundt played a minor role in the sensational hearings on Hollywood leftists.[27] Of greater interest to him was combatting the CPUSA. Working with Richard Nixon, he advanced the Mundt-Nixon Bill, the first piece of legislation to emerge from HUAC in a decade. As passed by the House, it required the registration of CPUSA members with the Attorney General and denied groups designated as front organizations from using mail or radio without revealing the sources of their print and broadcast materials.[28] The bill died in the Senate but was resurrected as the McCarran Act, passed by Congress, and enacted over President Truman's veto in 1950.[29]

Fittingly, the Mundt-Nixon Bill is the only legislation that bears Nixon's name. Equally fitting was the introduction of the legislation in 1948, the year Alger Hiss testified before HUAC. The chain of events that culminated in his conviction for perjury, the only successful prosecution of a government official for Communist activities in American history, began on July 31, when Elizabeth Bentley appeared before HUAC. In describing how she directed Communist spy rings during World War II, Bentley identified government officials—including prominent New Dealers—who provided her with classified documents which she passed to Soviet operatives.[30]

Hoping to corroborate Bentley's charges during an election year in which he was running for the Senate, Mundt demanded committee access to government personnel files.[31] He moved with trepidation since some Republicans had criticized the committee for its mismanagement of the investigation of Dr. Robert Condon, a prominent physicist and the head of the National Bureau of Standards. When the committee demanded that the Commerce Department turn over its Federal Bureau of Investigation (FBI) report on Condon, Truman invoked executive privilege, denied the request, and ordered his staff to draft legislation abolishing HUAC. Elizabeth Bentley's testimony swung the momentum back toward HUAC, whereupon Mundt, acting on a tip from a reporter, recommended inviting Whittaker Chambers, senior editor of *TIME* magazine—and a self-confessed former Communist—to appear before the committee.[32]

No witness would provide more substantive evidence of espionage than Chambers, who, prior to his appearance on August 3, knew little about the composition of the committee and had "no impression" of Mundt. He was, however, aware of HUAC's reputation in Washington social circles, where its members were described as "uncouth, undignified, and ungrammatical." To Chambers's surprise, "none of those charges proved to be true." The *TIME* editor formed a friendship with Nixon and developed "a most cordial feeling" toward Mundt.[33]

Chambers's opening remarks were made in executive session in the Old House Office Building, where chief investigator Robert Stripling posed a series of questions regarding the Communist spy apparatus. In response, the witness described the function of a clandestine organization, designated the Ware Group after its leader, Harold Ware, a farm policy specialist who placed Communists in the offices of the Agricultural Adjustment Administration (AAA). In a meticulous fashion that became the trademark of his testimony, Chambers identified members of the "top committee" recruited by Ware.[34]

According to a Nixon biographer, "HUAC sprang awake" when Chambers identified prominent New Dealers with Communist connections.[35] Committee members were astonished when Chambers named Alger Hiss a "top" Ware Group operative, for Hiss was, in the words of Alistair Cooke, "a full-blooded New Dealer."[36] After graduating from Johns Hopkins University, Hiss earned a law degree from Harvard. A protégé of future Supreme Court Justice Felix Frankfurter and a clerk for Justice Oliver Wendell Holmes, he served as counsel to the AAA and the Nye Commission. He held a post in the Office of the Solicitor General and was a State Department aide to Roosevelt during the Yalta Conference. An architect of the United Nations, Hiss spearheaded the Conference of International Organization in San Francisco, and at the time of Chambers's testimony, was president of the Carnegie Endowment for International Peace. Friend and confidante of congressmen, diplomats, and judges, Hiss epitomized the liberal elite.[37]

He was also a Communist—or so claimed Chambers. When Representatives John Wood and John McDowell moved that the hearing be opened to the public, Stripling suggested relocating to the cavernous House Ways and Means Committee Hearing Room in the New Office Building. Mundt, serving as HUAC chairman in Parnell Thomas's absence and, in the words of a Chambers biographer, the committee's "ringmaster," agreed and thus assured that Chambers's testimony would make a splash in the evening newspapers.[38]

Reporters were struck by Chambers's disheveled appearance. "He was short and pudgy," Nixon recalled. "His clothes were unpressed. His shirt collar was curled up over his jacket. He spoke in a rather bored monotone."[39] Chambers's demeanor did not diminish the impact of his words, especially after he repeated the names of Communists—Hiss among them—who infiltrated federal offices with "the specific purpose of overthrowing the Government, at the opportune time, by any and all means."[40] As news correspondents scrambled to the telephones, Chambers revealed that though Ware had organized the Washington apparatus, the leader of the underground was a Hungarian agent ensconced in the United States. Mundt voiced his astonishment that espionage activities were "conducted by a man who was not an American citizen."[41] He received another shock when Chambers stated that he shared "specific names" of Communist conspirators, Hiss among them, with Roosevelt's intelligence liaison.[42]

Chambers insisted that Hiss was a Communist, that they had been close friends, and that when in 1937 he tried unsuccessfully to get his friend to sever ties with his Communist handlers, Hiss "cried when we separated." Before gaveling the hearing to a close, Mundt thanked Chambers, whose testimony appeared to corroborate Mundt's charge that, due to security lapses by the Roosevelt administration, "a serious menace" had infiltrated the Washington bureaucracy.[43]

Mundt's satisfaction was short-lived. The next day Hiss sent him a telegraph denying knowing Chambers, doubted he had "laid eyes on him," and insisted that Chambers's allegations were baseless. Hiss asked that the telegram be entered into the record and requested an appearance before the committee.[44] His request was honored and on 5 August, he appeared before HUAC in the House Caucus Room, the largest hearing chamber in the Capitol. Inside was a contingent of Hiss's defenders emboldened by a *Washington Post* cartoon that depicted Hiss as a victim of "Smear Statements."[45]

The physical differences between Chambers and Hiss were pronounced. Historian David Halberstam describes Hiss as "strikingly patrician and handsome. His aristocratic bearing seemed to confirm his political legitimacy," and, seated before the committee, he became "imposing, almost imperious, a paragon of the establishment."[46] Hiss smiled frequently, spoke crisply, and displayed an effortlessness that contrasted with Chambers's nervous mannerisms. And in his opening remarks he denied "unqualifiedly" ever being a member of the Communist Party or having adhered to the tenets of Marxism. He insisted that the name Whittaker Chambers was unknown to him before 1947, when FBI officials referenced him during an interview. As far as he knew, he had "never laid eyes" on Chambers.[47]

Hiss, writes biographer Thomas C. Reeves, was representative of "the 'bright young men' who flocked to Washington during the New Deal to save the republic, and he was thus the symbol of almost everything most Republicans, particularly in the Midwest, despised." Should Republicans unmask him, "the political harvest might be enormous," for if Hiss was "a Communist, then any New Dealer might have been."[48] Nixon suspected that Hiss, whom he found to be "coldly courteous and, at times, almost condescending," was connected to the Ware Group, an allegation Hiss denied. Canadian and French agents, several Truman officials, a Soviet defector, and Representative Walter Judd of Minnesota all voiced suspicions about Hiss. Father John Cronin, an investigator for the National Conference on Catholic Welfare and an ally in the FBI's war on espionage, informed Nixon that Hiss was "the most influential Communist" in the State Department.[49]

During his testimony, Hiss insulted Mundt, who, despite having earned a graduate degree from Columbia University, fulfilled Hiss's stereotype of the crude midwesterner.[50] When Mundt, described by Nixon as "an experienced and skillful investigator," read the list of those whom he believed were the seven individuals in the Ware Group, Hiss rudely corrected him: "That is eight."[51] After telling Stripling that the name Whittaker Chambers "means absolutely nothing to me," Hiss was shown a photograph of his accuser and asked if the man in the image resembled anyone he knew. "If this is a picture of Mr. Chambers," Hiss remarked, "he is not particularly unusual looking. He looks like a lot of people. I might even mistake him for the chairman of this committee." As his supporters erupted in laughter, a grinning Hiss turned toward them to acknowledge their amusement, and, according to Nixon, "tilted his head in a courtly bow . . ." Mundt, who, like Chambers, was overweight, replied, "I hope you are wrong in that."[52] Nixon found the witness's mocking behavior "insulting in the extreme," while David Halberstam referred to the ridiculing of Mundt as "the high-water mark for [Hiss] in the case."[53]

Mundt regained his composure and, before closing the hearing, thanked Hiss for his cooperation.[54] The normally disapproving John Rankin hurried to the witness table to shake hands with Hiss, who, Nixon admitted, gave "a virtuoso performance." Hiss's supporters "surged around him, to . . . congratulate him . . . and to commiserate with him on the damage the committee had done to him."[55] Hiss had, it appeared, put to rest questions about his ties to Communism.

Mundt was perplexed. At best, it appeared Chambers had mistaken Hiss for another acquaintance. At worst, Chambers was lying. Hiss reinforced in the minds of his defenders the totality of his innocence and convinced nearly everyone in attendance at the two separate hearings that he was the more credible witness. His performance delighted President Truman, who characterized the "Capitol Hill spy scare" as a "red herring" that diverted the "do-nothing" Republicans from performing their duty.[56] Truman denied HUAC access to the files of federal employees and exhorted Americans to acknowledge FBI investigations and grand jury proceedings—not congressional hearings—as the best means of fighting espionage.[57]

When HUAC reconvened, the consensus among its members was to drop the investigation. Mundt worried that HUAC risked permanent damage if it did not "take the minds of the public off of the Hiss case."[58] Alone among committee members, Nixon resisted the urge to scotch the hearings. Hiss's examination of the photograph struck him as phony, and, moreover, the witness never stated categorically that he did not know Chambers, only that he did not recall a man "by the name of Whittaker Chambers" or that the name meant "absolutely nothing" to him. Though linking Hiss to the CPUSA might prove "impossible," Nixon insisted that HUAC could determine whether the two men knew one another. If Hiss was lying about his association with Chambers, then he "might also be lying about whether or not he was a communist."[59] Moved by Nixon's reasoning yet impressed by the verve with which Hiss asserted his innocence, Mundt appointed Nixon to head a subcommittee to question Chambers about his relationship with Hiss. This crucial decision, by expanding the investigatory mission of the committee, would disclose the truth about Hiss's past.[60]

While speaking with his wife Mary that evening, Karl Mundt expressed his fear that HUAC had "gotten hold of the wrong man."[61] Several hours later, John Peurifoy, Assistant Secretary of State for Security Affairs, defied Truman's orders and met with Karl to share a State Department file on Hiss. According to journalist Tom Wicker, the contents of the file convinced Karl that Hiss had been a Communist informant.[62] Yet by the time of the Peurifoy meeting, Mary had already encouraged her husband to persist with the probe. The Mundts' first encounter with Communists occurred in 1934 during a Writers' Colony retreat in Colorado where the couple "infiltrated" a CPUSA meeting chaired by a professor who, Mary recalled, outlined "a communist plan for seizing control of the government . . . [by] tak[ing] it from within." Mary believed that Hiss was part of that plan. In the days following the Chambers-Hiss testimonies, during which time her Washington acquaintances urged her to persuade her husband to halt the investigation, Mary's suspicions mounted. She was certain that Hiss "was guilty, and oddly enough the very qualities that recommended him to the society matrons incriminated him in my estimation." Hiss's self-control shook Karl's faith in Chambers. It had the opposite effect on Mary, who found Hiss "too smooth, too suave, too much the picture of outraged innocence."[63]

Three weeks later, toward the conclusion of the televised hearing on the Hiss investigation, Karl Mundt referenced the impact his wife had on his judgment. While he acknowledged that Hiss had been "persuasive and convincing," his wife decided that her husband "had been taken in by his suavity." Mary steadied Karl and restored his faith in HUAC's mission. "Perhaps a woman's intuition is better than a man's," he mused.[64]

Nixon's subcommittee, meanwhile, had surged ahead. Their interviews of Chambers on 7 August, Hiss on 16 August, and the two men together on 17 August revealed that Hiss knew Chambers under the latter's alias of "George Crosley." Chambers impressed the subcommittee with recollections of minute details about Hiss's hobbies and home life. Two memories in particular—of a Model A Ford owned by Hiss, and of Hiss's excitement at sighting a prothonotary warbler on an ornithology outing—exposed the depth of Chambers's association with Hiss.[65] On 16 August, the subcommittee queried Hiss about his private life. "He sensed the danger," writes John A. Farrell, "and tried, too late, to recast the controversy."[66] Hiss suddenly recalled a writer with "very bad teeth" by the name of George Crosley who sublet his apartment in 1935 and to whom he gave a rug, some furniture, and an "old Ford we had kept for sentimental reasons." The car, which he "threw in with the apartment," had hand-operated windshield wipers, a detail that Chambers highlighted in his 7 August testimony. Time and again, Hiss's accounts of events aligned precisely with Chambers's testimony, including Hiss recounting the day when, while birdwatching on the Potomac River, he sighted a prothonotary warbler.[67]

Chambers and Hiss confronted one another in subcommittee on 17 August. In what Nixon called "one of the most unconvincing acts that I have ever seen put on by a supposedly intelligent man," Hiss inspected Chambers's teeth to confirm that he was the man he knew as George Crosley.[68] Throughout the hearing, Hiss clashed with HUAC's members, who decided to bring the controversy to a climax in the form of a public confrontation between the two witnesses.[69]

On the morning of 25 August, some twelve hundred spectators squeezed into the House Caucus Room. Dozens of photographers, radio broadcasters, and reporters were present, but the new medium of television dominated the event. "Confrontation Day" was the first televised hearing, and it introduced, writes biographer Sam Tanenhaus, "a new age of political spectacle. After Hiss-Chambers would come the Army-McCarthy hearings, Watergate, Oliver North, Clarence Thomas-Anita Hill." Though less than one in ten Americans owned a television in 1948, it is estimated that millions watched the hearing.[70] And whereas up to this point Nixon and Stripling had served as HUAC's lead cross-examiners, on 25 August they shared the limelight with Mundt. Alger Hiss discovered that the ordinary-looking former professor from an undistinguished college in the insignificant state of South Dakota was a spirited orator. Mundt would expose Hiss as a liar and humble those who ridiculed midwesterners' "obsession" with Communism.

On a day when Hiss uttered phrases like "to the best of my recollection" nearly two hundred times, Mundt declared that HUAC's patience was exhausted.[71] Hiss's ever-changing recollections of the terms of use for the supposedly cherished automobile he provided Chambers—at different times he claimed to have sold, rented, or loaned it—damaged his credibility. During a particularly icy exchange, Mundt urged Hiss to "make a statement and stand by it."[72] Hiss retorted that he was offended by "the nature" of the comment and "the embellishments" that accompanied it. Mundt countered that Hiss had routinely changed his story and, significantly, that there were multiple transactions involving Chambers and the Model A, a sequence that suggested a long-term association between the two men and raised questions as to why Hiss suppressed evidence about the car. Confident that Hiss remembered specific details surrounding the transactions, Mundt pressed him to answer truthfully. He parried Hiss's caustic reply—"You know a great deal, Mr. Mundt"—by remarking that the witness's "evasive type of testimony" made it difficult "to get at the truth."[73]

Tedious as it was to follow, Mundt outlined the ownership history of the automobile because it laid bare Hiss's involvement in the Communist underground. Suggesting that the matter could be resolved "by a very simple question," Mundt posed a question for which Hiss would "not have to consult the records." Demanding a "yes or no" response, Mundt asked Hiss if he had,

> ever dispose[d] of that 1929 automobile to anybody else in any way besides Mr. Crosley?
>
> Mr. HISS: Mr. Mundt, I would hate to disappoint you in any expectation.
>
> Mr. MUNDT: You have already done that, but answer the question.
>
> Mr. HISS: I am not able, without consulting the records, to testify with exactness or finality as to the way in which I ultimately completely disposed of my interest in that automobile.[74]

The more Mundt focused on the final transaction involving the Ford, the more evasive Hiss became. The once imposing witness had been replaced by a vacillator who could not "recall with such aids to memory as I possibly can take." Mundt remarked that Hiss "would stretch the credulity" of HUAC if its members were asked to accept his claim that he had no memory of the automobile's destination. "I am not an expert on the credulity of this committee," Hiss responded.[75]

That was certain enough, as was the certainty that Hiss had surreptitiously transferred the automobile to another Communist conspirator by way of a Communist middleman employed at a local car dealership. Hiss's loyalty to fellow Communists was so complete that in defiance of orders that he avoid transactions that might link him to covert operations, he sold his Ford to a Communist in need of assistance. He arranged the transfer in 1936, a fact that undermined his testimony that Chambers might have disposed of the automobile in 1935, the year Hiss claimed to have last seen Chambers. Armed with evidence about the transactions, Mundt lured Hiss into a trap wherein the witness would be forced to admit his long-term relationship with Chambers or conceal it. He chose to conceal it.

Minutes after the exchange on the "credulity" of HUAC, Stripling produced a smoking gun, a copy of a title from the Washington-area Department of Motor Vehicles (DMV) revealing that on 23 July 1936, Hiss, in collusion with a Communist employee of Cherner Motor Company, a local dealership, signed over the car to the company. To cover Hiss's tracks, the salesman did not enter the sale in the company records, and then, a few hours later, transferred the title to William Rosen, a Communist organizer who listed a false address on the transfer papers. As Chambers later emphasized, "[t]he fact that Hiss had turned over his car to an unknown intermediary in a clandestine way was beyond question, while his elaborate efforts to cover up called into question the whole tissue of his story."[76]

Hiss struggled to regain the upper hand. After examining the copy of the title, he requested to see the original but was told that it could not be removed from DMV offices. Hiss claimed that "the outline of the letters" in the copy prevented him from verifying his handwriting. "Could you be sure if you saw the original document?" Mundt asked. When Hiss responded, "I could be surer," laughter rippled through the House Caucus Room. Congressman Thomas elicited additional laughter when he asked Hiss if his signature on the original "would . . . look any more like your signature?"[77]

Mundt read a summary of the investigation that highlighted "points in agreement" that had been reached. Hiss knew Chambers well. He housed and fed Chambers, lent him furniture and an automobile, and drove him to New York and Washington, where he "bought him lunches in the Senate Restaurant." Hiss even extended to Chambers "a series of small loans. There seems no question about that. In other words, there seems no question about your associations with a man who told this committee that he associated with you."[78] Mundt reminded Hiss that Chamber's testimony "stands unchallenged," whereas his was "clouded by a strangely deficient memory."[79] He finished his summation by highlighting the assumptions foremost in the minds of HUAC members: that the witness "telling the truth on the verifiable data" was "telling the truth on all of it," and that the witness "concealing the truth . . . on verifiable data . . . [was] concealing . . . the truth on obviously the points that we cannot prove," to wit, Hiss's role as a Communist.[80]

It was a devastatingly effective summary. David Halberstam referred to it as "a damning moment" in the hearings.[81] Hiss retreated to his last line of defense, a prepared statement that included a roster of dignitaries who, Hiss insisted, would vouch for his innocence. He lashed out at Mundt for being "trigger quick" to discredit him and criticized HUAC for not "penetrating to the bedrock of the facts relevant to the charge which you have publicized—that I am or have been a Communist."[82]

It was an unconvincing argument. "When Alger Hiss left his first public hearing, people crowded around him," Chambers recalled. "When he left the hearing room on 25 August, no one crowded around him. In the nine hours of the hearing, the tide of sentiment in the room, which had run deeply for him, had turned against him."[83] Nixon observed how Hiss and his attorney "made their solitary way out of the hearing room," and James Reston of the *New York Times* concluded that the witness's cautious responses, "in the opinion even of his friends, hurt his case."[84]

A few days later, HUAC issued an interim report, likely drafted by Mundt, that stressed that while Hiss would have the opportunity to clarify his recollection of events, the hearings had "definitely shifted the burden of proof from Chambers to Hiss, in the opinion of this committee."[85] At an appearance in Youngstown, Ohio, Mundt defended HUAC, noting that its opponents "can never make the American public believe that weeding Communists and their dupes out of government is not in the public interest." In response to an audience member's comment that the FBI, rather than Congress, should be investigating domestic Communism, Mundt expressed his homespun attitude toward government oversight. He replied that in his home state, "the great productive farming state of South Dakota, we have what is known as the volunteer fire departments that do a wonderful job—sometimes a lot better than these professionals do." He received applause after declaring that one of Congress's functions was to present facts and then trust "the good judgment of the people . . . to deal with whatever facts there are."[86]

When Chambers suggested during a radio broadcast that his onetime friend might still be a Communist collaborator, Hiss sued him for libel on the assumption that if Chambers had evidence to support the charge he would have produced it. Chambers did have evidence, and he produced it in two installments, the first a collection of State Department papers that had passed through Hiss's office, and the second the celebrated "pumpkin papers," several rolls of microfilmed State Department documents that Chambers had concealed in a carved-out pumpkin on his Maryland farm. Taken collectively, the documents in Hiss's handwriting and evidence that Hiss's typewriter had been used in duplicating classified files confirmed Chambers's allegation that Hiss had spied for Soviet intelligence. Of troubling significance was the discovery that documents obtained by Hiss later assisted Soviet cryptologists in breaking codes that disclosed additional state secrets.[87]

Mundt gloated. In the face of criticism from Truman, the press, and Hiss's defenders, HUAC had prevailed. On behalf of the committee, Mundt issued a press release that described the secret documents as "the object of a ten-year search by agents of the United States government." In the end, a congressional committee—not the FBI—exposed Hiss. Furthermore, the public supported HUAC probes, a Gallup poll revealing that even three out of four Democrats approved of the committee's work.[88]

On 15 December 1948, a federal grand jury indicted Hiss. Since the statute of limitations for espionage had expired, he was tried on two counts of perjury. Nevertheless, Thomas C. Reeves writes, "everyone understood that the real issue in question was whether or not the genteel, sophisticated, self-assured, influential, Ivy League New Dealer had once been a Communist spy."[89] In January 1950, Hiss was convicted and sentenced to five years in prison. He served forty-four months in the federal penitentiary in Lewisburg, Pennsylvania, during which time additional evidence confirmed his membership in a Communist cell in the 1930s. After being paroled, he slipped into obscurity as a stationery and printing supplies salesman in New York, maintaining his innocence until his death in 1996.[90]

In reflecting on the Hiss case, Whittaker Chambers underscored "the jagged fissure" exposed by the HUAC hearings. On one side of the fissure stood "the plain men and women of the nation." Opposite those ordinary Americans were "those who affected to act, think, and speak for them." At the height of the investigation, it was "the 'best people' who were for Alger Hiss and who were prepared to go to almost any length to protect and defend him," whereas the nation's majority maintained an "open mind." Average Americans, Chambers concluded, "suspected what forces disastrous to the nation were at work . . . while most of the forces of enlightenment were poohpoohing the Communist danger and calling . . . it a witch hunt."[91]

Historian Allen Weinstein, a leading authority on the Hiss Case, argues that for the liberals who defended Hiss, his conviction on perjury related to espionage was "a disaster" because he was "converted into a symbol of the New Deal's treachery, particularly in the State Department."[92] Scholar Richard M. Fried writes that Hiss's conviction marked the condemnation of "an era, a party, and a political style." Since the 1930s, the Republicans had been critical of "the smug urbanity of the New Dealers." Among the GOP faithful, the finality of the Hiss verdict "permitted a resounding chorus of I-told-you-so's."[93]

Leading the chorus was Mundt, now a U.S. senator, who, just days after the Hiss verdict, took to the floor to explain its significance. While emphasizing that the espionage activities of "disloyal men" were a threat to freedom, Mundt likewise expressed concern with the policies instituted by the Roosevelt administration. Alluding to the ideological divisions hardened by the Hiss investigation, Mundt commented that, despite Hiss's conviction, there remained those who "feel it inconceivable that a man who looks as smooth and so intelligent and speaks such an effective Harvard accent, could be considered guilty of such a charge." He blamed the White House for obstructing justice, speculated on Hiss's influence in the State Department, and blasted Hiss's associates and "the left-wing press" for issuing "critical and castigating statements" about HUAC. Even Truman's secretary of state, "poor, befuddled Dean Acheson," a chief defender of Hiss, had been duped.[94]

Back home, Mundt was hailed a hero, the *Sioux Falls Daily Argus-Leader* lauding the congressman who "took the leadership . . . to expose Hiss." Midwest attitudes toward Communism, once a target of derision, prevailed. The Roosevelt administration, asserted the *Argus-Leader*, allowed "men with extreme liberal and pinkish trends of thought to enter Federal office" where they were "welcomed and promoted."[95] That they were welcomed and promoted was confirmed in 1995 when declassified and decrypted Soviet cables collected through the "Venona" counterintelligence project proved that some 350 Americans spied for the USSR. An historian who analyzed the Venona records concluded that espionage in federal offices was a "serious problem and needed to be dealt with."[96]

Mundt summarized what he judged to be the legacy of eighteen years of Democratic dominance. The United States had been "run by New Dealers, Fair Dealers, Misdealers, and Hiss dealers, who have shuttled back and forth between freedom and Red Fascism like a pendulum on a cuckoo clock."[97] His over-the-top rhetoric aside, Mundt's characterization captured the sentiments of his constituents, whose attitude toward Communism, Mundt maintained, was neither obstinate nor narrow-minded. In their minds, Hiss had been protected by East Coast opinion shapers who spurned the sensibilities of Main Street. Additionally, the Hiss controversy made South Dakotans painfully aware of the establishment's disdain for inland congressmen, who the Groton, Yale, and Harvard educated Dean Acheson referred to as "the primitives," a species of political opportunists "eager to exploit the issue of domestic Communism."[98]

As was demonstrated by his efforts to repair the reputation of HUAC and his initial acceptance of Hiss's claim to innocence, Karl Mundt was not a primitive or opportunistic Communist witch hunter. But neither was he satisfied with the Roosevelt administration's oversight of a loosely monitored bureaucracy that concealed the treasonous activities of Communist spies. Mundt found it in the nation's interest to uncover the truth in the Hiss Case. He succeeded and did so in a fair and judicious manner that chastened Hiss, and, by association, the elite class he represented.

NOTES

1. Roger Morris, *Richard Milhous Nixon: The Rise of an American Politician* (New York: Henry Holt and Company, 1990), p. 344.

2. Jon K. Lauck, *From Warm Center to Ragged Edge: The Erosion of Midwestern Literary and Historical Regionalism, 1920–1965* (Iowa City: University of Iowa Press, 2017), pp. 60–61.

3. Karl E. Mundt, "International Relations," an address before the Kiwanis Club of Hibbing, Minn., 1933, folder 2, box 1209, record group VIII, Karl E.

Mundt Archives, Dakota State University, Madison, S.Dak. Mundt was professor of speech at Eastern State Normal College, now Dakota State University, from 1927 to 1936.

4. Ibid.; Scott N. Heidepriem, *A Fair Chance for a Free People: A Biography of Karl E. Mundt, United States Senator* (Madison, S.Dak.: Leader Printing Company, 1988), pp. 18–21.

5. John E. Miller, "McCarthyism before McCarthy: The 1938 Election in South Dakota," *Heritage of the Great Plains* 15 (Summer 1982): 2, 6–8; Lisle A. Rose, *The Cold War Comes to Main Street: America in the 1950s* (Lawrence: University Press of Kansas, 1999), p. 47; Ellen Schrecker, *Many Are the Crimes: McCarthyism in America* (Boston: Little, Brown and Co., 1998), p. 90; Alistair Cooke, *A Generation on Trial: U.S.A. v. Alger Hiss* (Baltimore: Penguin Books, 1968), pp. 7, 21; Richard M. Fried, *Nightmare in Red: The McCarthy Era in Perspective* (New York: Oxford University Press, 1990), p. 17.

6. Jon Lauck, "Dorothea Lange and the Limits of the Liberal Narrative: A Review Essay," *Heritage of the Great Plains* 45, no. 1 (2012): 5–11, 22–4.

7. Walter Goodman, *The Committee: The Extraordinary Career of the House Committee on Un-American Activities* (New York: Farrar, Straus and Giroux, 1968), p. 248.

8. Earl Latham, *The Communist Controversy in Washington: From the New Deal to McCarthy* (Cambridge: Harvard University Press, 1966), pp. 75–77, 94.

9. William Manchester and Paul Reid, *The Last Lion: Winston Spencer Churchill: Defender of the Realm, 1940–1965* (New York: Bantam Books, 2012), p. 297.

10. Donald T. Critchlow, *The Conservative Ascendancy: How the GOP Right Made Political History* (Cambridge: Harvard University Press, 2007), p. 12.

11. Lewis L. Gould, *Grand Old Party: A History of the Republicans* (New York: Random House, 2003), p. 289; Selig Adler, *The Isolationist Impulse: Its Twentieth-Century Reaction* (New York: Abelard-Schuman, 1957), pp. 43–45; David Caute, *The Great Fear: The Anti-Communist Purge Under Truman and Eisenhower* (New York: Simon and Schuster, 1978), p. 41.

12. Jon K. Lauck, "Karl Mundt's Foreign Policy from 1938–1947: Portrait of an American Transformation," *Papers of the Twenty-Fifth Annual Dakota History Conference, 3–5 June 1993* (Sioux Falls: Center for Western Studies, 1993), pp. 480–81; Manfred Jonas, *Isolationism in America, 1935–1941* (Ithaca: Cornell University Press, 1966), pp. 71, 86–87, 94–98; Seymour M. Hersh, *The Dark Side of Camelot* (Boston: Little, Brown and Company, 1997), p. 63.

13. Goodman, *The Committee*, pp. 16–23.

14. Ted Morgan, *Reds: McCarthyism in Twentieth-Century America* (New York: Random House, 2003), pp. 188–90.

15. Cong. Rec., 76th Cong., 3rd sess., 1940, 86, pt. 8: 8551.

16. R. Alton Lee, "'New Dealers, Fair Dealers, Misdealers, and Hiss Dealers':

Karl Mundt and the Internal Security Act of 1950," *South Dakota History* 10 (Fall 1980): 278.

17. Latham, *The Communist Controversy*, p. 8.

18. Goodman, *The Committee*, p. 163.

19. Thomas C. Reeves, *The Life and Times of Joe McCarthy: A Biography* (New York: Stein and Day, 1982), p. 209.

20. Karl Mundt, "Your Washington and You" (newsletter from the office of Congressman Mundt), 25 Jan. 1940, folder 1a, box 1246, record group IX, Mundt Archives; Karl E. Mundt, "The Spirit of 1776," address before the Executives' Club of Chicago, 28 Feb. 1941, in *The Executives' Club News* 17 (14 Mar. 1941): 3–8; Heidepriem, *A Fair Chance for a Free People*, pp. 38–39.

21. Lauck, "Karl Mundt's Foreign Policy," pp. 492–99.

22. Heidepriem, *A Fair Chance for a Free People*, pp. 48–53; "Your Washington and You," 8 Feb., 14 June 1945, folder 4, box 1247, record group IX, Mundt Archives.

23. Heidepriem, *A Fair Chance for a Free People*, p. 67.

24. Ibid., pp. 76–79; *Minneapolis Morning Tribune*, 12 May 1947; "Your Washington and You," 28 May 1947, folder 4, box 1247, record group IX, Mundt Archives.

25. Karl Mundt to M. Q. Sharpe, 12 Jan. 1945 (copy), folder 3, box 678, record group III, Mundt Archives; Ray A. Stratton to Karl Mundt, 5 Jan. 1945, in ibid.

26. *Life*, 26 Mar. 1945, p. 30.

27. *Chicago Daily Tribune*, 28 Mar. 1947.

28. Sean J. Flynn, "From HUAC to EROS: How the Mundt-Nixon Association Impacted South Dakota and the Nation" (lecture, Karl Mundt Library, Dakota State University, Madison, S.Dak., 7 Nov. 2019); Lee, "Mundt and the Internal Security Act," p. 282.

29. Richard Nixon, *RN: The Memoirs of Richard Nixon* (New York: Grosset & Dunlap, 1978), p. 47; John A. Farrell, *Richard Nixon: The Life* (New York: Doubleday, 2017), p. 103; Herbert S. Parmet, *Richard Nixon and His America* (New York: Konecky & Konecky, 1990), pp. 160–61; Lee, "Mundt and the Internal Security Act," pp. 288–89.

30. Richard Nixon, *Six Crises* (New York: Pyramid Books, 1968), p. 2; Sam Tanenhaus, *Whittaker Chambers: A Biography* (New York: Random House, 1997), p. 210; Goodman, *The Committee*, pp. 244–45; Caute, *Great Fear*, pp. 56–57.

31. Farrell, *Richard Nixon*, p. 106.

32. Allen Weinstein, *Perjury: The Hiss-Chambers Case* (New York: Alfred A. Knopf, 1978), pp. 4–5; Parmet, *Richard Nixon*, pp. 162–65; Farrell, *Richard Nixon*, pp. 102–3; Cooke, *A Generation on Trial*, p. 47; Fried, *Nightmare in Red*, pp. 80–81.

33. Whittaker Chambers, *Witness* (New York: Random House, 1952), pp. 536–37.

34. Ibid., p. 538; Harvey Klehr, John Earl Haynes, and Fridrikh Igorevich Firsov, *The Secret World of American Communism* (New Haven, Conn.: Yale University Press, 1995), p. 82; Morris, *Richard Milhouse Nixon*, p. 393; Tanenhaus, *Whittaker Chambers*, pp. 215–18.

35. Morris, *Richard Milhous Nixon*, p. 394.

36. Cooke, *A Generation on Trial*, p. 8.

37. Flynn, "From HUAC to EROS."

38. Tanenhaus, *Whittaker Chambers*, pp. 218–19.

39. Nixon, *Six Crises*, p. 2.

40. House Committee on Un-American Activities: Hearings Regarding Communist Espionage in the United States Government, 80th Cong., 2nd sess., 1948, pp. 563–64, hereafter cited as Hearings Regarding Communist Espionage; Cooke, *Generation on Trial*, p. 57; Tanenhaus, *Whittaker Chambers*, pp. 219–21.

41. Hearings Regarding Communist Espionage, 570; Chambers, *Witness*, pp. 543–44; Evan Thomas, *Being Nixon: A Man Divided* (New York: Random House, 2016), p. 45; Cooke, *Generation on Trial*, p. 57.

42. Hearings Regarding Communist Espionage, pp. 580–81; Tanenhaus, *Whitaker Chambers*, pp. 160–62, 222.

43. Hearings Regarding Communist Espionage, pp. 572, 584; Karl E. Mundt, "World Affairs—A Look Ahead," address before the 36th Annual Meeting of the Chamber of Commerce of the United States, 28 Apr. 1948, folder 4, box 1209, record group VIII, Mundt Archives.

44. Hearings Regarding Communist Espionage, pp. 585–86.

45. Cooke, *A Generation on Trial*, pp. 59–60; Morris, *Richard Milhouse Nixon*, p. 398; Tanenhaus, *Whittaker Chambers*, pp. 224–25.

46. David Halberstam, *The Fifties* (New York: Random House, 1993), pp. 11–12.

47. Hearings Regarding Communist Espionage, pp. 642–43; Weinstein, *Perjury*, pp. 11–12; Nixon, *RN*, pp. 53–54; Cooke, *A Generation on Trial*, pp. 60–61.

48. Reeves, *The Life and Times of Joe McCarthy*, p. 212.

49. Stephen E. Ambrose, *Nixon: The Education of a Politician, 1913–1962* (New York: Simon and Schuster, 1987), p. 171; Fried, *Nightmare in Red*, p. 19; Tom Wicker, *One of Us: Richard Nixon and the American Dream* (New York: Random House, 1991), pp. 53–54.

50. Morris, *Richard Milhouse Nixon*, pp. 398–99.

51. Hearings Regarding Communist Espionage, pp. 646-47; Nixon, *Six Crises*, p. 8.

52. Hearings Regarding Communist Espionage, p. 647; Chambers, *Witness*, pp. 552–55; Ambrose, *Nixon*, p. 171; Thomas, *Being Nixon*, p. 48; Nixon, *RN*, p. 54; Nixon, *Six Crises*, pp. 7–9; Weinstein, *Perjury*, p. 12; Morris, *Richard Milhouse Nixon*, p. 399.

53. Tanenhaus, *Whittaker Chambers*, p. 234; Morris, *Richard Milhouse Nixon*, p. 399; Halberstam, *Fifties*, p. 13.

54. Hearings Regarding Communist Espionage, p. 659; Cooke, *Generation on Trial*, p. 64.

55. Nixon, *Six Crises*, p. 8; Nixon, *RN*, p. 54; Tanenhaus, *Whittaker Chambers*, p. 227.

56. Robert J. Donovan, *Conflict and Crisis: The Presidency of Harry S. Truman, 1945–1948* (New York: W. W. Norton, 1977), p. 414; Flynn, "From HUAC to EROS"; Weinstein, *Perjury*, p. 15; Nixon, *RN*, p. 54.

57. Alonzo L. Hamby, *Man of the People: A Life of Harry S. Truman* (New York: Oxford University Press, 1995), p. 453; Donovan, *Conflict and Crisis*, p. 414; Wicker, *One of Us*, p. 55.

58. Weinstein, *Perjury*, p. 15; Nixon, *Six Crises*, pp. 10–11; Tanenhaus, *Whittaker Chambers*, p. 228; Ambrose, *Nixon*, pp. 172–73.

59. Nixon, *Six Crises*, p. 11; Thomas, *Being Nixon*, p. 46; Farrell, *Richard Nixon*, pp. 112–13; Tanenhaus, *Whittaker Chambers*, pp. 232–35; Weinstein, *Perjury*, p. 39.

60. Nixon, *Six Crises*, pp. 11–12; Weinstein, *Perjury*, pp. 15–16.

61. Farrell, *Richard Nixon*, p. 112.

62. Wicker, *One of Us*, p. 56.

63. Heidepriem, *A Fair Chance for a Free People*, pp. 15–16, 112; David M. Oshinsky, *A Conspiracy So Immense: The World of Joe McCarthy* (New York: The Free Press, 1983), p. 407.

64. Hearings Regarding Communist Espionage, pp. 1175–76.

65. Ibid., 664-69; Farrell, *Richard Nixon*, p. 115; Ambrose, *Nixon*, p. 174.

66. Farrell, *Richard Nixon*, p. 117.

67. Hearings Regarding Communist Espionage, pp. 955–62.

68. Ibid., 978-79, 986; Farrell, *Richard Nixon*, pp. 117–18.

69. Hearings Regarding Communist Espionage, 987.

70. Tanenhaus, *Whittaker Chambers*, pp. 265–66.

71. Morris, *Richard Milhous Nixon*, p. 435.

72. Hearings Regarding Communist Espionage, pp. 1097–98; Nixon, *RN*, p. 64.

73. Hearings Regarding Communist Espionage, p. 1098.

74. Ibid., p. 1106.

75. Ibid., p. 1107.

76. Ibid., pp. 1110–14; Chambers, *Witness*, pp. 664–70, 673; Nixon, *RN*, pp. 64–65; Cooke, *Generation on Trial*, p. 88; Tanenhaus, *Whittaker Chambers*, pp. 268–69.

77. Hearings Regarding Communist Espionage, pp. 1115–21, 1131.

78. Ibid., pp. 1157–59.

79. Ibid., pp. 1159–60.

80. Ibid., p. 1160.

81. Halberstam, *Fifties*, p. 14.

82. Hearings Regarding Communist Espionage, pp. 1162–64.

83. Chambers, *Witness*, p. 695.

84. Nixon, *RN*, p. 65.

85. Heidepriem, *A Fair Chance for a Free People*, p. 115; Hearings Regarding Communist Espionage, pp. 1347–57.

86. "Are the Congressional Spy Investigations Serving the National Interest," *Town Meeting* 14 (7 Sept. 1948): 8–23, in folder 7, box 1213, record group VIII, Mundt Archives.

87. John Earl Haynes, *Red Scare or Red Menace? American Communism and Anticommunism in the Cold War Era* (Chicago: Ivan R. Dee, 1996), pp. 84–85; Flynn, "From HUAC to EROS"; Cooke, *A Generation on Trial*, pp. 91–94; Nixon, *RN*, p. 69; Fried, *Nightmare in Red*, pp. 20–21; Reeves, *The Life and Times of Joe McCarthy*, p. 214.

88. Tanenhaus, *Whittaker Chambers*, p. 303; Oshinsky, *Conspiracy So Immense*, p. 100.

89. Reeves, *The Life and Times of Joe McCarthy*, p. 214.

90. Executive Sessions of the Senate Permanent Subcommittee on Investigations of the Committee on Government Operations, 83rd Cong., 1st sess., 1953, 619; Morgan, *Reds*, p. 274; Thomas, *Being Nixon*, p. 53; Nixon, *RN*, pp. 69–70; Farrell, *Richard Nixon*, p. 124; Klehr, et al., *Secret World of American Communism*, p. 321.

91. Chambers, *Witness*, pp. 793–94.

92. Weinstein, *Perjury*, p. 513.

93. Fried, *Nightmare in Red*, pp. 21–22.

94. "What the Hiss Trial Actually Means: Speech of Hon. Karl E. Mundt of South Dakota in the Senate of the United States, January 25, 1950," pp. 5–7, 25–31, folder 7, box 1210, record group VIII, Mundt Archives; Weinstein, *Perjury*, pp. 506, 510.

95. "What the Hiss Trial Actually Means," p. 39.

96. Larry Tye, *Demagogue: The Life and Long Shadow of Senator Joe McCarthy* (Boston: Houghton Mifflin Harcourt, 2020), p. 135.

97. Lee, "Karl Mundt and the Internal Security Act," p. 285.

98. Halberstam, *Fifties*, p. 56.

PAUL HIGBEE

7 | TWO SENATORS AND SOUTH DAKOTA POLITICS IN COMPARATIVE PERSPECTIVE: LYNDON B. JOHNSON VERSUS FRANCIS H. CASE

• • •

Francis H. Case, U.S. representative and senator from South Dakota for twenty-five years in the middle of the twentieth century, told a story about growing up on the semi-arid Great Plains. He was one of Herbert and Mary Case's five children, a teenager living on the family's recently acquired homestead below Bear Butte, Meade County, when, in 1910 or 1911, his parents enlisted the services of a crew to drill a well. Francis was asked to prepare a noon meal for the crew and knew the family routine: he heated wieners in a pot of water, used the same water to make coffee, and finally washed dishes in left-over coffee. Not a drop could be wasted. If living in drought conditions wore people down, those circumstances were harder still on livestock, sometimes trailed for miles by the Cases to open ponds. The family knew that most Americans didn't live this way, but they themselves did so by choice. In 1909, they left relatively lush Iowa, rode the rails west across the one hundredth meridian (traditionally considered the line where the Midwest segues into the dry Great Plains) and on to Sturgis, South Dakota. There Herbert had accepted a position as a Methodist pastor. Herbert and Mary's farming skills would help sustain their family, and be put to the test.[1]

"South Dakota's greatest economic problem—water!" Francis Case would write.[2] But that deficit never seemed to dim his rapidly developing love for the state, where he would scale Bear Butte and explore the adjacent Black Hills, build businesses, and launch a national political career.[3] He sometimes referred to himself as a "water and roads" senator, and if that didn't always make sense to distant outsiders, South Dakotans got it. Whatever other responsibilities might be thrust on Congress, it held power to improve economies with infrastructure in isolated regions. Up and down the Great Plains, early in the twentieth century, plenty of other emerging political leaders understood, too.

Twelve-hundred miles south of Sturgis in central Texas's Hill Country, Lyndon B. Johnson was born the year before the Cases moved west, into a family sustaining itself by agriculture in a similar semi-arid environment. They hauled water, and also dealt with soil compromised by earlier Texans who failed to rotate crops and overgrazed cattle.[4] Yet, like western South Dakota, the Hill Country was ruggedly beautiful. Johnson would always love it, and it seldom failed to nurture his spirit when he pushed himself too hard.[5] At a young age, he launched a political career. Both his father and grandfather had been Texas state legislators. Johnson's innate competitiveness seemed to make it impossible for him not to consider elected service attractive, and at age twenty-eight, in a special vote forced by a U.S. representative's death, Johnson won election to congress. He represented Texas's Tenth District and took his seat in May 1937.[6] Just four months earlier, fellow congressional freshman Francis Case of South Dakota's Second District had been sworn in; like Johnson, elected service in state government never appealed to him.[7] Johnson's early efforts in Congress included development of dams and hydroelectric plants on Texas's Colorado and Pedernales rivers. Simultaneously, Congressman Case planned irrigation dams on Rapid Creek and the Cheyenne River and soon grew intrigued by the possibility of generating hydroelectricity on South Dakota's stretch of the Missouri River.[8] The challenging landscapes that Case and Johnson called home and their districts' mostly rural and conservative constituents, for whom they expressed strong allegiance, regularly put the two men on the same page early in their careers. Later, they stood aligned in their commitments to curbing union power, advancing military preparedness, and voting rights. There were even some personal similarities: back home each made money in media and Hereford cattle, and late in their careers, both would find an adversary in South Dakota's George McGovern.[9] Each would die relatively young—in their mid-sixties—from heart disease.

Yet their contemporaries in Washington, D.C., would likely have laughed had anyone proposed listing similarities between Case and Johnson. South Dakota was mostly Republican during Case's tenure—as was he himself. Johnson was a Democrat in an era when his party dominated Texas, part of a sweep of Democratic states across the American South. Each man was intensely loyal to his party and threw himself into partisan national politics, most notably for Case when he followed a Harry S. Truman railway "Whistle-Stop Tour" through seventeen states to repudiate the president's claims, and in Johnson's case when he dedicated himself to raising election funding for Democratic congressional candidates nationally with Texas oil dollars.[10] The fact that Texas was southern and South Dakota northern shaped historical perspectives and family lore. South Dakota wasn't yet a state when the Civil War raged, but Case's grandfather, Samuel Grannis, served the Union as part of the First Minnesota Heavy Artillery Company F, sent into Tennessee, where Case's great-uncle died as part of the same company.[11] Confederate private Sam Ealy Johnson, Sr., Lyndon's grandfather, distinguished himself at the Battle of Pleasant Hill, after he continued to carry a wounded comrade from the field despite the death of his horse.[12]

But more than anything, it was the central makeup of the men that clearly distinguished one from the other. Case was a short, perpetually trim man, described by *TIME* as "wispy, upright." Another journalist observed, "At work Case is as self-effacing as a Marine private—his rating in the first world war—in the presence of the commandant. He has the retiring manner of a shy Westerner and speaks in a flat voice." Of Case's reserved nature, George McGovern remarked that, "if Francis ever bared his soul to anyone, I am unaware of it."[13] Six-foot-three Johnson, meanwhile, regularly bared every emotion at his disposal. He spoke firmly in a Texas drawl and his moods, upbeat or depressed, seemed to saturate a room. Case and Johnson personified a general contrast between South Dakota and Texas political cultures across the decades—low-key as opposed to brash.

Colleagues described "the Johnson treatment," when he stood face to face, jabbing his finger, sometimes barking commands and sometimes berating the other individual. Case recognized another persuasive strategy Johnson used: flattery. Even someone who knew that Johnson's smooth compliments had designs, Case noted, could fall under his spell.[14]

By no means did Case's reticence stem from hesitancy. Sometimes he startled colleagues with frank assessments from the Senate floor, and he possessed a command of language that distinguished him among national legislators. Case first saw Washington, D.C., in 1916, after winning a national college oratorical contest as a Dakota Wesleyan College student. Woodrow Wilson was president. Case, rather surprisingly for a man who would always consider himself a conservative Republican, drew inspiration from the Democratic president. He believed the president led with high morals. When Wilson took the United States into World War I in 1917, despite campaigning for re-election as the president who kept America out of war in 1916, Case stuck with him and was prepared to fight in a "war to end all wars." He enlisted in the Marines but didn't see combat. Rather, he served as a drill instructor for new recruits in California.[15]

After the war, Case returned to college—this time Northwestern University at Evanston, Illinois, where he earned a master's degree in history. Lyndon Johnson would remember his own college experience (Southwest Texas State Teachers College at San Marcos, Texas) as a time when he learned to organize fellow students in order to lead. Francis Case in college honed writing skills that allowed him to persuade and lead.[16]

Case decided to make newspapers his career, and as a twenty-four-year-old Northwestern graduate, he returned to South Dakota and bought an interest in the *Rapid City Daily Journal*. He sold his shares in 1925 and bought the *Hot Springs Star* and later the *Custer Chronicle*. All were major avenues for South Dakotans seeking news and commentary, in an era when papers regularly re-printed editorials from other newspapers across the state. Case found himself with a statewide voice, and he used it especially to advocate for economic development related to Black Hills mining and tourism.[17] He married Rapid City High School Latin teacher Myrle Graves, and they shared a dislike for the social scene—especially that of Washington, D.C. Case never ceased thinking of himself as a writer and editor by profession, and in Washington earned the sobriquet "Senator Comma," because he was willing to edit his colleagues' bills. That was true even for bills he didn't endorse if he thought better written expression would enhance the quality of debate.[18] "I always feel better about a project," Johnson wrote to Case late in their congressional careers, "when it has had the benefit of your careful, conscientious scrutiny."[19]

While Case had admired President Wilson, he did not extend that sentiment to Wilson's fellow Democrat, President Franklin D. Roosevelt. He considered Roosevelt's New Deal, implemented immediately after the New Yorker's ascendency to the presidency in March 1933, as overreach by federal government. "No nation," he said, "can endure half on the tax roll and half on the pay roll."[20] South Dakotans, however, used New Deal services widely, in line with Democrat governor Tom Berry's belief that the programs were the state's best shot at pulling through the Depression of the 1930s, and for rehabilitating agricultural lands simultaneously devastated by the Dust Bowl. Roosevelt, Berry and the New Deal were so favored by South Dakotans in 1934 that Democrats swept all statewide constitutional elections.[21] Case committed himself to rebuilding the Republican party as part-time congressional district director. That positioned him for a successful run for Congress in 1936. In Washington he found himself part of an 88–347 Republican minority.[22] South Dakota wasn't the only place the party required rebuilding (nationally, in 1946, Republicans won control of Congress for the first time in Case's career).

Lyndon Johnson watched the New Deal take form while serving as administrative aide to Democratic congressman Dick Kleberg (Texas's Fourteenth Congressional District). Johnson left a Houston high school speech and debate teaching position to take the job, and first saw Washington, D.C., in December 1931. He would shortly idolize Roosevelt, and believe in and understand the New Deal so well that he briefly returned to Austin to coordinate one of its statewide job services, the National Youth Administration of Texas. But at first it could be hard for those around him to know where Johnson stood on issues. He seemed inclined to agree with whomever he perceived to be leading a discussion.[23] Broadcast journalist Eric Sevareid, who covered national politics for virtually all of Johnson's Washington career, called him "liberal by instinct and intellect, and conservative by geography." Helping Johnson chart those treacherous waters, Sevareid noted, was U.S. representative and fellow Texan and Democrat Sam Rayburn, soon to become Speaker of the House.[24] Johnson made Rayburn's acquaintance while an aide, and a deep friendship developed.

In Rayburn, Johnson saw how great political action emanates largely from those governing near the top of the legislative structure. He also understood what made Rayburn tick: intense dislike for banks that applied impossible interest rates that buried farmers, and for railroads whose freight fees cut deeply into farmers' revenue, and electric power companies that made good profits yet didn't run lines far enough to reach farms and ranches.[25] If the New Deal could help alleviate those grievances, Johnson decided, he was a New Dealer.

Johnson would never be a writer of Case's caliber, and during the

Kleberg years he sometimes asked fellow staffers for help with grammar and punctuation as he labored over letters he wrote to a young woman he met on a trip back to Texas. "You know, Bird's got a journalism degree," he explained. Bird was short for Lady Bird, Claudia Taylor's lifelong nickname derived because she had looked dainty as a child. Johnson had seldom dated in college or as a teacher in Houston, but suddenly married a life partner able to consistently detect her husband's doubts and help him move beyond them,[26] and who never hesitated to express her thinking on political matters. In contrast, Myrle Case (who became friends with Lady Bird after the women arrived in Washington) focused on family life and kept it mostly separate from politics.[27] Lady Bird came from enough family wealth to finance her husband's first run for Congress and possessed business skills to parlay her inheritance into successful enterprises, including Texas radio stations.[28]

Case, a harbinger in 1937 of a strong South Dakota Republican Party yet to be realized, had no mentor similar to what Johnson found in Rayburn. Fred Hildebrandt, the state's only other representative, was a Democrat, as were Senators William Bulow and newly appointed Herbert Hitchcock. Just two weeks before Case entered Congress, South Dakota's highly respected third-term senator, Republican Peter Norbeck, died in office.[29]

Had Case found a mentor well attuned to both Congress and the state's diversity, that person might have told him to be sensitive to perspectives from eastern South Dakota, called East River, should he decide to seek the Senate and need votes from both sides of the state (not that Case hinted of any interest in the Senate in the 1930s). East River was agrarian in a midwestern way, as opposed to wide cattle and sheep grazing lands and the mineral rich Black Hills of West River. Mention of minerals would have brought up Homestake Gold Mine, the nation's top producer, located in the Second District and employing two thousand constituents.[30] A good advisor could have warned Case to be cautious in dealing with Homestake. Gold was a complex matter in South Dakota through the 1930s. The mine prospered like few other corporations in the nation after President Roosevelt took the United States off the gold standard in 1933. At the same time, South Dakota farmers felt the crushing effects of the Depression. The South Dakota Farmers Union came up with a slogan that resonated: "Tax Gold, Not

Poverty." The 1935 state legislature did just that, imposing a 4 percent industrial profits tax that substantially boosted state revenue.[31]

Homestake protested mightily but to no avail. The mine was a California corporation—capitalized and incorporated in 1877 and 1878 by a future U.S. senator from that state, George Hearst. The 1935 tax alarmed Black Hills people because Homestake said it might force employment and pension cuts. The very next year, Case's pro-mining positions as a journalist—he kept files on the potential for mica, aluminum, feldspar, and other Black Hills minerals—was certainly a key to his congressional election. Case won by 2,300 votes and 1,900 of them came from Lawrence County, site of Homestake Mine.[32] Yet being seen as a friend to mining in general was preferable to a perceived coziness with Homestake. In East River, the industrial profits tax was popular. Case appreciated that the mine had successfully fought to keep itself union free, and in coming years he would be accused of reciting from a Homestake script when speaking about organized labor.

Twenty-five years after Homestake's incorporation in 1877, the great Spindletop well gushed oil south of Beaumont, Texas. That moved Texas out of an era of exploration and small operations to one of a booming oil and natural gas industry, led by characters fully as colorful as the gold rushers and mining industrialists who populated Black Hills history.[33] Much more than gold in South Dakota, oil in Texas claimed an out-sized role in influencing politics. Lyndon Johnson, at age thirty, created an identity for himself by demonstrating an unusual and instant ability to relate to oil company heads and independent operators. He could help them expand, he promised, during the national emergency declared by President Roosevelt in the months leading up to World War II. Military preparedness would require lots of fuel—for mobilizing citizens, transporting war goods, and powering military craft across land, sea, and through the air. What's more, the oil and gas pipelines and refineries that the federal government could build would surely remain in place after the national emergency. In return for his help, the young congressman advised, there was a metaphorical form of re-fueling that Texas oil might tackle: dollar contributions to the nearly depleted Democratic Congressional Campaign Committee. Sure enough, contributions flowed, and as the prime collector of funds, Johnson had a great say in determining specifically where they went nationally. If Democratic congressmen knew nothing else about

Johnson (although his big personality made that unlikely), they understood that he could help them at re-election time.[34] Republicans in Congress—Case included—knew Texas oil dollars might hurt them. As it developed in South Dakota, however, Johnson's novel campaign finance plan had no impact. A suddenly vigorous Republican Party there, led by Case, Karl Mundt and Chan Gurney, wouldn't lose a congressional race for nearly twenty years.[35]

The day after Japanese planes struck Pearl Harbor, Hawaii, Case and Johnson each voted in favor of President Roosevelt's declaration of war on 8 December 1941. Both were thinking the same thing: that they should make themselves available for military service. Case was forty-five years old, Johnson thirty-one.

Case remained in the Marine Reserve and offered to enter active duty. But Lieutenant-General Thomas Holcomb told him younger officers were well qualified, and that the work Case performed in Congress was more important than any Marines assignment.[36] Johnson, meanwhile, was a member of the House Naval Affairs Committee and had enlisted in the Naval Reserve. Within hours of his vote for war, Johnson walked into Admiral Chester Nimitz's Washington office and requested his status be changed to active. Nimitz, a fellow Texan, complied. It was hard for friends to imagine Johnson, always physically awkward, handling gunnery or fighting in any other way. But he proved himself an organized bureaucrat during his National Youth Administration tenure, and there was a need for those in the Navy. He was assigned to inspect West Coast bases, especially training methods, through early 1942. In April, Roosevelt named him to represent the Navy on a three-member observation team that flew to the South Pacific. Near New Guinea on 9 June, Johnson was aboard an Army B-26 that developed engine trouble and was targeted by Japanese Zeros, and he was in the thick of combat for thirteen minutes. That qualified him for a Silver Star, the Army's third highest service honor. The adventure set up an encounter between two giants of twentieth century American history several days later. An annoyed General Douglas MacArthur asked Johnson how it had been appropriate for a Navy observer to risk his life aboard an Army plane. Johnson replied he believed there were Texans in that squadron and that they should see how their congressman wouldn't expect them to face dangers that he himself would not. The general ended the conversation by stating that no medals were at hand; Johnson bought his Silver Star at an Army-Navy store back in the States and wore it on his lapel for the rest of his life. President Roosevelt ordered all members of Congress out of military assignments and back to Washington in July. In Washington and Texas, Johnson regularly referenced his combat experience in speeches, which led to scrutiny in the press. Reporter Marshall McNeil said of Johnson's medal, "He got it for a flight, not a fight." The congressman ignored his critics, kept the Silver Star in view, and continued describing his service over the Pacific.[37] Understanding Lyndon Johnson, it's possible that as early as 1942 he considered how Silver Star status could enhance his credibility should he ever meet soldiers as their commander-in-chief.

All congressmen, before and throughout World War II, worked to bring military installations and training missions to their states. Few states were more successful than Texas, home to long-established infantry, flight, and naval operations. Case's Second District, by contrast, claimed a National Guard camp at Rapid City and a frontier Army fort that dated back to 1878. But Case rolled up his sleeves and secured an Army air base outside of Rapid City (today's Ellsworth Air Force Base). Its first mission in 1942 was training B-17 Flying Fortress crews.[38] Case also successfully endorsed an Army aviation training detachment at Spearfish, won funding for a munitions depot at Provo, led the establishment of Black Hills National Cemetery for veterans and spouses on the eastern edge of the Black Hills near Sturgis, and brought new life to the 1878 fort.[39] He knew that post, Fort Meade, well. Like his family's long-ago dry homestead, it sat near Bear Butte. Case led Fort Meade's transformation into a Veterans Administration Hospital, a role it retains to this day.

Case was proud to note that his 1940s military building projects in South Dakota were built without unionized construction crews. Organized labor was widely criticized during World War II. Critics feared that labor demands and the recent, federally mandated 40-hour work week could slow weapons production and military facilities construction. As the *Dallas Morning News* claimed, "Factories which can turn out 1,000 instruments of war a week are turning out 500."[40] Case seized on that thinking and expanded on it post-war, making it a key to his national identity. On 29 January 1946, he introduced the Case Labor

Bill (HR 5262) mere days after 750,000 steel workers went on strike. Case's bill sought to make unions liable when strikes made it impossible to fulfill contracts, forbid unionized supervising staff, and set up a labor-management board authorized to enforce a thirty-day cooling off period after a union announced strike intentions.[41]

Newsweek magazine noted that, "The Second District, which Case represents, is predominantly agricultural. Labor problems seldom disturb the 150,000 people who live in the vast stretches of grazing and wooded lands as big as Kentucky . . . the 20,000 Indians Case represents outnumber his labor-union constituency."[42] That theme—that Case didn't have to answer to union members—was repeated elsewhere, and Thomas Stokes, a columnist syndicated nationally through Scripps-Howard, guessed that Homestake was behind Case's thinking.[43] *Newsweek*'s offhand comment about South Dakota's American Indians, implying they couldn't be relevant to a discussion about labor, was typical of the way the 1940s national press characterized one-eighth of Case's constituency.[44]

"You never know when you're going to make a ripple," Case told a reporter, and his labor bill did, winning attention throughout Congress.[45] It set the tone for a Senate version, the landmark Taft-Hartley Bill, that passed both Houses and, to the surprise of many, won Lyndon Johnson's vote. Johnson was generally loyal to Roosevelt's prolabor philosophies, but the president had been dead for nine months when Case's bill began forcing debate. It seemed that Johnson was demonstrating more of his "conservative by region" persona. President Harry S. Truman vetoed Taft-Hartley, but Congress overrode the veto and the bill became law in 1947.[46]

The 1940s made it clear what drove Johnson. He would always seek higher elected office. Case, by contrast, admitted it was pleasant to consider returning with Myrle and their daughter Jane to South Dakota. When "the Black Hills come into conversation, his deep-set eyes brighten behind his gold-framed glasses," *Newsweek* noted, adding that, "riding horses he hires from Washington stables are no match for his Arabian stallions and favorite mare at home." Meanwhile, few watching Texas politics when Johnson voted for Taft-Hartley doubted that the Tenth District representative would reach for the Senate in 1948.

On 2 November 1948 Lyndon Johnson won 66 percent of the vote over Republican Jack Porter to be elected senator.[47] But that wasn't even the big story. The bigger news was Johnson's victory over popular former governor Coke Stevensen in a primary runoff for the Democratic nomination two months earlier, since at the time Democrats always won statewide elections in Texas. Johnson had tried for the senate once before, in a special election in 1941, but narrowly lost the nomination. He claimed that his opponent's team stole votes. In 1948, it was Johnson who, Texas critics would always believe, benefitted from stuffed ballot boxes and dead people on registration lists to eke out an eighty-seven-vote primary win. At question was a missing ballot box from tiny Alice, Texas, near the Mexican border, and a tally sheet from that precinct containing irregularities and two hundred votes for Johnson. A joke circulated, and no one was better telling it than Johnson himself, making use of a Hispanic accent. As the joke went, a questioner asked a boy why he was crying. Because, the boy replied, his father passed through town but didn't visit him. But wasn't his father dead? wondered the questioner. "Si," said the boy. "He has been dead for ten years but he came to town last Saturday to vote for Lyndon Johnson, and he did not come to see me!"[48]

Johnson, telling the joke in his over-the-top style (by contrast it was hard for most acquaintances to imagine Case telling jokes in any style) seemed to challenge Texans who took the stolen election idea seriously. The point was that he was a now seated senator. In unprecedented fashion he moved quickly to become the senate's most powerful member—minority leader in four years and majority leader six years after his election.[49]

Case in the 1940s, along with advancing his military projects within the Second District, delved into the issue that took more of his time than any other throughout his Washington tenure: the Flood Control Act of 1944. Through that Act's authority, the Pick-Sloan Plan brought together the Bureau of Reclamation and the Army Corps of Engineers to build four dams across South Dakota's section of the Missouri River. The dams would substantially reduce—but not eliminate—spring flooding that had devastated South Dakota river towns since territorial days. More than that, the dams would generate hydroelectricity for South Dakota and the national grid, attract boaters and fishermen to the reservoirs (to a greater extent than projected), and irrigate croplands (to a lesser extent than projected). Water that Case once identified as the state's number one economic problem now appeared to hold potential as a great asset.[50] Most South Dakotans appreciated Case's vision and leadership related to the river, and Army Corps of Engineers major general Lewis Pick held him in high esteem. In that political climate, Case decided a senate seat might help him to continue shepherding the Pick-Sloan Plan, and he announced his candidacy for the 1950 race. That meant challenging two-term Republican senator Chan Gurney for their party's nomination. The move surprised observers, not the least Gurney, who had worked closely with Case over the years. But Case now viewed Gurney's consistent efforts related to national defense as mirroring "the opinions of the military and the administration" (Truman), and he appealed to war-weary South Dakotans by focusing on local issues. The strategy worked. In the primary, Case defeated Gurney by taking 58 percent of the vote, then went on to defeat Democrat John Engel with 64 percent in November.[51] Two months later, Case was sworn in, one of seven new Senate Republicans.

In South Dakota, for the rest of Case's years in Washington, components of the Pick-Sloan Plan took form, submerging 611,164 acres underwater in the state. More than half, 309,584 acres, were American Indian reservation lands that included towns, naturally watered agricultural lands, and, especially painful, cemeteries where bodies were disinterred and reburied elsewhere. Case and other leaders promised reimbursements. Those payments were made.[52] Still, some families were put in positions far from the river, where they had to haul water, dig wells, and drive cattle across the plains to stock dams—the same conditions Case and his family knew at Bear Butte half a century before. In the nineteenth and twentieth centuries the ways South Dakota prospered—agriculture, gold, and railroads—often deprived American Indian peoples of land. The Pick-Sloan Plan continued that pattern. Later historians sometimes criticized the plan, most notably Michael L. Lawson. Although he considered Case somewhat "paternalistic" in his dealings with tribes, Lawson credited him as the only politician "who voiced concern about how the army intended to acquire the Indian lands," and called Case's communications with federal American Indian agencies and tribal leaders "the only known instance in which tribal governments were informed by a federal representative of the possible adverse effects of the Pick-Sloan Plan prior to its enactment."[53]

In the U.S. Senate, as individuals of a governing club of just ninety-six members, Case and Johnson interacted as never before. The 1950s—the era of McCarthyism, the Cold War, civil rights, and the space race—had the pair often thinking far beyond the prairies and hills of South Dakota and Texas. Johnson's party leadership was so strong that when it came time to meet with the Republican senate leader (usually California's William Knowland) to choose members for committees, he often in effect designated Republican members as well as Democrats.[54] Johnson made it his job to learn everything he could about all senators, and that led him to become a master at predicting senate voting well before a vote was called.[55] In 1954, Case was named to a six-member select committee charged with deciding whether or not to recommend censure of Wisconsin senator Joseph McCarthy. Case sat on the committee because Johnson wanted him there.[56]

McCarthy believed, as did Case, that the threat of Communism stemmed not only from the Soviet Union, but was likely rooted in the United States. McCarthy, in fact, believed Communists worked within the U.S. government under the Roosevelt and Truman administrations (he later included the Eisenhower administration too). The senator captivated the nation in hearings that charged government employees, military members, and individuals in private industry with being "card carrying" communists.[57] Johnson knew that Case believed McCarthy's quest for evidence of internal infiltration was good for the nation, as it was opening eyes. But Johnson also understood Case to be offended by McCarthy's uncivil personal attacks during the hearings, considering them beneath the dignity of the Senate. In particular, McCarthy called New Jersey Republican senator Robert Hendricks—a veteran of both world wars and the Korean War—"a living miracle who has lived so long without brains or guts."[58] As a member of the select committee, Case would ask McCarthy if he would like to retract or modify the insult.

In choosing members of the committee, chaired by Utah Republican Arthur Watkins, Johnson and Knowland sought conservative senators without a hint of scandal in their pasts. They succeeded; *New York Daily Post* columnist John O'Donnell considered the men so colorless that he branded them the "Six Sad Sacks."[59] Early on, Case successfully moved to ban television from committee meetings, depriving McCarthy of an outlet for his well-rehearsed dramatics.

McCarthy declined Case's offer to back away from the insult aimed at Hendricks.[60] Case saw that as evidence of contempt of the Senate, and on that count alone endorsed recommending censure to the full Senate. The decision wasn't easy; he knew from his mail that most South Dakotans supported McCarthy. In the future, Case's stand, combined with the fact that South Dakota's other senator, Karl Mundt, was an anti-Communist crusader in the same league as senators McCarthy and Richard Nixon, led some observers to think Case wasn't much worried about Communism. In fact, he found it abhorrent because it established atheistic regimes. But Case saw no room in government for a crude man like McCarthy, who was indeed censured by the full Senate.[61]

Meanwhile in 1954, Johnson campaigned across Texas for what proved to be an easy Senate re-election. He won more than 70 percent of the vote in the Democratic primary and more than 80 percent in the general election.[62] Johnson remained an advocate for the oil and gas industry. By early 1956 he was advancing the Harris-Fulbright Bill, which aimed to nullify the Federal Power Commission's authority, granted in 1938, to regulate interstate pipelines and pricing for natural gas. The 1956 bill would significantly boost gas company profits. But on 3 February, Senator Case rose on the Senate floor and said, "I cannot vote for the bill as it stands before us. In the light of evidence personal to me that the bill has prospects of unusual monetary profit to some and with that profit would go the means for a continuing effort to influence the course of government for private gain, I must vote to maintain in people's government the opportunity to control the profits from a monopoly product."[63]

Case's personal issue stemmed from twenty-five one-hundred-dollar bills, delivered to him in Sioux Falls by an attorney for Superior Oil Company of California. Case considered it a bribe for his Harris-Fulbright vote in the Senate. An angry Johnson accused Case of misconstruing a simple campaign contribution as something nefarious and quipped that he thought it time "to investigate the morals of some people in South Dakota for bringing this up."[64] The Senate vote moved ahead and Harris-Fulbright passed 53–38. However, at the other end of

Pennsylvania Avenue, President Dwight D. Eisenhower decided to veto it because of what Case revealed. The president wrote that the natural gas incident was the "most flagrant kind of lobbying that has been brought to my attention in three years."[65] If Case, perhaps predictably, defined a high standard for conducting senate business, as he had regarding McCarthy, it's certain that Johnson didn't see it that way.

Later in 1956, Case was re-elected to the Senate, but this time with just 4,620 more votes (of a quarter million cast) than Democrat Kenneth Holum. President Eisenhower's unpopular Secretary of Agriculture, Ezra Taft Benson, was a problem for all congressional Republicans. Farmers believed the Secretary aligned with food processing corporations rather than with those who grew produce, and Case asked Eisenhower to dismiss Benson, but to no avail. George McGovern astutely seized upon farmers' mistrust of Benson to begin rebuilding the state's Democratic party, and was himself elected to the U.S. House of Representatives in 1956—the first Democrat to be part of South Dakota's congressional delegation since 1943.[66]

Briefly, the state Democratic Party considered complaints that Case benefitted by stuffed ballot boxes in Pennington County. It was revealed that about one hundred sample ballots were cast, a legal procedure if not enough regular ballots were supplied. Election officials said that was indeed the situation but Washington journalist Drew Pearson (the nationally syndicated *Merry-Go-Round* columnist) took up the story. It briefly appeared possible Case might face an Alice, Texas, scandal of his own. But state Democrats acknowledged the legality of the substitute ballots and noted that one hundred votes weren't enough to sway the outcome, even in tight 1956.[67]

Case and Johnson alike supported Cold War-era military preparedness, meaning developing technology that would out-pace anything the Soviets might deploy. Both sat on the Senate Preparedness Committee. The 1957 launch of Sputnik, the Soviet satellite, put space and rocketry into play. Johnson became an architect of the American space program and never forgot his underlying motivation, stating that, "we are not reaching for prestige in space; we are reaching for peace . . . to default the exploration of the universe of space would be as catastrophic in its consequences as if we had defaulted exploration of the universe of the atom."[68] Each man regarded the sparsely populated Great Plains as the best location for launching intercontinental ballistic missiles.[69] While Texas sat too far south for Minuteman missile launch facilities (the thermonuclear weapons, if ever launched, would fly over the Arctic toward Soviet targets), South Dakota was well positioned. Eventually 150 Minuteman missiles sat in silos beneath the South Dakota plains, from the 1960s until the mid-1990s, when they were deactivated under the Strategic Arms Reduction Treaty.[70]

Meanwhile, both senators were competing with the rest of Congress in acquiring miles in their states for the developing Dwight D. Eisenhower National System of Interstate and Defense Highways. Case had a great say, as a member of the Senate Public Works Committee and ranking Republican on its Roads Subcommittee, in shaping construction financing with a federal gasoline tax rather than local bonds.[71] That metropolises like Houston, Dallas, and San Antonio would be linked to the four-lane highways surprised no one (Texas eventually acquired 3,340 miles). But South Dakota's two interstates and 678 miles without a major American city in sight is testimony to Case's funding formula and understanding that the highways were for moving military equipment wherever it might be needed, not only civilian traffic. Senator Johnson's aide, Harry McPherson, credited Case for "a monument which archaeologists a millennium from now may find to be proof of our production genius or madness, or both—the Interstate Highway System."[72]

Case's thinking about civil rights in the 1950s was shaped by his deep belief that all Americans deserved unimpeded access to the voting booth (he was part of the District of Columbia Committee that won District residents the right to vote in presidential elections under the Twenty-Third Amendment) and also by his observation that federal programs intended to aid his American Indian constituents sometimes interfered with their rights.[73] Civil rights overall, as indicated by Case's South Dakota correspondence, did not "reflect the intense interest it has commanded in the East and South," Case wrote in 1957.[74] Meanwhile Johnson, longtime aide Joseph Califano recalled, was deeply moved by African Americans he saw forced into inferior, segregated hotels and restaurants in the South—including members of his staff as they drove between Washington and Texas.[75] In summer 1957, in a bold move for a southerner and one that transformed his national image, Johnson decided to advance the first federal civil rights legislation since 1875. Johnson knew he had Case's support in guaranteeing voting rights, and likely guessed that his South Dakota colleague would identify some complicating matter that most others missed.

Indeed, Case did. He feared empowering a future U.S. attorney general who could hypothetically enforce inclusion through injunctions against individuals; remembering 1920s history, Case wrote that would be "a bit reminiscent of using prohibition agents for local law enforcement."[76] When the Civil Rights Act of 1957 passed the Senate on 7 August, it emphasized voting rights, and Johnson saw Case's handiwork there. The next day Johnson wrote to Case: "For the courage of your convictions and the precision of your mind, the country should always be grateful. You played a major role in bringing about an effective bill that honorable men can accept."[77] Johnson would work to expand civil rights for the rest of his career, understanding that the 1957 Act set a precedent for further federal action, including integrating Southern hotels and restaurants.[78]

In Lyndon Johnson, Case saw that a man could suffer a major heart attack yet bounce back, apparently as vigorous as before. Johnson experienced his first at age forty-nine, in 1955. Case suffered his first at age sixty-five in March 1962, as he prepared to run for a third Senate term. In early June he easily won his party's nomination and learned he was set to face the young, increasingly popular George McGovern in the general election.[79] But on the morning of 22 June, in Washington, Case was hit by a fatal heart attack.[80] Four days later Johnson led a sixteen-member congressional delegation that flew to Rapid City for the funeral, but not as a senator. He served as President John F. Kennedy's vice president, from 1961 to 1963—a difficult period that Lady Bird remarked "was somewhat limiting to the capacities of Lyndon."[81]

In Rapid City, recalling their congressional service, Johnson described Case as "a man of rugged and uncompromising independence. He insisted on thinking all problems through and on coming to his own independent conclusion. This is the type of intellectual integrity that has made America strong."[82]

McGovern defeated Case's governor-appointed replacement, Joseph Bottum, in November.[83] A year later, Johnson became president when Kennedy was assassinated in Dallas. When he won a term as president in his own right in 1964, Johnson became the first Democratic presidential candidate to capture South Dakota's electoral votes since 1936—and the last to date.[84] McGovern's rebuilding of the South Dakota Democratic Party helped, and it's certain that Johnson appreciated McGovern's support early in his presidency as he advanced civil rights and Great Society programs. But it's equally certain that Johnson saw McGovern as a persistent problem as his administration was more and more defined by his unpopular Vietnam War policy. McGovern stood out nationally as a war critic. Vietnam, more than anything, drove Johnson out of presidential politics in 1968. He died of a heart attack at his ranch, at age sixty-four, on 22 January 1973.[85]

NOTES

1. Richard R. Chenoweth, "Francis Case: A Political Biography" in *South Dakota Historical Collections*, Vol. 39 (Pierre: South Dakota State Historical Society, 1978), pp. 295–96. For insight into farming with less than twenty inches of precipitation annually, see *The Interior Borderlands*, ed. Jon Lauck (Sioux Falls: Center for Western Studies, 2019), pp. 1–20, 188–200.

2. Chenoweth, "Francis Case," p. 296.

3. Jarvis Harriman, *The Man from the Hills: A Biography of Leland D. Case* (Tucson: Westerners International, 1994), pp. 1–20.

4. Robert A. Caro, *The Path to Power*, Vol. 1, *The Years of Lyndon Johnson* (New York: Vintage Books, 1990), pp. 21–32.

5. Clint Hill with Lisa McCubbin, *Five Presidents—My Extraordinary Journey with Eisenhower, Kennedy, Johnson, Nixon, and Ford* (New York: Simon and Schuster, 2016), p. 219. Hill was a secret service agent assigned to Johnson from 1965 to 1969.

6. Caro, *The Path to Power*, p. 452.

7. Chenoweth, "Francis Case," pp. 315–16.

8. Caro, *The Path to Power*, pp. 459–68, 527–28; Chenoweth, "Francis Case," pp. 319–20.

9. No other industry linked western South Dakota and Texas like beef cattle. Texas cattle companies began trailing livestock north to Dakota Territory's public domain, open range grasslands in the late 1870s. These entrepreneurs escaped overgrazed ranges and southern bovine diseases. Some cattlemen, their families, and their working cowboys remained to build an agricultural economy distinct from eastern South Dakota croplands. See Herbert Schell and John Miller, *History of South Dakota* (Pierre: South Dakota Historical Society Press, 2004), pp. 155–56; Richard Slatta, "Afterword" in *Cowboy Life*, ed. Cathie Draine (Pierre: South Dakota Historical Society Press, 2007), pp. 297–307.

10. Chenoweth, "Francis Case," pp. 379–80.

11. Leland D. Case and Edith E. H. Grannis, eds., *New Hampshire to Minnesota: Memoirs of Samuel Higbee Grannis* (Tucson: published by Edith E.H. Higbee, 1962), pp. 59–72.

12. Caro, *The Path to Power*, p. 19.

13. For descriptions of Case by journalists who were his contemporaries, see "Milestones," *Time*, 29 June 1962, p. 29, and "The Ripple Maker", *Newsweek*, 10 June 1946, p. 34. McGovern's quote was recorded by Chenoweth on 14 July 1974, and used in "Francis Case," p. 292.

14. Descriptions of "the Johnson Treatment" are legion. See especially Caro, *Master of the Senate*, Vol. 3, *The Years of Lyndon Johnson* (New York: Vintage Books, 2002), pp. 126–27, 139–40; and Hill and McCubbin, *Five Presidents*, p. 188. Case's observation about Johnson's flattery is from the author's interview with Jane Case (daughter), 6 Oct. 2019.

15. Chenoweth, "Francis Case," pp. 300–302.

16. Ibid.; Caro, *The Path to Power*, pp. 174–201.

17. Chenoweth, "Francis Case," p. 303.

18. Author's interview with Jane Case, 11 Apr. 2021; Chenoweth, "Francis Case," pp. 304, 430–33.

19. Letter, Johnson to Case, 29 Jan. 1958, Drawer 184 Senator Francis H. Case Collection, Dakota Wesleyan University (DWU) Archives, Mitchell, S.Dak.

20. Chenoweth, "Francis Case," pp. 314–15.

21. "Berry Sweeps State Ticket to Victory," *Pierre Capital Journal*, 7 Nov. 1934.

22. Case never forgot entering congress as part of a small minority, "scarcely one member in five," and he used the experience to stress the importance of congressional rules that protect voting and speaking for all members. See his senate speech, 20 June 1954, "Rules Are For the Protection of Minorities," drawer 2, Senator Francis H. Case Collection, DWU Archives.

23. Caro, *The Path to Power*, pp. 213–77.

24. Eric Sevareid commentary, *CBS Evening News with Walter Cronkite*, 22 Nov. 1963.

25. Caro, *The Path to Power*, pp. 306–40.

26. Julia Sweig, *Lady Bird Johnson, Hiding in Plain Sight* (New York: Random House, 2021), pp. xviii—xx.

27. Interview with Jane Case, 11 Apr. 2021.

28. "Some Day You'll Be Sitting in That Chair," *Time*, 29 Nov. 1963, pp. 32–33.

29. Larry Pressler, *U.S. Senators from the Prairie* (Vermillion: University of South Dakota Press, 1982), pp. 77–89, 97–111.

30. Schell, *History of South Dakota*, p. 382.

31. Elizabeth Williams, *Emil Loriks: Builder of a New Economic Order* (Sioux Falls: Center for Western Studies, 1987), pp. 45–52.

32. Chenoweth, p. 316.

33. Bruce Wells, "Spindletop Launches Modern Petroleum Industry," American Oil and Gas Historical Society, 31 Dec. 2009, https://aoghs.org/petroleum-pioneers/spindletop-launches-modern-oil-industry/.

34. Caro, *The Path to Power*, pp. 606–26.

35. *The Plains Political Tradition*, Vol. 1, ed. Jon Lauck, John Miller, and Donald Simmons (Pierre: South Dakota Historical Press, 2011), pp. 343–45.

36. Chenoweth, "Francis Case," pp. 336–44.

37. Caro, *Means of Ascent*, Vol. 2, *The Years of Lyndon Johnson* (New York: Vintage Books, 1990), pp. 20–45.

38. Bart Pfankuch, *Ellsworth Air Force Base: 75 Years of Guarding Freedom*, (Rapid City: Pediment Publishing, 2017), pp. 7–43.

39. Neil Lyon King and Joan Sunderland King Collection, Leland D. Case Library for Western Historical Studies, Black Hills State University, Spearfish, S.Dak; Chenoweth, "Francis Case," p. 328.

40. "The 40-Hour Week," *Time*, 30 Mar. 1942, p. 9.

41. Chenoweth, "Francis Case," pp. 345–49, and "Labor Policy Failure Puts Nation Close to Perils of General Strike," *Newsweek*, 18 Jan. 1946.

42. "The Ripple Maker," *Newsweek*, 10 June 1946, p. 34.

43. Chenoweth, "Francis Case," pp. 348–49.

44. Case was proud of his understanding of and constituent services for American Indians who, as a voting block, leaned Republican in South Dakota until the 1950s. He championed the career of his friend, Republican Ben Reifel, the first American Indian to represent South Dakota in Congress from 1961 to 1971. See Sean Flynn, *Without Reservation: Benjamin Reifel and American Indian Acculturation* (Pierre: South Dakota Historical Society Press, 2018), pp. 122, 133.

45. "The Ripple Maker"; See also Matthew Pehl, "The Frustrations of Organized Labor in South Dakota and the Making of a Conservative Coalition in the Midcentury United States," *The Plains Political Tradition*, Vol. 2, ed. Jon Lauck, John Miller, and Donald C. Simmons, Jr. (Pierre: South Dakota Historical Society Press, 2014), pp. 103–25.

46. Caro, *Means of Ascent*, p. 125

47. "1948 United States Senate election in Texas," *Wikipedia*, https://en.wikipedia.org/wiki/1948_United_States_Senate_election_in_Texas.

48. Caro, *Means of Ascent*, pp. 303–99.

49. Ibid., p. 412.

50. John Ferrell, "Developing the Missouri: South Dakota and the Pick-Sloan Plan," *South Dakota History* 19 (Fall 1989): 306–41.

51. Pressler, *U.S. Senators*, p. 116; Chenoweth, "Francis Case," pp. 369–87.

52. Ferrell, "Developing the Missouri."

53. Michael L. Lawson, *Dammed Indians Revisited: The Continuing History of the Pick-Sloan Plan and the Missouri River Sioux* (Pierre: South Dakota Historical Society Press, 2009), pp. 40, 123.

54. Robert Dallek, *Lyndon Johnson and His Times, 1908–1960* (New York: Oxford University Press, 1991), p. 457.

55. Caro, *Means of Ascent*, p. 13.

56. Dallek, *Lyndon Johnson*, p. 457. Dallek's source was journalist William S. White, in Knowland's office as select committee members were designated.

57. "McCarthy Is Dead of Liver Ailment at The Age Of 47," *New York Times*, 3 May 1957.

58. "Committee Findings on McCarthy," *U.S. News and World Report*, 8 Oct. 1954, p. 69.

59. "The Congress—Censure of Joe McCarthy," *Time*, 4 Oct. 1954. This includes John O'Donnell's characterization.

60. "Committee Findings on McCarthy."

61. Chenoweth, "Francis Case," pp. 391–97.

62. "1954 United States Senate Election in Texas", *Wikipedia*, https://en.wikipedia.org/wiki/1954_United_States_Senate_election_in_Texas.

63. Pressler, *U.S. Senators*, pp. 145–47.

64. Caro, *Master of The Senate*, p. 667.

65. Dallek, *Lyndon Johnson*, pp. 498–99.

66. Jon Lauck, "George McGovern and the Farmer: South Dakota Politics, 1953–1962," *South Dakota History* 32 (Winter 2002): 331–53.

67. Chenoweth, "Francis Case," pp. 425–27.

68. "Some Day You'll Be Sitting in That Chair."

69. Case was deeply involved in helping South Dakotans, especially landowners who might yield land to Minuteman facilities, understand the program. See File 34, Drawer 136, Senator Francis Case Collection, DWU.

70. Interpretation of the Minuteman program, locally and nationally, is found at the Minuteman Missile Historic Site, Philip, S.Dak.

71. Chenoweth, "Francis Case," p. 414.

72. Ibid.

73. Pressler, *U.S. Senators*, p. 143; Interview with Jane Case, 11 Apr. 2021; Chenoweth, "Francis Case," p. 324.

74. *Senator Francis Case Reports* (constituent newsletter), 5 Aug. 1957, Drawer 1, series 5, Senator Francis Case Collection, DWU.

75. Joseph A. Califano, Jr., *The Triumph and Tragedy of Lyndon Johnson—The White House Years* (New York: Touchstone, 1991), p. 41.

76. *Senator Francis Case Reports* (constituent newsletter), 22 July 1957, drawer 1, series 5, Senator Francis Case Collection, DWU.

77. Letter, Johnson to Case, 8 Aug. 1957, drawer 179, ibid.

78. Caro, *Master of The Senate*, pp. 1009–11.

79. "Case Handily Captures Primary; Nauman Wins," *Huron Daily Plainsman*, 6 June 1962.

80. Chenoweth, "Francis Case," pp. 428–29.

81. Sweig, *Lady Bird Johnson*, p. 16.

82. "Sen. Case Buried at Foot Of His Beloved Hills," *Aberdeen American News*, 27 June 1962.

83. The race was close; McGovern won by 597 votes in an election with a quarter million votes cast. Pressler, U.S. Senators, pp. 150–51.

84. *The Plains Political Tradition*, Vol. 1, pp. 351–56.

85. "Lyndon Johnson, 36th President, Is Dead; Was Architect of 'Great Society' Program," *New York Times*, 23 Jan. 1973.

PAUL WILSON

8 | THE POLITICAL STRATEGIES OF GEORGE MICKELSON

• • •

My mother was a precinct committee woman in Kansas City, Missouri, and she took me along, going door-to-door. I loved the buttons, stickers, and yard signs and so I came to love politics. At age six, I teamed up with other kids in my neighborhood to have our own election. We ran the Disney characters for office and I had Bambi for President. I campaigned on my bike with playing cards clipped to the frame to make a loud clacking sound as I pedaled. The neighbors came and voted in a makeshift polling place in a neighbor's garage and Bambi won! That's how I got into politics. From that unusual start, I became obsessed and studied "how to campaign" in every class by asking annoying campaign related questions that would improve my skills. I remember in middle school staying long after school to practice my typing skills, reasoning that I would need to write a lot in my future profession. After college I went to work for one of the first campaign firms, Bailey Deardourff & Associates. I called them up while finishing my master's degree and boldly announced, "Well, I'll be coming to work for you." They seemed happy to have me and kept me so busy that I packed one bag in June and did not fully unpack it until November. After a decade, I left and formed my own firm. We started working out of my basement with the dryer blasting away. It was so hot that my two employees had to strip off their shirts as we worked. We moved out of that basement as fast as we could, which was my wife's plan all along. In mid-1985, I surveyed the country for possible clients and I reasoned that South Dakota, with four candidates for governor, would provide an excellent opportunity.

I thought about working for the Secretary of State of South Dakota, Alice Kundert, a grandmotherly political success story. I knew her campaign manager and called him, having never met Alice. "No, no, no, Paul! Alice is not who you want to help," the manager surprisingly said.

"Alice isn't going to win. You want to work for the one who is dead last in the primary: George Mickelson, the former Speaker of the House." So began the journey of helping George Mickelson go from dead last to governor. Up to this point in my "you're on-your-own" career, I had never had the campaign manager of one candidate tell me to work for another. Not just tell me but actually plead with me to work for someone else. But I took his advice, and I am glad I did. Because George Mickelson became one of my all-time favorite candidates to work for. Someone in describing Mickelson to me said, "Mickelson played football in high school and college." I asked why that made any difference. He said, "Mickelson is eminently 'coachable.' You tell him the play and he will execute." It was 1985 when we got started. No email. No internet. Commercials back then were still only shot on film. We were off to the races against three formidable Republican opponents.

Clint Roberts was a former member of the United States House of Representatives from South Dakota's Second District and former Agriculture Secretary. Dubbed the "Marlboro Man" for his good looks and western way, rumor had it that Clint, with his western mustache, was almost picked to be the original Marlboro Man for the famous cigarette ad campaign. He didn't get that job but over the course of his career, his Western rugged good looks and cowboy boots won him many television commercial gigs. No sooner did Clint get in the race than he dropped a bombshell poll on 15 October 1985, showing that he would win a Republican primary with 47 percent of the vote in a four-way race. Mickelson was dead last in the poll in single digits.

Also running was Lowell Hansen, the incumbent lieutenant governor to Governor Bill Janklow and the wealthiest in the field, thanks to family money earned with an intra-state bus line called Jack Rabbit Lines. Lowell knew state government, came from Sioux Falls, the largest voting bloc, and had befriended the country club crowd in Sioux Falls.

Alice Kundert was the South Dakota Secretary of State. Alice was not the favorite in the race, far from it. She worked on the theory that the men in the race would split the field and she would shoot up the middle as the only woman in the race. Alice was competent, extremely well-known among Republican voters, hard-working, and friendly, but did not have widespread support.

George Mickelson was the fourth candidate and former Speaker of the South Dakota House of Representatives and a Vietnam veteran. Mickelson was the personification of the rugged, larger-than-life candidate. He was a lawyer from Brookings. Fortunately, his law partner was highly supportive and carried the practice while Mickelson campaigned. Mickelson and Roberts both embodied the strong frontier image more so than Hansen or Kundert.

It was August 1985 and to save money and time for both Mickelson and me, we agreed to meet in Minneapolis to discuss my advertising firm being hired. When I met Mickelson, I was put off a little. True, he was a big man as a former football player, but what bothered me was that he was a "mouth breather." To breathe through your mouth you must keep your mouth open—making you look dumb as a post. Combine that "look" with the stereotype of a football player and, well, that's not a good combination. Mickelson was my first major client after I left Bailey Deardourff & Associates to start my own firm. Mickelson was 6'5" and 250 pounds. I showed up at 5'8" (well maybe 5'7"). So it was a bit of an odd pairing. Mickelson said he had a man in mind to be manager: Dwight Adams, who was in his early sixties. Dwight turned out to be deadly serious and a superb organizer and manager. Dwight was a retired military man with combat experience in three wars. You knew this because Dwight would routinely wear a small rifle pin on his lapel signifying his combat service. Mickelson wanted him as campaign manager; they were both from Brookings. I got to know Dwight quite well and over the years we became close friends. I remember staying in his basement recreational room when I was in Brookings. There on the far wall in a corner was a small proclamation awarding Dwight the highest honor for bravery. It read something like this: "Dwight Adams, when his platoon was pinned down by enemy machine gun fire, did run across an open field, in clear view of the enemy, and circled around behind the machine gun installation and with grenades did single handedly neutralize the opposing force."

As luck would have it, our triumvirate made a good team. Dwight Adams was used to having a battle plan and carrying out the orders. Mickelson was the old football player who preferred to have the play called and then he would execute. My background was as one of the campaign industry's first ad firms. I was accustomed to writing large, two-hundred-page campaign battle plans, with detailed budgets and with nearly every single detail mapped out, including which television spots to produce. I was ably helped by Jamie Pound, a veteran of Senator John Chaffee's office. Jamie brought a charming sense of humor to the effort, which helps in a high-tension campaign.

My company was allowed, under our contract, to bill the campaign for expenses. Dwight Adams called once and said, "You owe the campaign seven stamps. I saw where you had used 93 stamps, but you billed us for a full 100-stamp roll so kindly return the other seven." That level of detail and oversight was Adams's trademark. In fact, Dwight organized the campaign to such an extent that almost every night the headquarters closed by 5 p.m. That never happens in a campaign.

The plan would say, for example, go to Brookings and walk a specific precinct. Dwight Adams would check the schedule and bring Mickelson to Brookings, being careful that every second was used but not wasting extra time. Mickelson would do his part, grinding out a door-to-door effort even though it was a statewide primary. The extra effort served to show Mickelson's strength. He went door-to-door even at five degrees below zero. Having a plan, a battle-tested military commander, and an extremely hard-working candidate was a combination that was needed to win a primary with three other better-known Republicans.

George S. Mickelson's middle name was Speaker. It was given to him by his father, who had served first as Speaker of the House before becoming governor. But the problem for the campaign was that it was so long ago that only centurions remembered the father as governor. It was not an advantage, but neither was it a disadvantage. George Mickelson's work in the community and the legislature seemed to resonate better. The campaign from day one had the mindset that there was a strong feeling that Mickelson could have great difficulty getting elected: he was last in the polls, he had never run in a statewide election, he held no statewide office, and had been out of any office for almost six years. Plus, he was just not well-known. As the campaign plan laid out, "These facts make George Mickelson's campaign difficult. They do not make it impossible."[1] The campaign set out with some incredibly specific numerical goals. Mickelson's challenge in the primary race was to: 1) Identify and win 37,238 votes [Mickelson actually won 40,979 votes]; 2) Raise $357,000; 3) Pull equal in name identification by 1 April and build a strong organization in seventy-three precincts in the top forty-three counties.[2] Fortunately, Mickelson eked out a few thousand more votes because the goal in the plan would have been a few votes shy of what Clint Roberts received.

Clint Roberts' Total	Mickelson's Goal	Mickelson's Vote
37,250	37,238	**40,979**

The campaign predicted a turnout weighted toward East River for Mickelson but with Clint Roberts winning an overwhelming number of West River votes in the area he had won as a congressman. The state is divided politically by the Missouri River. East River is Minnehaha County (Sioux Falls) and all other rural areas east of the Missouri. West River includes Pennington County (Rapid City) and all land out west of the Missouri River. With the primary on 3 June, the goal was to pull even by 1 April 1986. The campaign had a great plan for media but was also committed to having a major organizational push that we termed the "ground game." This included parades, door-to-door canvassing, and campaigning on college campuses. The campaign consisted of targeting precincts with five hundred or more registered Republicans. Many people asked, "why would you go door-to-door in a statewide contest?" The answer: there were a limited number of Republican voters and they were geographically located in two corridors in the eastern and western parts of the state. As laid out in the campaign plan, "Going door-to-door demonstrated the strength and determination that Mickelson had to be Governor."[3] The campaign clearly believed that making the massive door-to-door effort reinforced the overall message of highlighting Mickelson's strength.

Throughout the primary, one figure loomed large: Governor William Janklow, the two-term, tough-as-nails governor. Polling showed 80 percent of primary voters had a favorable impression of Janklow's time as governor and they liked how he stood up to everyone, especially to Washington, D.C. Janklow personified the wild west culture of South Dakota and Mickelson wanted to fit right in. A duality existed in voters' appreciation of Janklow. On the one hand, Republican primary voters loved the job he had done as governor, but they also worshiped their beloved U.S. senator Jim Abdnor, who was being challenged by Janklow in the senate primary. The Mickelson campaign had its hands full trying to match the bravado of Janklow. Voters wanted a strong governor again. So the Mickelson campaign did everything it could to emphasize his fortitude.

As the campaign plan noted, "Nothing does more to convince people of the seriousness of a candidate than plain hard work."[4] The advantages to portraying Mickelson as strong were many. It emphasized the rugged Western ethos of South Dakota's heritage. It also showed Mickelson as a leader willing and capable of continuing the progress made under Governor Janklow. Fortunately, Mickelson fit the perception both physically and as a character trait. A number of issues played directly into this narrative of strength. Top among them, Mickelson opposed unions, whereas Lowell Hansen caved in on right-to-work laws and appeared willing to accept unions gaining a toe hold in South Dakota.[5] On 16 October 1985, Mickelson announced his candidacy for governor. He relied on a rhetorical device that Senator Bob Dole used—speaking of himself in the third person. It was different and effective and helped his lagging name identification. Mickelson would say: "As governor, I can tell you no one will be stronger, no one more experienced, no one more committed to continuing our success than George Mickelson." This self-referential speaking style allowed Mickelson to use his name more. It also sounded stronger. "I am here today because I want to help choose which road we take for the next four years. I want your help in leading this state down the road of opportunity."[6]

One of Mickelson's most formidable competitors was Clint Roberts, the former congressman from western South Dakota. Clint was an original to be sure. Clint once rode his horse into the State Capitol and frequently wore his cowboy boots to Washington. As the editorial writer of the *Sioux Falls Argus Leader* put it in his obituary for Clint, "No South Dakota politician's facial hair had taken him further than that of Roberts, who rode his unmistakably Western-style 'stache to jobs as a commercial actor and narrowly missed being chosen as the Marlboro Man."[7]

The Mickelson campaign had a major problem from day one and no one outside the inner circle knew it. George Mickelson was trying to become governor in a farm state during a national farm crisis and the campaign came to learn that Mickelson knew almost nothing about agriculture or ranching. He could ride a horse, but that and hunting were about as close to the farm that Mickelson got. The campaign staff was extremely worried that running against Clint Roberts, a cowboy from out west, would expose our candidate's deficiency. Mickelson was, after all, a well-heeled lawyer who had spent the previous five plus years practicing law. To address the problem, the campaign carved out a significant chunk of time for a program dubbed "Farm Hard Work Days." In the mid-80's the idea was relatively unique. But what made Mickelson's take on the idea a little better was that it was secret. No one in the press knew the campaign had started months before having Mickelson go to a farm to work. The plan had a little more punch to it. After Mickelson had gone to eighteen farms, the campaign started retracing Mickelson's steps and went back to many of the farms he had worked. Only on the second visit did a camera crew come along. Mickelson did what he had done before: sweep out the barn, ride the tractor, and feed the cattle. There was a sweet surprise at one farm. In early February, Mickelson had been in a farmer's barn and was asked to help "pull a calf" that was being birthed. It was a pretty gruesome sight to the non-farmer types. The calf's hind legs were grabbed by Mickelson as it was coming out and Mickelson gave a mighty yank until the calf slithered out of its mother's womb. The campaign debated not using the footage but decided to air the commercial to pick up much needed attention and name identification. It produced the desired effect. Some argued that this was a farm state and voters could "handle" the image. The "calf pulling spot" only aired for about one week (of course around the dinner hour) but it generated huge publicity with people arguing on both sides whether the campaign should show the calf pulling or not. In the end, the spot jump-started the campaign and got people talking about Mickelson.

Although the original plan was to hold the strategy of working on farms secret until a little later in the primary, the decision changed with the cow birthing spot to reveal the entire Farm Hard Work program earlier than originally planned. The footage was not only riveting, but even shocking to some and it showed literally that Mickelson would get his hands dirty.

"I'm Not A Farmer"

George Mickelson: *My name's George Mickelson. I'm not a farmer and I don't pretend to be, but when our farmers and ranchers are hurt, the rest of us are too. That's why I've taken time during this campaign to work shoulder to shoulder with our farmers. On dairy farms, grain and cattle farms, successful farms, and farms which need our help. And the one thing I've learned from these brave people is that we need a governor who fights for our farmer. And that's the kind of governor I intend to be.* Announcer: *Mickelson. George Mickelson. Republican for governor.*

The campaign also highlighted Mickelson's physical strength "bucking bales" into a truck. This spot played well during the early winter months of the campaign and boosted Mickelson's awareness among agricultural bonafides.[8] The campaign had another great surprise. By the time the campaign circled back to farms in the fall of 1986 with another film crew, Mickelson and his team came across the same ranch and the same calf. Only we came to learn that the calf Mickelson had pulled had won first place at the state fair in his class. Priceless. Although a general election spot, it fits in better here:

"Blue Ribbon Cow"
Testimonial #1: *George Mickelson came on a cold day. Came about 7:30 in the morning and shoveled out the feed bunks.*
Testimonial #2: *Went with us and helped feed the cattle.*
Testimonial #3: *He rode in the combine with us.*
Testimonial #4: *We were putting some dry straw in the sheds.*
Testimonial #5: *George helped us sort heifers off.*
Testimonial #6: *He also helped us with some smaller calves.*
Testimonial #7: *He helped pull this heifer that day and it created quite a stir. But George went on to win the primary in June. This heifer went on to win her class at the state Holstein show.*
Announcer: *George Mickelson. He'll deliver for South Dakota.*

Airing this spot in the fall with the winning calf gave the Mickelson team a small sense of destiny. This may seem quite strange, but it felt like we were supposed to win because of that calf. We wanted to humanize Mickelson in the primary and this next introductory spot did that. It summarized his life, which was about as much as anyone knew about the other candidates.

"Ready to be Your Governor"
George Mickelson: *I'm George Mickelson. To me, there's more to being governor than just having been in government. It takes*

understanding how people live. So after serving as speaker of the house and chairman of four committees, I took the time to build my own legal business. Worked to improve my community. And with my wife Linda, raised our three children, Mark, Amy and David. And with this experience, I can truly say, George Mickelson is ready to be your governor.

The spot "Ready to be your Governor" turned out to be a very solid introductory spot in the primary for Mickelson. It established that Mickelson was Speaker of the House but expanded his resume to give it a more human dimension by introducing his wife Linda and their three children. The spot ran in the spring long before the primary. The goal remained unchanged. Mickelson had to pull even with the other candidates in terms of name identification by April of the election year. The best spot for laying out the campaign to voters was this one, since it emphasized how tough the weather is and how hard Mickelson was going to work.

"Weather is Tough Here"

Announcer: *Our weather is tough here in South Dakota, but so is George Mickelson, Republican candidate for governor.* George Mickelson: *No one deserves to be governor. You have to earn the job every day. And that's what I intend to do in this campaign. That means going door-to-door to meet 55,000 voters. And it means working side-by-side with our farmers. I worked hard when I was speaker of the house and chairman of four committees. Now I'm working even harder to be your governor.* Announcer*: George Mickelson, Republican for governor.*

To display Mickelson's ruggedness and his desire to be governor, the campaign featured Mickelson outside going door-to-door in the dead of winter. At minus five degrees on the day of the shoot, Mickelson's breath was visible as he crunched his way through the frozen snow. The cold and the snow were a metaphor for how hard Mickelson would work to become governor. It also beautifully showcased the spot's opening line: "Our weather is tough here in South Dakota." The next spot tried to remind voters that their governor could impact the economy in very real terms. Yes, farmers depended on Washington, but there were many ways the governor could help.

"Fight for Farmers"

George Mickelson: *I'm George Mickelson. Some people feel all of our farmers' problems must be solved in Washington. I don't agree. It isn't Washington, it's the governor that will help South Dakota farmers who no longer have a farm. It isn't Washington, it's the governor that will attract food processing plants to South Dakota. And it isn't Washington that will save our railroads and keep our transportation costs low. We need a governor who's not afraid to fight for our farmers. And that's the kind of Governor George Mickelson will be.* Announcer: *George Mickelson. He's ready for governor.*

With the U.S. Senate race remaining highly contested during Mickelson's primary, the decision was made to create space between what could be accomplished in Washington versus South Dakota. The spot took an indirect swipe at Representative Tom Daschle and made the case that a strong governor has a lot to say about the future of the state.

As Mickelson gained name recognition, we drew upon his close friends who were the legislative leaders to make the point that Mickelson could get things done. Many primary voters were still on the fence as the campaign came into the final stretch. This spot used legislative leaders—filmed authentically in the Senate and House chambers—to endorse Mickelson. The result was a spot that looked credible and was also a crushing endorsement. All of the leaders were persuasive, but no one was "over the top." In a word, they appeared credible.

"Colleagues"

Announcer: *Those who know the candidates best endorse Mickelson for Governor.* Testimonial #1: *I know all of the candidates quite well, but I'm choosing George Mickelson.* Testimonial #2: *I've served in the legislature twenty years, and of all the people that I've had the opportunity to serve with, George Mickelson has superior qualities.* Testimonial #3: *George Mickelson would be an excellent governor for South Dakota.* Testimonial #4: *He is a true leader and the person that should be leading the state of South Dakota.* Testimonial #5: *George Mickelson is ready to be governor.* Testimonial #6: *The person who can carry out the office of governor more effectively than anyone else, is George Mickelson.*

Each person had credibility and sincerity, and each delivered a sledgehammer of an endorsement. As the primary drew near, Lowell Hansen, the lieutenant governor, attacked. Mickelson was gaining and was within striking distance of winning the primary. Clint Roberts was hoping his prior experience and awareness would carry the day. But he was, and continued to be, impecunious. So the task of knocking down George Mickelson fell to Lieutenant Governor Lowell Hansen, who possessed money and two powerful arguments. His first attack was to spread the rumor that Mickelson secretly supported an income tax. In this Republican primary, such an accusation, if true, was the kiss of death.

"Misleading Opponent"

George Mickelson: *I'm George Mickelson. One of my opponents, Lowell Hansen, is misleading voters by saying I support an income tax. He's wrong. Anyone who examines my record can see that I voted against an income tax twenty-one times. That's where I stand. In fact, as former Speaker of the House, I'm proud of my record of keeping taxes low. My opponent may want to mislead you, but you can count on this, as long as George Mickelson is governor, this state won't have an income tax.* Announcer: *Mickelson for governor. He's ready for the job.*

Mickelson's record was strong: he had voted against an income tax twenty-one times. Hansen had mistakenly used an answer to a reporter's question as the basis for the charge. Mickelson had built a high level of credibility up to this point in the primary and that combined with his voting record carried the day. Plus, Mickelson emphatically stating that if he became governor, South Dakota wouldn't have an income tax was an excellent punctuation mark.

Two weeks before the primary, Lieutenant Governor Lowell Hansen dropped his second bombshell on George Mickelson. Hansen attacked Mickelson for going on an extravagant hunting trip with Citibank executives, the state's largest employer. Governor Bill Janklow and Lieutenant Governor Lowell Hansen disagreed over whether George Mickelson's hunting trip to South America was improper. Hansen criticized Mickelson in the primary for being the guest of Citibank on a quail hunting trip to South America in 1984. The bill for the five-day trip for four people was $86,000, including the cost of a private jet. At the time of the trip, Mickelson was not in public office and was not an announced candidate, although he had publicly said he was thinking about running for governor. Janklow said he was disappointed in Hansen for bringing up the hunting trip (and this was Janklow's own lieutenant governor). Janklow did not endorse Hansen. That is not to say he was outwardly against him, but he certainly never helped him, despite Hansen being his second-in-command for eight years. This incident exposed the naked fact: Janklow was not pro-Hansen. Internally in the Mickelson campaign, the hunting trip was clearly viewed as one of the major problems Mickelson had as a candidate. The hunting trip debacle attacked the honesty and integrity of Mickelson. It besmirched his otherwise super-clean image. Some in the campaign had the fatalistic view that this was the poison arrow. Mickelson had clearly gone on the trip, which cost a small fortune, so many thought Mickelson was guilty as charged. But in the television defense, the campaign took the unusual step of agreeing with the critics. Instead of running from the issue, Mickelson turned and ran right at it. Mickelson sat outside on a large stump holding his shotgun.

"Where the Ducks Are"

George Mickelson: *As a lifelong hunter, one of the first things I taught my sons was to go hunting where the ducks are. And when it comes to bringing jobs to South Dakota, that means going to the business leaders that can bring jobs here. To try to save his campaign, Lowell Hansen is now criticizing Citibank, one of our state's largest employers, for inviting me as a guest on a hunting trip. That's the difference between us. I know where to hunt for jobs. I think the people of South Dakota want a governor who knows the business leaders that can bring jobs to South Dakota. And that's the kind of governor I'll be.*

Mickelson knew the attack by Hansen looked very bad. But Mickelson believed South Dakota voters should want their governor to be on excellent terms with corporate leaders. After all, this was a Republican primary. So, with shotgun in hand, Mickelson pronounced that the extravagant hunting trip was a good thing. Voters agreed and the crisis was averted.[9]

The primary was in the first week of June 1986. At the time, there were only three television stations on the air in Sioux Falls. Fox TV

Table 1. Republican Primary Results

	Candidate	*Votes*	*%*
Republican	George S. Mickelson	40,979	35.30
Republican	Clint Roberts	37,250	32.08
Republican	Lowell Hansen	21,884	18.85
Republican	Alice Kundert	15,985	13.77
Total votes		116,098	100.00

Primary Election Results—Top Candidates

Candidate	*Votes*	*%*
George S. Mickelson	40,979	35.30
Clint Roberts	37,250	32.08

The primary election result appeared like Mickelson had won relatively easily: Mickelson 35.30% and Roberts 32.08%.

had barely started anywhere in the country and had only a little programming in prime time. All television network heads in Sioux Falls said there wasn't room in the market for an independent television network and certainly not before the Fall of 1987. In 1986, three dominant stations existed in Sioux Falls. The result of this small media pool was that it was far easier to communicate one message to the entire electorate very quickly. The outcome was that Mickelson rebuffed the Hansen attack.[10]

But the vagaries of election law played a part. South Dakota had an election codicil to complicate the primary election night. Even though Mickelson won the most votes, the state required that the outright winner had to have *over* 35 percent. Fortunately, Mickelson had 35.30%, avoiding the dreaded runoff by only 0.3 percent.

In addition to the gubernatorial election, 1986 proved to be a highly charged news year, which stole attention away from the governor's race. Number one was the Farm Crisis. Farmers were in a terrible tailspin. Agriculture prices were depressed, and farmers faced foreclosure for defaulting on loans. But three other blockbuster news events distracted voters. First, as noted earlier, Governor Bill Janklow had decided after eight years as governor to challenge Senator James Abdnor in the Republican primary. Janklow was unsuccessful in the primary. Abdnor beat Janklow surprisingly handily 54 to 46 percent. Secondly, Tom Daschle, the four-term congressman, challenged Senator Jim Abdnor, the Mr. Nice Guy of the Republican Party, in the general election. Daschle and Abdnor, backed by Washington D.C., money, spent millions in the race, to the surprise of all. Without question, the Senate race overshadowed the governor's race and Daschle beat Abdnor in a tight race: Daschle received 51.6 percent of the vote to Abdnor's 48.4 percent. Third, the Challenger space shuttle had exploded in January, killing all seven of the astronauts and the first civilian schoolteacher astronaut. Finally, Chernobyl had shocked the world by failing on 26 April 1986. This was the Soviet Union's four-unit nuclear power plant. The world knew it was a calamity as radiation sensors had gone haywire. Decades later, the site is still too dangerous to visit without radiation suits, and then only for brief periods of time.

On the Democratic side of the ledger, State Representative Lars Herseth had been in office for twelve years, eight as the Legislature's minority leader. Ken Stofferahn, a public utilities commissioner, took office in 1978. Richard Kneip, president of Nelson's Laboratories, spent seven and a half years in the governor's seat. It was as competitive a race as the Republicans were having.[11] Herseth and Stofferahn both worked to erode Kneip's early overwhelming lead.[12] Herseth, the more personable of candidates, went on to win the Democratic primary, snuffing out Kneip's attempt at a fourth term as governor.

Mickelson had celebrated his primary victory in his hometown of Brookings on election night and his plan was to drive to Sioux Falls to capture interviews on all three television stations. Mickelson looked terrible. He was sick, hoarse, and absolutely exhausted. Mickelson had put everything into the race. I remember joking: "Now that's how I like 'em. Totally spent." Mickelson had won by the smallest of margins and was victorious but worn out. The region's biggest newspaper, the *Minneapolis Tribune*, reported: "Primary Victory Barely Avoids Runoff." Mickelson had exceeded the runoff margin by 344 votes.[13]

The general election became a battle between two smart, knowledgeable candidates who had each served in the legislature for years. Lars Herseth, a farmer and Democratic legislative leader hailed from the Democrat bastion of Brown County in northeastern South Dakota. Mickelson was from Brookings. In the general election there were four

Table 2. Mickelson/Herseth Polling Data and Actual Vote 1986

	Percent	% Difference	Votes
June 1986			
George Mickelson	52	+16	
Lars Herseth	36		
Undecided	12		
September 1986			
George Mickelson	49	+13	
Lars Herseth	36		
Undecided	15		
October 14–16th 1986			
George Mickelson	46	+16	
Lars Herseth	30		
Undecided	25		
October 26–28th 1986			
George Mickelson	48	+12	
Lars Herseth	36		
Undecided	17		
Election Day			
George Mickelson	51.81	+3.63	152,543
Lars Herseth	48.19		141,898
TOTAL VOTES			294,441

surviving polls from the Mickelson campaign, all from the general election of 1986. Shown below is a chart displaying results of the four polls and the actual election day results.

An analysis of the polling taken by Market Strategies from June to late October shows that Mickelson appeared to hold a comfortable lead throughout the 1986 election. But a closer look shows an alarmingly high number of undecided voters. Days before the general election, Mickelson appears to have a comfortable lead of 12 percent. But by election day, Mickelson's lead disappeared to a margin of only 3.63 percent.[14] The Mickelson camp viewed the high percentage of unde-

Table 3. Final Election Results General Election 1986

Party	Republican	Democrat
Candidate	George Mickelson	Lars Herseth
Popular vote	152,543	141,898
Percentage	51.8%	48.2%

cided voters as a warning sign. In mid-October, Mickelson was ahead by a very favorable 16 percent. But at the same time, an alarming one in four voters were still undecided. The race was not over. "By most accounts, Mickelson is in the driver's seat in his bid to become Governor," the *Argus Leader* journalist Dave Kranz wrote. "But Herseth will disagree pointing to his in-house poll showing he now leads the Brookings lawyer by nine points."[15] Both Mickelson and Herseth had been around a long time in state government. Both campaigned hard. During the campaign, Miceklson had learned how to be outgoing and friendly. But Herseth was a natural politician and the more people who met him, the more they liked him, and so the race tightened considerably. Plus, Herseth was a real farmer in this hard-hit farm state. The other giant factor was the draw Daschle had on independent and undecided voters. Many went with Daschle for the Senate and Mickelson for governor. Speculation still surrounds the race with the Herseth supporters accusing Daschle of actively pushing Daschle/Mickelson voters to the polls to the detriment of Herseth. At the finish line, Mickelson edged Herseth by 10,645 votes—not a photo finish but still quite close.

The Democrats during the gubernatorial primary and general election period simply could not put together the resources that Republicans had mustered. Herseth was outspent two to one. Mickelson had three thousand contributors and won a contribution from the Republican National Committee totaling $45,000. The best summary of the race came from the *Argus Leader* editorial page in its endorsement of Mickelson: "The race comes down to which candidate can most articulately, forcefully and successfully pursue the interests of South Dakota. We believe Mickelson is that candidate. He has a refined talent to lead."[16]

South Dakota had one of the country's fiercest fire fights in its U.S. Senate race. This senate race easily overshadowed the governor's race in terms of interest and dollars spent. It began in the most contentious of ways. Incumbent governor Bill Janklow, rarely a team player, decided to face off in the primary against beloved Republican U.S. senator Jim Abdnor. Janklow assumed Abdnor was too old. It turned out, at least for the primary, he was not. Abdnor was loved by South Dakota Republicans, and they surprisingly turned their back on their eight-year Governor Bill Janklow and gave Abdnor a handy victory. Janklow was both a proud and arrogant man, but someone capable of one day returning to election success against Mickelson's West River lieutenant governor and then Governor Walt Miller. In fact, Janklow won two more terms as governor and a term in Congress before having to resign after killing a motorcyclist near his home while driving well over the speed limit. Abdnor's opponent in the November general election was Democrat Tom Daschle—a strikingly good-looking veteran, who along with Abdnor's Republican friends, turned the race into a financial blood bath. They made the race one of the most expensive in the country. The very popular President Reagan traveled to the state twice but to no avail. Daschle served from 1987 to 2005, becoming Senate Minority Leader in 1995 and later the Majority Leader in 2001. Daschle hailed from the Democratic base of Aberdeen. He served four terms in the House after serving three years in the Air Force during the Vietnam War. State Representative Lars Herseth had been in office for twelve years, eight as the Legislature's Minority Leader. Ken Stofferahn, a public utilities commissioner, took office in 1978. Richard Kneip, president of Nelson's Laboratories, spent seven and a half years in the governor's seat. Herseth and Stofferahn eroded Kneip's early overwhelming lead and Herseth easily won the primary. People recognized Herseth as the better candidate.[17]

The most persistent and pernicious issue was the wage scale in South Dakota. From teachers to timber workers, everyone thought that wages were too low. It was clear people were starved for more money. The Mickelson campaign engaged on that issue. Admittedly, it was an unusual start to the General Election to have economic theory of supply and demand being the starting point.

"Wages Up"
Announcer: *Too many of us aren't paid enough for what we do. George Mickelson knows this, and he has a plan.* George

> Mickelson: *The way that we can increase wages for South Dakota workers is by increasing the competition for jobs. I can cite an example of a company that came to South Dakota and hired welders. Another company came in a couple of years later. Suddenly the wage scale for welders went up. Competition builds wages. I think the people of South Dakota want a governor that can bring jobs to South Dakota. And that's the kind of governor I'll be.* Announcer: *Mickelson. Ready for governor.*

The campaign used a simple economic principle to argue the Mickelson case: demand will drive up wages. An odd start to a gubernatorial campaign but it was the single biggest issue. People wanted to make more money.

Later, after Abdnor fended off Janklow's primary challenge, Janklow was freed of restraints. He did not want his record besmirched by Herseth, so after a special trip by Mickelson to Pierre to formally ask the governor to record a commercial, he agreed. It was a good one.

> *"Income Tax Friend"*
> Governor William Janklow: *As governor, I've worked here with both George Mickelson and Lars Herseth, and there's a big difference in their records. While Lars Herseth sat in this chair, on four occasions he sponsored state income taxes and on 10 occasions he voted for them. Those votes could be costing your family over a thousand dollars a year. George Mickelson has never sponsored an income tax and 21 times he's voted against one. If you don't want an income tax in South Dakota, then like me, you want George Mickelson sitting in this chair.*

It was a bit touchy to approach Janklow to do an ad for Mickelson since he had lost his primary race in June. But Mickelson persuaded him, and the governor probably figured it would be restorative to his wounded reputation. Bill Janklow went on to defeat Walt Miller for governor in 1994 after Mickelson died in an airplane crash. Nonetheless, Janklow was licking his wounds from his primary dust up against Senator Jim Abdnor. The campaign filmed this spot using the prop of the governor's actual chair. It was a masterful spot because it had the strength of Janklow combined with Herseth's votes for an income tax and Mickelson's opposition to one.

South Dakota is thought of as an "old" state because much of its population is older. This was true in 1986. The campaign played to seniors on television and through direct mail. Seniors were a group Mickelson needed. If any group still remembered Mickelson's father, the former governor, this was the group. But as polling came to show, it was Mickelson's campaign, rather than his father's legacy, that won over this critical voting-block.

"Golden Seniors"

Announcer: *One out of five of us in South Dakota is a senior citizen. So, we need a governor who listens. Who cares. Who helps.* George Mickelson*: I'm going to form a golden pheasant fund where senior citizens can sign up to get issued a golden pheasant card. And then it would just identify you as being entitled to a senior citizen discount at any participating merchant.* Cashier: *That'll be two dollars off.* George Mickelson: *Absolutely free. It's on a volunteer basis. Doesn't cost anything and I think that's the least I can do as governor.* Announcer: *The golden pheasant discount card. Mickelson. Ready for governor.*

This spot made a direct play for senior citizens who could be easily targeted on daytime television. The idea eventually became adopted in Mickelson's first term. Seniors, of course, liked the idea and merchants did not object since offering the discount was voluntary. Polling comparing Mickelson's support going up from 55 percent to 63 percent was due in large part to the increase in support from seniors. The message got through. No other age group increased support as much. Seniors' support for Mickelson went from 42 percent in April 1990 to 71 percent in mid-October—a blockbuster rise.[18]

At this time in the general election, we rolled out the mildly humorous spot called Blue Ribbon Cow described earlier. It showcased the calf that had been pulled by Mickelson in the winter and the Blue Ribbon-winning grown up calf.

"Don't Have to be a Farmer"

Testimonial #1 Farmer: *You don't have to be a farmer to be governor of South Dakota.*

Testimonial #2: *I don't feel like you have to be a farmer to be the governor.*

Testimonial #3: *A basic knowledge of agriculture would be pretty important. And George has that.*

Testimonial #4: *Our governor can be the number one salesperson, number one ambassador for our products.*

Testimonial #5: *As a farmer and a businessman, I think George Mickelson will make a great governor.*

Testimonial #6: *We're not sending George Mickelson to Pierre to pitch hay or to ride a tractor. We need a man who can help agriculture. And George Mickelson can do that.* Announcer: *George Mickelson. He's ready for governor.*

This spot was key to selling Mickelson the lawyer as acceptable to the farm community. It was one of the most persuasive spots of the campaign. Of course, not even 10 percent of South Dakotans were farmers, but everyone identified with the land or had come from the land. Each farmer's testimonial explained in a logical way why Mickelson was both acceptable to farmers and would actually help the farm community. This whole message was artfully delivered by the farmer who said, "We are not sending George Mickelson to Pierre to pitch hay or ride a tractor. We need a man who can help agriculture." There it was. The perfect embodiment of why Mickelson should be governor—even as a lawyer, even with a very credible farmer running against him. Nearly everyone in South Dakota it seemed had family that had come from the farm. Mickelson hooked his wagon to the image, and it carried him across the finish line.

As the campaign was nearing the end, the Mickelson team was nervous about the progress our polling showed Herseth making. To hamper that progress, an attack on Lars Herseth's record was needed. Mickelson's long-standing opposition to an income tax and Herseth's sponsorship of one was the contrasting issue to close the campaign.

"Business Climate"

Announcer: *Companies don't come here for our weather. They come for our business climate. But the record of Lars Herseth has them worried. After years of voting for an income tax, in 1980 Herseth started sponsoring one. And nine months before his campaign, he still favored an income tax. Now he says he's against one. Would you move jobs here on what Lars says or on George Mickelson's record of never sponsoring an income tax and voting twenty-one times against one? Mickelson for jobs.*

This ad was the hardest hitting of the campaign even though it rehashed the same issues. The ad directly compared the steadfast opposition of Mickelson to an income tax versus Herseth's record of sponsoring one.

Mickelson's victory over Herseth was a combination of hard work and advertising that convinced voters that Mickelson would do a better job of protecting and improving their economic futures. The closing spot harkened back to the image of Mickelson's pioneer grandfather. It was a perfect image to end on for the campaign.

"Close"

George Mickelson: *When my grandfather came to South Dakota, he had to clear the rocks from his land with his bare hands. And that same kind of hard work is what I put into this campaign. Working on farms and ranches. Defining my program to save family farms. And market our new products. And I've worked just as hard outlining how I'll bring jobs here.* Linda Mickelson: *Both of us want to thank everyone who's helped this year.* George Mickelson: *And the hard work I've shown during this campaign is the same hard work I'll give you as governor. On Tuesday, I'd appreciate your vote.*

This was a very nice "ask for the order" spot. Mickelson subtly invoked his family's pioneer roots and equates in metaphorical style his hard work in the campaign to the hard work of his ancestors. It was also the right time to show off Linda Mickelson, George's wife. This proved the whole family was supportive and in the game. By this late point in the campaign, Mickelson had become excellent on camera. It paid off in this spot.

In 1990, the path to reelection for Mickelson was clear and substantially easier than his election in 1986. The campaign produced thirteen ads that aired from mid-August through election day. Some of those ads are shown below. In February 1990, Democrat Bob Samuelson, preparing his campaign, was buoyed by a poll taken by the Democratic Party. It offered him real hope. It was quite encouraging to him and no doubt helped him decide to get into the race. It did appear to run contrary to prevailing opinion. Mickelson's popularity was a shaky 34.2 percent. Typically, incumbents like to be over 40 percent in their re-election year. When voters were asked "will you consider voting for someone else, or do you think you will vote to replace Mickelson," 46.8 percent of respondents in the Samuelson poll wanted someone else.[19]

However, other metrics in the poll were not at all encouraging for Samuelson—only 3.7 percent of respondents said "experienced" described Samuelson. The poll also showed Mickelson with a very strong positive rating: 72.6 percent very favorable or somewhat favorable opinion versus 22.3 percent with a less than favorable impression.[20]

The first spot of the reelection campaign summarized all of the positives of Mickelson's first term. The campaign and the first spot emphasized how new jobs were coming to South Dakota.

"New Jobs"

Announcer: *Across South Dakota, more people are working, and new jobs are still coming. New opportunities and better wages. Through the "REDI Fund" Governor George Mickelson is creating thousands of new jobs. Better paying jobs! And South Dakota is moving forward.*

George Mickelson: *New jobs like these are coming to South Dakota, and that's a fact. This is only the beginning. Together we can build an even brighter economic future.* Announcer: *Re-elect Governor Mickelson. He's moving South Dakota forward.*

The upbeat jobs message played well to Mickelson's base. The campaign slogan of "he's moving South Dakota forward" emphasized the progress the state had made compared to four years earlier.

But the second ad of the campaign stressed an issue that was unusual for South Dakota: crime. To film this spot the campaign went to the state prison—an ancient relic near a hog processing plant. The stench was so horrible that crew members covered their face with handkerchiefs. The culprit in the rising crime rate in 1990 was drugs. Like the rest of the nation, the drug crisis hit South Dakota hard enough to push the issue near to the top of the campaign.

"Prison"

George Mickelson: *We're simply not going to tolerate drug abuse. Because the people who live in South Dakota will live safe and*

I'm dead serious about that. As governor, I fought for tougher sentencing for drug pushers and drug prevention programs for our school children. So now children at risk of drug abuse can be helped earlier before they're in trouble. But the people who break our drug laws are gonna do time. Hard time! And I'm making sure we're building the prison cells to lock 'em up. Announcer: *Re-elect Governor Mickelson.*

Mickelson looked tough in the spot helped by a guard who was thirty yards away and holding a shotgun looming over Mickelson's shoulder throughout the spot, Mickelson looked convincing and talked about modernizing the prison in front of the ancient one.

Another surprising ad for a Republican was a full out pro-environment spot. The campaign went to the expense of moving the crew to far Western South Dakota and trudged around the Black Hills.

"Environment"
Announcer: *A new day is dawning in South Dakota's Black Hills. People are working harder to preserve these hills and Governor Mickelson has worked to make sure this natural treasure will be here for generations. He passed a two-year moratorium on new mines and toughened environmental regulations to keep our groundwater safe and clean.* George Mickelson: *I grew up admiring the beauty of these hills and I still come here often. As governor I've made it my job to protect our Black Hills.* Announcer: *Re-elect Governor Mickelson.*

The political mood had changed over four years and even Republicans in growing numbers supported protecting the Black Hills from strip mining and the use of dangerous chemicals in the mining process. Even though Mickelson's lieutenant governor came from out West, where mining was somewhat more popular, Mickelson took credit for the unthinkable: ordering a two-year moratorium on new mines. Mickelson himself confided privately that he hated the strip-mining techniques used in his beloved Hills. The farm crisis was easing and Mickelson reaped the benefits. Farm foreclosures by banks were down and Mickelson had worked hard in the legislature to freeze property tax increases.

"Agriculture"

Announcer: *Governor George Mickelson and Lieutenant Governor Walt Miller have worked hard for South Dakota's ranchers and farmers. With their programs, farm bankruptcies have decreased 81% since 1987.* Testimonial #1: *Well, they worked to save the family farmer. That's what counts most to me.* Announcer: *Mickelson's "REDI Fund" has attracted new ag processing plants for oats and ethanol.* Walt Miller: *The governor put a freeze on property taxes and also proposed a permanent cap.* George Mickelson: *When agriculture moves forward, all of South Dakota moves with it.*

Mickelson was well on top of the agriculture issue with four solid years under his belt as governor. He didn't have to go work the farms in this campaign.

One of the most unbelievable accomplishments, if compared to present-day politics, was winning the South Dakota Education Association's endorsement because it is usually a very reliable Democrat organization. But Mickelson's support of higher teacher salaries carried the day. The campaign was made so much easier because it could lean on the credible work of the previous four years. Internal polls in mid-October, as depicted in Chart 5 below, showed Mickelson winning with 63 percent to Samuelson's 26 percent with 11 percent undecided.[21]

"Vision"

Announcer: *Governor Mickelson has a record of improving education. Bob Samuelson has no plan. So educators endorse Mickelson.*

Testimonial Clyde Clausen, SDEA: *It is a pleasure for me today to announce the SDEA endorsement of Governor George Mickelson for re-election.* Announcer: *Governor Mickelson's improving rural health care. Samuelson has no plan. And Mickelson's shown he can bring jobs here. But there's NO Samuelson plan. He can't even list his priorities. Re-elect Governor Mickelson. He's moving South Dakota forward.*

The Mickelson/Samuelson battle toughened up with this ad accusing Samuelson of having no plan for education. Mickelson touted the endorsement from the South Dakota Education Association. Compared to negative commercials of the 2020 campaign season, the attack on Samuelson is mild and largely unsubstantiated. The campaign, however, was not over. Mickelson had a three-issue power play: the endorsement by teachers and his work on a jobs program and an environmental program.

"Day One"

Announcer: *Governor Mickelson's has a plan for South Dakota from day one. The Winner Advocate says Mickelson's job program has been an undebatable success. Mickelson's plan for education: endorsed by teachers. Mickelson's protected our environment and defended our water.* George Mickelson: *We have to fight for this water because if we don't, they're going to take it from us.* Announcer: *A plan for South Dakota that works. Re-elect governor Mickelson. He's moving South Dakota forward.*

A new issue was introduced, albeit briefly: the issue of water. The ad alluded to the on-going war with the federal government over water rights. Few things, if any, are more important to ranchers and farmers than access to water. The campaign also used a very small newspaper's testimonial at the top of the ad to tout Mickelson's job program.

"Close"

Announcer: *From his first day in office through our Centennial Celebration, George Mickelson has brought to the job of governor, the energy and skill to improve South Dakota. Creating more jobs at higher wages. Protecting our Black Hills. Improving education for our children.*

George Mickelson: *Since taking office, I fulfilled my commitment to bring more jobs to South Dakota and improve education. We're moving South Dakota forward.* Announcer: *On Tuesday, re-elect Governor Mickelson.*

Initially this spot called "Close" was intended to be the closing ad. Frequently, with a heavy television buy, two spots are run, one positive and one critical of the opponent. This "Close" spot is a simple listing of key accomplishments, but it lets Mickelson deliver the final appeal for support. But the best "Close" spot was right around the corner. A beautiful quote from Senator Daschle became the perfect ending spot.

"Samuelson No Plan"

Announcer: *While Governor Mickelson works hard to bring better paying jobs to South Dakota, Bob Samuelson sits back claiming he can do better. But Samuelson has no plan. He never has. In the legislature Bob Samuelson introduced only one bill. Governor Mickelson doesn't sit back, he produces. A record so remarkable Senator Tom Daschle said, "I am one Democrat who thinks this Governor has done a heck of a job in leading South Dakota economic development. He's been the leader." Re-elect Governor Mickelson. He's moving South Dakota forward.*

This ad, run in the last week of the campaign, was a bit of a surprise because it quoted the popular Democratic senator Tom Daschle. Although Daschle's full quote is not available, the excerpt appears genuine and no doubt levelled a kidney punch to Samuelson. The other knockout punch was the exposure of Samuelson's record in the legislature—he only introduced one bill. He failed to look like a leader. Of the three closing spots developed for Mickelson, this one was best, discrediting Samuelson's legislative record of only passing one bill and the devastating quote by Democratic senator Tom Daschle praising Mickelson.

The results upended the Democrats' early poll showing Mickelson weak and behind Samuelson. By the end of the campaign, Mickelson produced a commanding victory of nearly 20 percent, with Mickelson winning 58.9 percent and Samuelson barely breaking 40 percent at 41.1 percent. Polling by Fred Steeper of Market Strategies showed Mickelson comfortably ahead of Samuelson every month of the campaign and enhanced his support among seniors from 42 percent to over 71 percent by the end of the campaign—nearly a 30 percent improvement.[22]

The final results showed no similarity to the early February poll Samuelson received from his Democratic Party showing him ahead. In the end, Samuelson was totally outmatched by Mickelson. The 1990 South Dakota gubernatorial election took place on 6 November 1990. Republican governor George S. Mickelson was reelected, defeating Democratic nominee Bob L. Samuelson by nearly 20 percent.

In early January 1990, Mickelson summoned me to write his State of the State speech. In their den, the governor and first lady sat side-by-side in two retractable leather lounge chairs with a small table in

Table 4. Market Strategies Polling—All Voters

	Mickelson	*Samuelson*	*Don't Know*
Oct 12–17, 1990	63	26	11
Sept 28–30, 1990	57	33	10
July 1990	62	28	9
April 1990	55	34	10

Table 5. Market Strategies Polling—Voters Over 65

	Mickleson	*Samuelson*	*Don't Know*
Oct 12–17, 1990	71	17	12
Sept 28–30, 1990	51	37	12
July 1990	60	24	16
April 1990	42	40	18

Table 6. 1990 General Election Official Results

Nominee	Gov. Mickelson	Bob Samuelson
Party	Republican	Democratic
Running mate	Walter Dale Miller	Shirley Halleen
Popular vote	151,198	105,525
Percentage	58.9%	41.1%

between them. After pleasantries, the governor turned to me and said, "I'm thinking of doing something different." Most of what Mickelson had proposed up to then was preordained based on campaign promises he had made. But this year would be different. Kevin Woster, the long-time reporter for the *Argus Leader* and occasional tough critic of Mickelson, had pointed out that Mickelson had "opened the double doors between his office reception room and the second-floor hallway during working hours. It was a symbolic gesture that signaled his commitment to new ideas and different voices."[23]

The twenty-eighth governor had a new idea he had shared with his wife Linda and a few others. He clearly was ready to spring it on the entire state. Mickelson said he wanted to do something that would unite the state. He said he wanted to declare "The Year of Reconciliation" between American Indians and the white community. It was a stunner. The idea came from Tim Giago, publisher of the *Lakota Times.* It signaled to everyone that the state was changing. The Year of Reconciliation was blockbuster news. It was certainly unanticipated from Mickelson. The State of the State message was a perfect launching pad.

On 19 April 1993, while on an economic development trip, Governor George Mickelson, fifty-two, died in a tragic airplane crash along with seven other souls. After the funeral at the State Capitol, the casket was driven in a slow parade across the state from Pierre to Mickelson's hometown of Brookings where the funeral and burial were held. "As dusk settled in this eastern South Dakota farming town, everyone from Cub Scouts to war veterans stood in solemn silence as the body of their governor made its way toward a final resting place. The funeral cortege carrying the casket of Gov. George Mickelson drove through flag-lined De Smet at 7:38 pm. The only sound was wheels crunching on pavement, the engines of the vehicles—and nearby church bells pealing 'Ode to Joy' from Beethoven's Ninth Symphony. De Smet has a hundred American flags, and all were displayed Thursday atop aluminum polls along the route. About 300 people turned out. The cortege was on its way to Brookings for today's funeral. 'People of that stature and ability don't come along every day. It's hard to replace people who care that much,'" Todd Wilkenson, Kingsbury County State's Attorney said of Mickelson.[24]

NOTES

1. *Mickelson Campaign Plan,* 1986, p. 10, folder 1, box 05513C, George S. Mickelson Campaign Plans Collection, State Archives Collection, South Dakota State Historical Society, Pierre.

2. Ibid., pp. 12–20.

3. Ibid., p. 16.

4. Ibid., p. 18.

5. Ibid., p. 21.

6. *Rapid City Journal,* 16 Oct. 1985, p. 2.

7. "Former S.D. Congressman Clint Roberts dies," *Sioux Falls Argus Leader,* 13 Feb. 2017.

8. In 2014, U.S senator Joni Ernst of Iowa won a contentious primary in Iowa coming from far behind. She was boosted by her startling ad showing a pig castration to make the point "she would cut pork" from the budget if she was elected to the Senate (Wikipedia, https://en.wikipedia.org/wiki/Joni_Ernst).

9. *Rapid City Journal,* 23 May 1986.

10. "FOX not on the air in 1986," *Sioux Falls Argus Leader*, 7 May 1986.

11. *Rapid City Journal,* 23 Apr. 1993.

12. "GOP candidates boast years of experience," *Sioux Falls Argus Leader*, 2 June 1986.

13. "Primary Victory Barely Avoids Runoff," *Star Tribune (Minneapolis),* 10 June 1986.

14. Market Opinion Research polls and election results, June 1986–Election Day 1986, Fred Steeper, pollster. Copy in author's collection.

15. Dave Kranz, "Mickelson displaying political maturity," *Sioux Falls Argus Leader*, 31 Aug. 1986.

16. Ibid.

17. *Rapid City Journal,* 23 April 1993.

18. State Democratic Poll, Feb. 1990, question 8, folder 3, box 05513C, George S. Mickelson Campaign Plans Collection, State Archives Collection, South Dakota State Historical Society, Pierre.

19. Ibid., question 6.

20. Ibid., question 58.

21. State Democratic Poll Feb. 1990, question 87, folder 1, box 05513C, George S. Mickelson Campaign Plans Collection, State Archives Collection, South Dakota State Historical Society, Pierre.

22. Market Strategies polling Apr. 1990–Nov. 1990, Fred Steeper, pollster. Copy in author's possession.

23. *Sioux Falls Argus Leader*, 21 Apr. 1993.

24. *Rapid City Journal,* 23 Apr. 1993.

MARSHALL DAMGAARD

9 | POLITICAL "NOBODIES" OUT OF POLITICAL "NOWHERE": FROM WHERE HAVE SOUTH DAKOTA'S POLITICAL LEADERS COME?

• • •

The "Battle between the Legacies." That is how many South Dakota voters described the 1986 governor's race. Republican candidate George S. ("Speaker") Mickelson was the son of South Dakota's eighteenth governor, George T. ("Theodore") Mickelson. Democratic candidate R. ("Ralph") Lars Herseth was the son of South Dakota's twenty-first governor, Ralph Herseth, and South Dakota's twenty-third secretary of state, Lorna (Buntrock) Herseth.[1]

Voters ultimately elected Mickelson the state's twenty-eighth governor. His son Mark served three terms in the South Dakota Legislature, and, like his grandfather and father, served as speaker of the house. Lars Herseth's daughter, Stephanie, won one primary election, one special election, three general elections, and served over six years in the U.S. House of Representatives. She was the first woman elected to the House from South Dakota and the youngest woman serving in that institution during that time. Thus, the Mickelson and Herseth "political families" have both contributed extraordinary public service to South Dakota.[2]

"Legacies" is a term generally found in the lexicon of sororities and fraternities, but in South Dakota politics, not so much. Indeed, the 1986 gubernatorial campaign was the exception that proves a rule. Unlike several other states, South Dakota, at the statewide level, does not have many multi-generational political families.[3]

During the almost 132 years since statehood in 1889, thirty-two individuals have served as governor of South Dakota. George S. Mickelson, Lars Herseth, and Stephanie Herseth Sandlin are the only descendants of a South Dakota governor to be general election candidates for any statewide political office in South Dakota. Also, since 1889, no descendants of the state's thirty-seven members of the House or twenty-seven members of the Senate have ever been statewide general election candidates for governor or Congress in South Dakota. Today, not one of South Dakota's thirteen statewide elected officials has an ancestor who was ever elected to any statewide office in South Dakota—or in any other state.[4]

Many decades ago, South Dakota boasted several political families, including the Gambles, the Grigsbys, and the Pyles. New York-born brothers John Rankin Gamble and Robert Jackson Gamble of Yankton both represented South Dakota in the House. John served from 4 March 1891 until his death on 14 August 1891. Robert served from 1895 to 1897 and from 1899 to 1901. Robert also represented South Dakota in the Senate from 1901 to 1913. Robert's son, Yankton-born Ralph Abernathy Gamble, represented Westchester County, New York, in the House from 1937 to 1957.[5]

In 1896, South Dakota voters elected People's Party candidate Melvin Grigsby to be the state's next attorney general. Melvin's son Sioux Grigsby served in both houses of the state legislature and as lieutenant governor under both Merrill Sharpe and George T. Mickelson. During the 1950s, Sioux was known as "Mr. Republican" in South Dakota. Melvin's son John Grigsby of Redfield served as Democratic lieutenant governor of South Dakota under William Bulow. Melvin's son George Grigsby served as Democratic attorney general of Alaska Territory, mayor of Nome, and the Alaska Territory delegate to the U.S. House from 1920 to 1921. The Grigsby family thus included a Populist, two Democrats, and "Mr. Republican."[6]

Gladys Pyle's father, John Pyle of Huron, served as South Dakota's fourth attorney general from 1899 to 1902. Gladys's mother, Mamie Shields Pyle, and sisters, May and Nellie, were leaders in the woman suffrage movement. Gladys was the first woman appointed to a state commission in South Dakota, the first woman to serve on a grand jury in South Dakota, the first woman elected to a statewide office in South Dakota, the first woman elected as South Dakota secretary of state, the first woman elected to the South Dakota state legislature, and the first woman elected to the Senate who had not previously been appointed to that position At the 1940 National Republican Convention, she became the first woman to place a name in nomination for the presidency.[7]

Thus, the Gambles, Grigsbys, and Pyles certainly qualify as South

Dakota political families. Yet, the last time any member of those remarkable families held statewide elective office anywhere was sixty-four years ago. Given the paucity of political families, especially during recent years, where have South Dakota's political leaders come from? Frankly, in purely political and geographic contexts, these ultimately powerful and popular people started their public service careers as political "nobodies" from political "nowhere."

TOM BERRY

Thomas Matthew ("Tom") Berry was born the fifth of ten children on 23 April 1879 in Paddock, an unincorporated community in Holt County in north central Nebraska. In 1893, Berry's mother, Cynthia, died at forty-one, when Berry was only fourteen. In 1897, he moved northward across the Niobrara River and into South Dakota, working as a cowboy on a cattle ranch.[8]

In 1913, Berry, his wife, Lorena, and their four children moved to a cedar log house they built near Black Pipe Creek in Mellette County. There, about seventeen miles south of Belvidere, they operated what eventually became the thirty-thousand-acre Double X brand saddle horse and cattle ranch. Initially, just getting the mail involved a seven-mile horseback ride. The family's first car, a Buick with a rumble seat for the kids, arrived in 1918. Electricity did not arrive until the 1940s. Berry's experiments with new grasses and cattle breeding reflected his innate curiosity and business acumen. For example, in a single transaction, he and his brothers sold two million pounds of beef on the hoof.[9]

Berry was a registered Democrat, mostly because his parents were. He also saw the Democratic Party as the friend of the farmer and the party of the people. He did not run for any elective office until he was forty-five, but the political spark glowed much earlier than that. His daughter Faye saw him as a natural politician. "Everywhere he went he met people because he'd always go up and start talking to anybody. And he always listened to them. He always wanted to hear their side of how things were—what was going on."[10]

In 1924, District Fifty-Seven (Mellette and Bennett counties) voters elected Berry, at age forty-five, to his first of four terms in the State House. Eight years later, 158,058 South Dakota voters elected Berry the fourteenth governor, voting out Republican incumbent Warren Green.

During that campaign, Berry often delivered as many as twenty public speeches a day, well on his way to becoming known across the nation as the "Cowboy Governor." In 1934, the more conservative Berry won a gubernatorial primary against his fellow Democrat, progressive lieutenant governor Hans Ustrud, and then won reelection that autumn by over 50,000 votes.[11]

As governor, Berry battled against the twin tragedies of the Great Depression and the Dust Bowl. He ended Progressive Era financial bleeders, such as the state coal mine, the state bonding department, and state hail insurance. He increased state revenues with an income tax (initially with a gross tax and then with a net tax) and an ore tax. He called special sessions of the legislature to adopt unemployment insurance and to license and tax wine and beer. After wielding an array of axes during his 1932 campaign, he kept his promise to chop state government down to size by cutting its budget by 25 percent. A classic outsider, Berry used his Irish cowboy humor to score political points, once observing, "There is so much nepotism in Pierre that they could have a father and son banquet every night."[12]

In 2020, former U.S. senator James Abourezk told me the following story: "When I was about two years old, Governor Tom Berry visited my parents' home. I was running around the house wearing a big cloth diaper. Now, in those days, Prohibition was a big issue. If you supported the prohibition of alcohol, you were called a "dry." If you opposed prohibition, you were called a 'wet.' Tom said to me, 'Are you a wet or a dry?' I looked down at my dripping diaper and announced, 'I am a wet!' "[13]

BENJAMIN REIFEL

Benjamin ("Ben") Reifel (Wiyaka Wanjila, "Lone Feather") was born 19 September 1906 in a dirt roof log cabin near Parmelee, South Dakota, on the Rosebud Reservation. His mother, Lucy Burning Breast, was Lakota Sioux; his father, William "Shorty" Reifel, the younger brother of Lucy's day school teacher, was German. Lucy spoke little English, and William spoke little Lakota, but romance overcame the language barrier.[14]

Lucy implored Ben and his four younger brothers to learn to read, write, and speak English in addition to their fluency in Lakota. By Ben's own admission, though, he was an unfocused classroom student. He dropped into and out of public schools, government day schools, and the Rosebud boarding school. Eventually, in 1923, at the age of sixteen, he finally earned his eighth-grade diploma. By then, some local people—former teachers, Rosebud Superintendent James McGregor, and Swedish-American Rosebud photographer John Anderson and his wife Myrtle—saw promise in Ben that perhaps he did not see in himself. With the help of such visionary friends, he made the longest journey of his life: 290 miles to the secondary School of Agriculture at South Dakota State in Brookings.[15]

Reifel's congressional aide Vernon Loen later reminisced that on that journey, young Ben had his first train ride and his initial exposure to running water and electric lights. Unaware of the Brookings taxi service, he shoved his luggage trunk end-over-end seventeen blocks from the train station to the campus. Graduating a year early, he started college classes at South Dakota State, where he became, in the words of a local reporter, "one of the outstanding students of the institution." He graduated from South Dakota State in 1932.[16]

We do not know if a gradually awakening political ambition led to Reifel's election as South Dakota State Student Association president during his senior year, or if that election precipitated a slowly percolating interest in politics, or both. Another twenty-eight years would pass before he was first elected to statewide political office in 1960—the first of his five terms in the House—at the age of fifty-four.[17]

During those twenty-eight years, his life was an amalgamation of challenging jobs, military service, and post-secondary education. He worked as a counselor and handyman at the Episcopal Hare Vocational School near Mission, while his new wife, his college classmate Alice (Johnson) of Erwin, South Dakota, taught school at Parmelee. He later served the Bureau of Indian Affairs (BIA) as farm extension agent to the Oglala Lakota, a field agent in Pierre, a tribal relations officer, superintendent of the Fort Berthold Reservation in North Dakota, superintendent of the Pine Ridge Reservation in South Dakota, and finally area director of the BIA office in Aberdeen. During World War II, he finished active duty with the rank of lieutenant colonel. At Harvard, he earned his master's degree in public administration in 1949 and his Ph.D. in 1952.[18]

In 1960, South Dakota Republicans, stung by Democratic victories in 1958, were searching for articulate, hard-working candidates. Initially, virtually nobody knew for sure about Reifel's political registration. He was a Republican, in large part because Republican President Calvin Coolidge had signed the Indian Citizenship Act of 1924. The GOP recruiters inquired, but Reifel had many reasons to decline their offer. His wife and daughter were opposed. He was a well-paid and universally respected BIA leader. He would lose his pension if he left that service for a possibly unsuccessful political challenge. He started calling Republican leaders to decline their offer. All their phone lines were busy. Later, when he learned they were all on their phones energetically raising money for him, he changed his mind.[19]

Ben Reifel was the first person of Sioux descent to serve in the U.S. Congress. During the 1960s, he was the only American Indian among the 535 members of Congress.[20] After serving five terms, Reifel retired from Congress in 1971, but retirement did not mean relaxation. He chaired the National Capitol Planning Commission, served as special assistant for Indian programs to the director of the National Park Service, and served as interim commissioner of Indian Affairs. In 1977, he established, with most of his personal collection, the first Native American collection at the South Dakota Memorial Art Center in Brookings.[21]

JAMES ABDNOR

E. ("Ellis") James ("Jim") Abdnor was born 13 February 1923 in the tiny wheat farming and cattle ranching community of Kennebec in Lyman County, South Dakota. A nearby sign along Interstate 90 asks, "Where the heck is Kennebec?" The answer is that the community of 281 souls is about fifty-seven sparsely populated highway miles from Pierre, South Dakota, the second-smallest state capital in America.[22]

Jim Abdnor's parents, Lebanese immigrants Samuel Joseph and Mary (Wehby) Abdnor, raised him in the Kennebec home that remained his residence for most of his life. Samuel Abdnor, a Lyman County homesteader, operated a general store in Kennebec for many years while he and Mary raised Jim and Jim's older siblings, Joseph and Marina. At Kennebec High School, Jim played basketball, baseball, and football. He went on to play football at the University of Nebraska, and, after serving in the U.S. Army during World War II, graduated from that university in 1945 with a degree in business administration. He began a lifelong farming and ranching career in the

Kennebec area. He was runner-up for the South Dakota Outstanding Young Farmer award.[23]

Abdnor's more than three decades in politics and public service began when he was elected, at age thirty, as the chairman of the South Dakota Young Republicans. District Twenty-Nine (Haakon, Jones, Lyman, and Stanley counties) voters elected him to the State Senate in 1956. His colleagues elected the thirty-three-year-old freshman senator the chair of the Joint Appropriations Committee. Back home, his constituents re-elected him to five more terms in the State Senate. In 1968, statewide voters made him the state's lieutenant governor.[24]

Defeated in a run for Congress in 1970 (he lost in the primary), he bounced back with a victory in the 1972 Congressional race. Voters re-elected him three times. In the 1980 Senate race, the four-term congressman defeated three-term incumbent senator George McGovern, gaining over 58 percent of the vote. His service on the Senate Appropriations Committee was a valuable asset to his state, which, beginning in 1983, was represented by two senators and only one representative. He was the second U.S. senator of Lebanese descent after South Dakota U.S. senator James Abourezk. After Abdnor lost his Senate seat to Congressman Thomas Daschle in 1986, President Reagan appointed him to lead the U.S. Small Business Administration.[25]

Abdnor leased out his four-thousand-acre ranch while serving in the Senate. "I'm a farmer," he once said. "I've dug more field dirt out of my ears than anyone in Congress. I treasure that heritage."[26] When he said he got off his tractor and went to Washington, he was being literal. Soft-spoken and genuinely gregarious, he was not an orator. Often called "The Peoples' Senator," he admitted, "God didn't make me a flashy speaker; that's for sure. But we got a lot of flashy speakers in Congress. And if speeches solved problems, we wouldn't have any problems."[27] In a television ad, he once said, "So I'm not a great speaker. Heck, I'm not a great dancer, either, but I'm a great fighter for South Dakota."[28]

A lifelong bachelor with no children of his own, Abdnor "adopted" hundreds of young people. He taught history and coached in Kennebec and nearby Presho. He coached American Legion baseball for two decades. Later in his life, he became a passionate fan and financial supporter of the American Legion Post 22 baseball program in Rapid City. During his years in Congress, he relished recruiting many talented young people as interns and staff, including future U.S. senator John Thune. Year after year, he attended many South Dakota high school sporting events.[29]

JIM ABOUREZK

Democrat James George ("Jim") Abourezk, like Republican James Abdnor, is the son of Lebanese immigrants. Abdnor's mother, Mary, was Abourezk's godmother. Abourezk's mother, Juliana ("Lena"), a homemaker, and his father, Beshara Abu Rizk (later anglicized to Charles Thomas Abourezk), a traveling backpack peddler and later the owner of two general stores, were Lebanese Christians from the small village of Kfeir along the slopes of Mount Hermon. Born 24 February 1931, Jim Abourezk grew up on the Rosebud Reservation near the community of Wood, which is about twenty-nine miles away from Ben Reifel's hometown of Parmelee.[30]

After graduating from Wood High School, Abourezk served in the U.S. Navy during the Korean War. He earned a degree in civil engineering from the South Dakota School of Mines and a law degree from the University of South Dakota (USD) School of Law. While working his way through those two schools, Abourezk bartended at the American Legion in Rapid City and at the Gay Lady in Rockerville, taught judo classes, helped construct a Catholic school, labored in a cheese warehouse, (illegally) dealt blackjack, helped build Minuteman missile silos, and served as business manager for the Crazy Horse Pow Wow near Hot Springs.[31]

One of Abourezk's fellow USD Law School students was future South Dakota governor William ("Bill") Janklow. One summer, when Abourezk was managing the Gas Light (formerly the Gay Lady), he hired Janklow as a bartender. Abourezk recalls, "He didn't want to serve drinks; he wanted to talk. No lie. And I looked down at the end of the bar, there he was with two empty glasses, and he was going to pour a drink for somebody. His jaw was working a hundred miles an hour with the guy he was talking to. So when he got done talking, I fired him."[32]

Abourezk lost his first race for statewide office when he ran against fellow Navy veteran Gordon Mydland of Brookings for South Dakota attorney general in 1968. The year 1970, however, would be a watershed year in South Dakota politics, and Abourezk surfed the wave election. Both of South Dakota's incumbent Republican congressmen, Ben Reifel in the First District and E.Y. Berry in the Second District, had decided not to seek reelection. Abourezk, thirty-nine, won the three-way Democratic primary for Second District Congress by 657 votes. On the Republican side, Rapid City businessman Tom Brady upset Lieutenant Governor Abdnor by 1,726 votes.[33]

During the general election, Brady published a little color pamphlet titled, "This—I Believe." One of the ideas in which Brady believed was "Compulsory Citizenship Training." Brady wrote that young men and women would "enjoy" a mandatory summer camp at which they would have ". . . the opportunity to be properly disciplined." Some voters likened Brady's proposal to Hitler Youth Camps.[34] Beyond that controversial issue was good old-fashioned hard work. Abourezk says that "back then, we worked our butts off—because we were so far behind." He adds, "The hard work we did paid off, and I don't think the Democrats work that hard now."[35]

In 1970, while Abourezk captured the Second District seat (becoming the first Democrat to hold that seat since the 1930s), fellow Democrat and former FBI Agent Frank Denholm from Brookings took the First District seat, Democratic state senator Richard Kneip of Salem defeated incumbent Republican governor Frank Farrar of Britton, and Democratic Sioux Falls businessman Bill Dougherty won election to be lieutenant governor. In 1972, Abourezk, after garnering 57 percent of the vote to defeat Robert Hirsch of Yankton, replaced four-term Republican U.S. senator Karl Mundt of Madison. Mundt had suffered a severe stroke in November 1969 but remained in office through the conclusion of his final term in January 1973. Denholm, Kneip, and Dougherty won re-election. Abdnor salved Republican wounds by capturing the Second District Congressional seat Abourezk had left to run for the U.S. Senate.[36]

After the 1972 general election, of the ten statehouse offices in South Dakota, Democrats held all but three (auditor, treasurer, and one of three public utilities commissioners). For the first time since the New Deal era, Democrats controlled both houses of the state legislature.[37]

Abourezk, who has always brandished a fierce Populist streak, is an unapologetic, outspoken liberal in a conservative state. During the 1970s, when Abourezk and George McGovern represented South Dakota in the Senate, the state's delegation was probably the most liberal and iconoclastic in the entire one-hundred-member Senate, even more so than the famous Massachusetts tandem of Democrat Edward Kennedy and Republican Edward Brooke.[38]

After one tumultuous term in the U.S. Senate, during which he created the American Indian Policy Review Commission (AIPRC) and authored the landmark Indian Child Welfare Act (ICWA), Abourezk had had enough of elective office. After leaving the Senate, he founded the American-Arab Anti-Discrimination Committee, authored two provocative books, led many tours to the Middle East, and practiced law in Sioux Falls. He still holds court at his table in his wife Sanaa's restaurant in downtown Sioux Falls.[39]

DICK KNEIP

In 1960, when South Dakota Democratic congressman George McGovern was running against incumbent senator Karl Mundt, Massachusetts senator and Democratic presidential candidate John F. Kennedy campaigned in South Dakota alongside McGovern. That autumn, in South Dakota, Mundt narrowly defeated McGovern, while Republican Richard Nixon crushed Kennedy. A factor in Kennedy's lop-sided loss was an undercurrent of anti-Catholicism, and Kennedy sensed that sentiment hurt McGovern's campaign. He observed to his brother Robert, "I think we just cost that nice guy a Senate seat."[40]

During the 1960s, Richard Francis ("Dick") and Nancy (Pankey) Kneip were members of the Christian Family Movement, an organization of young married couples from St. Mary's Catholic Church in Salem, South Dakota. At one meeting of the group, a member opined that a Democrat could not get elected to the state legislature from McCook County. Dick Kneip, who at that time had zero political experience, saw the comment as a dare.[41]

Kneip, of Luxembourgish ancestry, was born 7 January 1933 in Tyler, Minnesota.[42] His parents, Frank and Bernice (Pederson) Kneip, lived just across the border in Elkton, South Dakota. Young Dick graduated from high school in nearby Arlington, South Dakota. After attending South Dakota State and St. John's University, he served four years in the U.S. Air Force. Following their marriage in 1957, Dick and Nancy Kneip moved to Salem, where he owned and operated a statewide wholesale dairy equipment distributorship and they raised their eight children—all boys.[43]

During Kneip's 1964 campaign for the State Senate, he appeared on the doorstep of every voter in the three-county (McCook, Hanson, and Sanborn) district—three times. The voters rewarded his work ethic with a victory and then reelected him in 1966 and 1968. After securing the 1970 Democratic nomination for governor, he threw himself into his energetic "People to People" campaign against incumbent Republican Governor Farrar. Lacking substantial statewide name recognition, he launched his campaign with clever ads inquiring, "What is a Kneip?" Come November, the answer was the twenty-fifth governor of South Dakota, the fourth (and last) South Dakota governor elected from the Democratic Party, the youngest person ever elected governor of South Dakota (taking office two days short of his thirty-eighth birthday), and the first Catholic governor of South Dakota.[44]

Voters reelected Kneip to a second two-year term in 1972. That year, voters also changed the term of office of governor to four years and further allowed a person to serve two consecutive terms totaling eight years. In 1974, after defeating his fellow Democrat, Lieutenant Governor Bill Dougherty, in a primary, Kneip won a third term.[45]

Kneip resigned the governorship in 1978 when President James Earl ("Jimmy") Carter appointed him ambassador to Singapore. His political career concluded in 1986 with a narrow defeat in the Democratic primary for governor—a contest Lars Herseth won.[46]

BILL JANKLOW

William John ("Bill") Janklow's Hungarian Jewish father, Arthur, prosecuted Nazi officials at the Nuremberg Trials in Germany during the aftermath of World War II. In 1950, after Arthur suddenly died, Bill's Norwegian mother, LouElla (who would later serve as a Christian missionary nurse in Liberia, Ethiopia, Eritrea, Somalia, Uganda, and Kenya and also smuggle Bibles into Russia before dying a few days short of her one hundredth and seventh birthday in 2020), moved their six young children back to Chicago. Bill had been born there on 13 September 1939. In 1954, LouElla moved the family to her hometown of Flandreau, South Dakota. A self-avowed juvenile delinquent, Bill dropped out of Flandreau High School following his sophomore year and enlisted in the U.S. Marine Corps.[47]

Honorably discharged in 1959, Janklow married his high school sweetheart, Mary Dean Thom, in 1960. That autumn, he enrolled in the University of South Dakota. University officials sought to expel him because he lacked a high school diploma. He somehow talked them into allowing him to continue if he got good grades. He graduated from USD with a degree in business administration in 1964 and received his law degree from the USD School of Law in 1966.[48]

Continuing an inability or disinclination to get along with authority figures, Janklow consistently parked his old car in the space reserved for the dean of the law school. According to legends, the first thing Dean Scarlett did every day was to direct his secretary to "go find out what Bill Janklow is doing, and tell him to quit it." Once, after the dean wrote a letter of reprimand to Janklow and copied Janklow's mother, Janklow wrote a letter of reprimand to the dean and copied the dean's mother.[49]

Immediately after graduating from law school, Janklow took a job as a Legal Services lawyer on the Rosebud Reservation. He soon became the director of the Legal Services program in South Dakota. Former South Dakota Circuit Court Judge William ("Bill") Srstka, who worked on the Rosebud Reservation with Janklow, said that when Janklow was defending Native Americans on the reservation, he was "completely unknown" across the state. Srstka added, "I know he thought he'd never be elected to anything back at Rosebud." For six and a half years, the Janklows lived in Mission, South Dakota, which is almost two hundred miles away from Rapid City.[50]

After handling over 4,300 requests for assistance from Native Americans and representing thirty-one individuals in federal or state court for murder or manslaughter, Janklow, in 1973, agreed to become the chief prosecutor in the office of South Dakota Attorney General Kermit Sande. In that position, Janklow convened a grand jury which handed down forty-five individual indictments against members of the American Indian Movement (AIM). In the 1974 race for state attorney general, Janklow defeated Sande, and the former juvenile delinquent became the twenty-fifth chief law enforcement officer of South Dakota.[51]

At one point during the 1974 Republican state convention, Srstka considered running for the Republican nomination for attorney general. Then, he decided against it. Sioux Falls attorney Rolly Samp, who was at the convention, says that after Srstka backed out, Janklow agreed to run as a "ticket-filler." Srstka says he talked Janklow into running. The thirty-four year-old Janklow was apparently not an ideal candidate. Samp recalls that Janklow was "a guy who refused to shake hands with anybody. He didn't want to raise money . . . He rode in the Augustana parade in Mary Carlsen's convertible, and when he got done, he said to me, he said, 'I'm never going to do that again. They parade you down the street like a hunk of meat.'"[52]

In 1978, voters elected the self-described thirty-nine-year-old "red-haired kid with braces" the twenty-seventh governor of the state. Voters reelected him in 1982. They elected him to a third term in 1994 and a fourth term in 1998. Thus, after being elected in 1994, Janklow became the thirtieth governor of South Dakota and the only governor to serve split tenures. His service as governor spanned four decades. He was thirty-nine when voters first elected him to that office; he was sixty-three when he left that office.[53] They elected him to Congress in 2002, but his public service career ended in 2004, when he resigned from office after killing Minnesota motorcyclist Randy Scott in a traffic accident near Flandreau.[54]

During Janklow's sixteen years as governor, critics called him a "dictator" and a "bully." Admirers called him "Governor Bill," as if he were somehow part of their family. Formal political polling consistently revealed a curious pattern. Those who voted against him said, "I admit he gets things done, but I sure don't like *how* he gets things done." Those who voted for him said, "I don't always like how he gets things done, but he sure does *get things done*."[55]

CONCLUSION

What do the political careers of Berry, Reifel, Abdnor, Abourezk, Kneip, and Janklow tell us about the political culture of a state whose entire population is smaller than the population of each of sixty-three American metropolitan areas?[56] Those lives suggest South Dakota is still the frontier. South Dakotans respect and elect people not for *what* they are, but for *who* they are. The state's political culture is remarkably nonjudgmental and egalitarian. Also, in South Dakota politics, hard work still works. In all their races—primary and general—all six candidates met voters' expectations by attempting to earn their votes by working hard. While all used the most modern media available, they focused their campaigns at the handshake level. That hard work continued after they were elected, demonstrating that their attitude toward public service in South Dakota was never "be somebody," but always "do something."

To top statewide offices, South Dakotans have elected people from remote ranches (Governor Tom Berry), tiny towns (U.S. senators Jim Abdnor and Jim Abourezk), and our largest city (Governors Joe Foss and Nils Boe and Lieutenant Governor Bill Dougherty). The voters have elected Catholics (Governor Dick Kneip, Congressman and Senator Tom Daschle, and Governor and Senator M. Michael Rounds); a Native American (Congressman Ben Reifel). Arab-Americans (Senators Abdnor and Abourezk); a Democratic woman (Congresswoman Stephanie Herseth Sandlin) and a Republican woman (Congresswoman and Governor Kristi Noem); a Populist-Democrat-Free-Silver-Republican "Fusionist" (Governor Andrew Lee); Populists (Attorney General Melvin Grigsby and Congressmen Freeman Tulley Knowles and John Edward Kelley); an Independent (Senator James Henderson Kyle); and a Chicago-born former juvenile delinquent (Attorney General, Governor, and Congressman Bill Janklow). In 1966, the state reelected sixty-six-year-old U.S. senator Karl Mundt to his fourth six-year term. South Dakotans also elected a thirty-seven-year-old (Dick Kneip) and three thirty-nine-year-olds (Joe Foss, Frank Farrar, and Bill Janklow) as governors. In 1972, when Dave Volk was only twenty-five, he won the election for state treasurer.[57]

The obvious question now arises. South Dakotans have, over the years, voted for an amazing array of different personalities, policies, and philosophies. Why, then, are there today no multi-generational political families on our statewide public service landscape? South Dakotans have voted for just about everybody and everything else, so why not dynasties? The last member of the Mickelson and Herseth families to hold statewide elective office in South Dakota—Stephanie Herseth Sandlin—last held office over a decade ago.

There are several reasons why South Dakota should be the perfect place for political dynasties to develop and flourish:

(1) South Dakota has a lot of government with many opportunities to serve. South Dakota is home to nine Native American tribes.[58] Our state has 311 municipalities, 66 counties, 914 townships, and 85 school districts.[59] We have 185 school districts.

(2) The state elects more statewide officials (thirteen) than do many states.[60] California has almost forty-five times the population of South Dakota, but California voters elect only eleven statewide officials.[61] New York has about twenty-two times the population of South Dakota, but New York voters elect only six statewide officials.[62]

(3) South Dakota is one big community with very few degrees of separation between and among people.[63] If one does not know somebody, one probably knows somebody else who does know that somebody or at the very least has heard of them. That augers to the advantage of people related to well-known public figures.

(4) Finally, in 1895, State Treasurer W. W. Taylor absconded to Central America, and $367,020.59 of the state treasury was missing.[64] Other than that admittedly glaring exception, our statewide elected officials have been personally untainted by the major corruption all too common in other states. Four of seven recent governors of Illinois went to prison on corruption charges.[65] Former Congressman Billy Tauzin often observed, "Half of Louisiana is under water, and the other half is under indictment."[66] By contrast, if you are related by blood or marriage to any historical or current statewide elected officeholder in South Dakota, your family connection is gold.

In conclusion, South Dakotans expect their elected officials to get into office by hard work and to continue those efforts once in office. No one gets to ride the coattails of a family name. South Dakota voters elected Tom Berry, Ben Reifel, Jim Abdnor, Jim Abourezk, Dick Kneip, and Bill Janklow—collectively—to nine terms as governor, one term as lieutenant governor, eleven terms in the House, and two terms in the Senate. Yet, not a single ancestor of theirs had ever been elected to a statewide political office anywhere. Neither have any of their siblings or descendants. Going forward, will that pattern hold or break?

NOTES

1. George T. Mickelson was one of ten children born to homesteaders in Walworth County, South Dakota. Orphaned at fifteen, he lived with older siblings. In 1927, he married Madge Turner, a former schoolmate at Selby High School, who had been a schoolteacher in Wakonda and Colton (Tonnis H. Venhuizen, "Governor George Theodore Mickelson," Trail of Governors, https://www.trailofgovernors.com/governor-george-theodore-mickelson/; Ellsworth Karrigan, "George T. Mickelson, 1947–1951," in *Over a Century of Leadership: South Dakota Territorial & State Governors,* ed. Lynwood E. Oyos [Sioux Falls: Center for Western Studies, 1987], pp. 149–50; Venhuizen, "Governor George Speaker Mickelson," Trail of Governors, https://www.trailofgovernors.com/governor-george-speaker-mickelson/). Lorna Buntrock was the youngest of eleven children in a Brown County German pioneer farm family. Ralph Herseth was the youngest of eight in a Brown County Norwegian pioneer farm family. Ralph courted his Columbia High School classmate Lorna for eleven years, including during the Great Depression, before they married in 1937 (https://www.findagrave.com/memorial/156011802/lorna-helene_bertha-herseth; Venhuizen, "Governor Ralph E. Herseth," Trail of Governors, https://trailofgovernors.com/governor-ralph-e-herseth/; Steve Barnett, Legislative Manual of South Dakota, 2019 [Pierre: Office of Secretary of State, 2019], https://sdsos.gov/general-information/assets/bluebook-docs/2019bluebook.pdf.) The 2020 population estimates: Selby, 610, and Columbia, 160 (www.census.gov).

2. Today, Mark Mickelson is the president and owner of Mickelson & Company, an entrepreneurial professional services firm in Sioux Falls (Tonnis H. Venhuizen, *The Governors of South Dakota* [n.p.: By the Author, 2016], pp. 186–95; Mickelson & Company, LLC, www.mickco.com). Stephanie Herseth Sandlin is president of Augustana University in Sioux Falls. ("Legacy Stephanie Herseth Sandlin," South Dakota Hall of Fame, https://sdexcellence.org/Stephanie_Herseth_Sandlin_2017; Venhuizen, "Herseth,"; South Dakota Election History, 2002, 2004, 2006, 2008, South Dakota Secretary of State, https://sdsos.gov/elections-voting/election-resources/election-history/2002, 2004, 2006, 2008).

3. America's political dynasties include the La Follettes, the Tafts, the Kennedys, the Bushes, the Lowells, and the Cabots.

4. Only four governors have had a child serve in the South Dakota Legislature: Coe Crawford, Ralph Herseth, George T. Mickelson, and George S. Mickelson. Author's conversation with and emails from Tony Venhuizen, 17 Dec. 2019; Venhuizen, *Governors*.

5. See the following entries in the Biographical Directory of the United States Congress: John Rankin Gamble, https://bioguideretro.congress.gov/Home/MemberDetails?memindex=G000030; Robert Jackson Gamble, https://

bioguideretro.congress.gov/Home/memberDetails?memindex=000032; Ralph Abernathy Gamble, https://bioguideretro.congress.gov/Home/Member Details?memindex=G000031.

6. Author's conversation with and emails from Tony Venhuizen, 5 Dec. 2019; George W. Kingsbury and George Martin Smith, *History of Dakota Territory,* Vol. 5 (Chicago: S. J. Clarke Publishing, 1915), pp. 314–18; Melvin Grigsby, https://grigsbyfoundation.org/wp-content/uploads/2020/01/24-Colonel-Melvin-Grigsby-1845-1917-and-Family.pdf; "Former State Lt. Gov Dies," *The Daily Plainsman (Huron)*, 22 Aug. 1968; *South Dakota Bar Journal.* 37 (1968).

7. Jeannette Kinyon and Jean Walz, *The Incredible Gladys Pyle* (Vermillion: Dakota Press, 1985); Cleata B. Thorpe, *The John L. Pyle Family: Dakotans Extraordinary 1882–1973* (Huron, S.Dak.: Creative Printing Company, 1973); Dorinda Riessen Reed, *The Woman Suffrage Movement in South Dakota* (Vermillion: Government Research Bureau, 1958); "Champion of Excellence: Gladys Pyle," South Dakota Hall of Fame, https://sdexcellence.org/Gladys_Pyle_1979.

8. Lisa Chamley, "Dakota Images: Tom Berry," *South Dakota History* 26 (Summer/Fall 1996): 194; Cynthia Berry, https://findagrave.com/memorial/40480820/cynthia-ann-berry; Paul J. Higbee, *South Dakota's Cowboy Governor, Tom Berry* (Charleston, S.C.: *History Press*, 2017), pp. 12–15. "The Rand McNally Atlas shows that Paddock had a population of 20 people in 1895 with a post office and no railroad service." https://roadsidethoughts.com/ne/paddock-xx-holt-profile.htm.

9. Chamley, "Tom Berry," 194; "South Dakota's New Executive is Termed Second Will Rogers," *Deseret News* (Salt Lake City, Utah), 16 Feb. 1933; Higbee, *Tom Berry,* pp. 14–25; Joseph V. Ryan, "Tom Berry, 1933–1937;" in *Over A Century of Leadership*, ed. Lynwood Oyos (Sioux Falls: Center for Western Studies, 1987), pp. 126–31; John E. Miller, "Our Cowboy Governor," *South Dakota Magazine* (Nov. 1986): 6–11. The Census Bureau's 2020 population estimate for Belvidere is 46 (www.census.gov).

10. Higbee, *Tom Berry*, pp. 27–28; Miller, "Our Cowboy Governor," p. 10.

11. Tom Berry, https://findagrave.com/memorial/38983651/thomas-matthew-berry; Ryan, "Tom Berry"; Higbee, *Tom Berry*, p. 10; Venhuizen, "Governor Tom Berry," Trail of Governors, https://www.trailofgovernors.com/governor-tom-berry/; Venhuizen, *Governors*, pp. 88–89; Bob Mercer, "Remembering when a Lt. Gov. stood on his own," *Pierre Capital Journal*, 5 July 2000; Chris Nelson, *2005 Legislative Manual* (Pierre: Office of Secretary of State, 20005), https://sdsos.gov/elections-voting/assets/ElectionsReturnsPre1972.pdf; also *see* footnote 24.

12. Ryan, "Tom Berry," pp. 127–31; Higbee, *Tom Berry*, pp. 41–94; https://www.trailofgovernors.com/governor-tom-berry/; Paul A. O'Rourke, "South Dakota Politics During the New Deal Years," *South Dakota History* 1 (Summer 1971): 231–

71; Matthew Cecil, "Democratic Party Politics and the South Dakota Income Tax, 1933–1942," *South Dakota History* 26 (Summer/Fall 1996): 137–69.

13. Author's conversation with James Abourezk, 6 Jan. 2020.

14. Benjamin Reifel Papers, Hilton M. Briggs Library, South Dakota State University Archives and Special Collections, Brookings, S.Dak.; Sean J. Flynn, *Without Reservation: Benjamin Reifel and American Indian Acculturation* (Pierre: South Dakota Historical Society Press, 2018), pp. 9–19; John S. Painter, "Traditional Sioux Leader: Benjamin Reifel" in *South Dakota Leaders from Pierre Chouteau, Jr., to Oscar Howe*, eds. Herbert T. Hoover and Larry J. Zimmerman, (Vermillion: University of South Dakota Press, 1989), pp. 331–33. The U.S. Census Bureau calls Parmelee a "census-designated place." Its 2020 population was 606, www.census.gov. Painter explains that the Burning Breast family name derived from the sun's reflection off a gold medallion on the chest of an ancestor. "Federal officials often issued such medals to participants in treaty councils" (pp. 331–32).

15. Flynn, *Without Reservation*, pp. 19–22; Painter, *Sioux Leader*, pp. 333–35. Flynn says there were no high schools on the Rosebud Reservation at that time.

16. Flynn, *Without Reservation*, pp. 22–24; Painter, *Sioux Leader*, pp. 334–35.

17. *2005 Legislative Manual*; Flynn, p. 23; Benjamin Reifel, Biographical Directory of the United States Congress, https://bioguideretro.congress.gov/Home/MemberDetails?memIndex=R000152.

18. Flynn, *Without Reservation*, pp. 24–124; Painter, *Sioux Leader*, pp. 335–51; Ben Reifel, https://bioguideretro.congress.gov/Home/MemberDetails?memIndex=R000152. Painter notes on p. 343 that the Fort Berthold Reservation is the home of the Three Affiliated Tribes: Arikara, Hidatsa, and Mandan. Alice Reifel died of pneumonia in February 1972. Ben remarried in August 1972 to Frances Colby of DeSmet, whom he had known at South Dakota State (Flynn, *Without Reservation*, pp. 201–5; Painter, p. 354n11). In that note, Painter states: "Ben's younger brothers all had successful careers. John was a carpenter and maintenance engineer prior to his death in an auto accident in 1969. George was an educator. Alexander was an engineer. Albert was a medical doctor." I can find no evidence any of them ever ran for statewide public office.

19. Flynn, *Without Reservation*, pp. 23–126; Painter, *Sioux Leader*, pp. 351–52.

20. "Ben Reifel, 83, Dies; Former Congressman," *New York Times*, 4 Jan. 1990.

21. Flynn, *Without Reservation*, pp. 197–220; Painter, *Sioux Leader*, p.353.

22. James Abdnor Collection, South Dakota State Archives, Pierre, S.Dak., https://history.sd.gov/archives/abdnor.aspx; Marshall Damgaard, "10 Things You Probably Did Not Know About Pierre & Fort Pierre," unpublished manuscript, 3 Feb. 2018; www.census.gov.

23. James Abdnor Collection, https://history.sd.gov/archives/abdnor.aspx; "Legacy James Abdnor," South Dakota Hall of Fame, https://sdexcellence.org

/James_Abdnor_1995; "James Abdnor, Former South Dakota Senator, Dies at 89," *New York Times*, 16 May 2012.

24. "James Abdnor," *New York Times*; *2005 Legislative Manual*. South Dakota voters in 1972 amended the State Constitution so that beginning with the 1974 general election, the state's governor and lieutenant governor would be "jointly elected." Thus, they ran together as a ticket. Prior to 1974, candidates for those two offices ran individually. See *South Dakota Constitution*, Article IV, Section 2, History.

25. "James Abdnor," *New York Times*.

26. Ibid.

27. Kevin Woster, "Jim Abdnor and his people," *Rapid City Journal*, 21 May 2010; "James Abdnor," *New York Times*.

28. Ibid.

29. Ibid.; The Census Bureau's 2020 population estimate for Presho is 472. www.census.gov. Abdnor was truly the youngest "old person" I ever met.

30. James G. Abourezk, *Advise & Dissent: Memoirs of South Dakota and the U.S. Senate* (Chicago: Lawrence Hill, 1989), pp. 7–23; Abourezk in conversation with the author on 6 Jan. 2020. The United States Supreme Court, in *Rosebud Sioux Tribe v. Kneip*, 1977, ruled that the Rosebud Reservation had been diminished. Thus, today, Wood is no longer on the Reservation. *See 430 US 584*. The Census Bureau's 2020 population estimate for Wood is 41. www.census.gov.

31. Abourezk, *Advise & Dissent*, pp. 25–79.

32. Quote is from James Abourezk interview with Joe de la Rosa and the author, 10 July 2014. Audio and transcription available at University of South Dakota Oral History Center in Vermillion. Tom Lawrence, "Tom Lawrence Recaps the Life And Career Of A Great South Dakota Democratic Stalwart, Jim Abourezk," *South Dakota Standard*, 23 Nov. 2019.

33. Abourezk, *Advise & Dissent*, pp. 79–91; Abourezk conversation, 6 Jan. 2020; *2005 Legislative Manual*.

34. Abourezk, *Advise & Dissent*, pp. 87–88. Abourezk interview with de la Rosa and the author, 10 July 2014.

35. Lawrence, "Abourezk."

36. Abourezk, *Advise & Dissent*, pp. 79–100; "James Abourezk," South Dakota Hall of Fame: https://sdexcellence.org/James_Abourezk_2012; *2005 Legislative Manual*; For the 1972 election: https://sdsos.gov/elections-voting/assets/72SDGEN.pdf; Jon K. Lauck, "'It disappeared as quickly as it came': The Democratic Surge and the Republican Comeback in South Dakota Politics, 1970–1980," *South Dakota History* 46 (Summer 2016): 105–21; Robert D. Sivertson, "The Rise and Fall of a Democratic Majority in the South Dakota Legislature: A Personal Account, " unpublished pamphlet, in author's possession. The Census Bureau's

2020 population estimate for Britton is 1,215 (www.census.gov); Venhuizen, "Governor Frank Leroy Farrar," Trail of Governors, https://www.trailofgovernors.com/governor-frank-leroy-farrar/.

37. Lauck, "It disappeared as quickly as it came," pp. 105–21; Sivertson, "Rise and Fall;" Venhuizen, *Governors*, p. 169; Abourezk conversation, 6 Jan. 2020.

38. Abourezk, *Advise & Dissent*, pp. 243–65. Abourezk conversation, 6 Jan. 2020.

39. Abourezk, "South Dakota Hall of Fame,"; Lawrence, "Abourezk;" Abourezk conversation, 6 Jan. 2020.

40. George McGovern, *Grassroots: The Autobiography of George McGovern* (New York: Random House, 1977), pp. 82–83; Robert Sam Anson, *McGovern: A Biography* (New York: Holt, Rinehart and Winston, 1972) pp. 95–96; Jon Lauck, "'You can't mix wheat and potatoes in the same bin': Anti-Catholicism in Early Dakota," *South Dakota History*, 38 (Spring 2008): 1–2. McGovern's political support from and personal friendship with the Catholic Kennedys was an issue with quite a few voters in 1960. Richard Kneip's Catholicism was an issue with a few voters in 1970. Yet, when voters elected Republican state senator M. Michael Rounds governor in 2002, the author does not recall hearing a single voter raise a concern about Senator Rounds's religion. By 2004, when U.S. senator Thomas Daschle ran for re-election, the Roman Catholic Bishop of Sioux Falls, Robert Carlson, had written to Daschle, and, citing Daschle's position on abortion, told Daschle he should cease identifying himself as a Catholic. Thus, for some voters, the political issue was not that Daschle was a Catholic, but that he was not a "real Catholic," (J. Bottum, "Tom Daschle's Duty to be Morally Coherent," *Weekly Standard*, 17 Apr. 2003,).

41. Daniel B. Garry, "Richard F. Kneip, 1971–1978," in *Over a Century of Leadership: South Dakota Territorial and State Governors*, ed. Lynwood E. Oyos (Sioux Falls: Center for Western Studies, 1987), p. 199; John Andrews, "What is a Kneip?" *South Dakota Magazine*, 3 June 2014. The Census Bureau's 2020 population estimate for Salem is 1,325 (www.census.gov).

42. Venhuizen, *Governors*, p. 163. In the 2000 census, the number of South Dakotans who were Luxembourgers was 1,184 (www.census.gov).

43. Garry, "Richard F. Kneip," p. 199; Venhuizen, "Governor Richard Francis Kneip," Trail of Governors, https://trailofgovernors.com/governor-richard-francis-kneip/. The Census Bureau's 2020 population estimate for Arlington is 915 (www.census.gov).

44. Garry, "Richard F. Kneip," pp. 199–200; Venhuizen, *Governors*, pp. 163–72; Andrews, "What is a Kneip?"

45. Venhuizen, *Governors*, pp. 170–71; *South Dakota Constitution*, Article IV, Section 2, History.

46. Venhuizen, "Kneip,"; Venhuizen, *Governors*, p. 168. Of South Dakota's thirty-two governors, six governors were subsequently unsuccessful candidates to reclaim their former job. Eight former or current governors ran unsuccessfully for the U.S. Senate. Two governors ran unsuccessfully for the U.S. House (Venhuizen, *Governors*).

47. The author worked with Bill Janklow from August 1980 to Janklow's death in January 2012 and began working on the Janklow Archival Project at the University of South Dakota in November 2010. Miller Funeral Home Funeral Bulletin for William J. Janklow, 18 Jan. 2012, box 19, William J. Janklow Staff Papers, Archives and Special Collections at the University of South Dakota in Vermillion. "South Dakota native LouElla Janklow Nace turns 96" in *Dakota Nurse Connection* (Summer 2010): 10–11, box 19, Janklow Staff Papers. There are fewer than one thousand residents of Hungarian descent in South Dakota (www.census.gov). The entire state has fewer than four hundred Jews and only one rabbi. Sharyn Jackson, "Meet South Dakota's lone rabbi," *Jerusalem Post*, 24 Sept. 2017, box 19. Janklow Staff Papers. The Census Bureau's 2020 population estimate for Flandreau is 2,372 (www.census.gov).

48. Venhuizen, "Governor William Janklow," Trail of Governors, https://trailofgovernors.com/governor-william-john-bill-janklow/; James Soyer, "William Janklow, 1979–1987," in *Over a Century of Leadership: South Dakota Territorial and State Governors,* ed. Lynwood E. Oyos (Sioux Falls: Center for Western Studies, 1987), p. 211; Venhuizen, *Governors*, p. 179.

49. Marshall Damgaard, "Governor William J. Janklow Archival Project at USD: Bill Janklow Biography," 19 Aug. 2013, box 19, Janklow Staff Papers.

50. Soyer, "William Janklow," p. 211; Funeral Bulletin in Janklow Staff Papers; William Srstka interview with Joe de la Rosa and the author, 10 July 2014. Audio and transcription available at the USD Oral History Center. The U.S. Census Bureau lists the 2020 population of Mission as 1,156 (www.census.gov).

51. Funeral Bulletin in Janklow Staff Papers; Damgaard, "Bill Janklow Biography"; Soyer, "William Janklow," p. 212.

52. William Srstka interview, 10 July 2014; Rolly Samp interview, 18 June 2014. Janklow himself was painfully aware of his inadequacies as a politician. About his run for attorney general in 1974, he once observed, "I had no money! I hate fundraising. I'm bashful. I don't sound like it. When I was younger, I didn't like asking for dates; it's very hard asking people to vote for me. To this day, I would not walk down the street shaking hands with people. I mean, they're sitting in a restaurant having something to eat; they've probably washed their hands, and some son-of-a-bitch wants to shake hands with them? People don't want to get pandered to by a politician." http://www.togovern.com/gov-bill-janklow.html.

53. Damgaard, "Bill Janklow Biography"; Venhuizen, *Governors*, pp. 180, 203.

54. "Bill Janklow, a Four-Term Governor of South Dakota, dies," *New York Times*, 13 Jan. 2012; Venhuizen, *Governors*, pp. 206–7.

55. Damgaard, "Bill Janklow Biography,"; Jon Walker, "Larger Than Life to the End," *Sioux Falls Argus Leader*, 13 Jan. 2012; Jon Walker, "One man can, did change the world,'" *Sioux Falls Argus Leader*, 18 Jan. 2012. In September 1978, when Attorney General Janklow was a candidate for governor, his approval rating among all voters was 69 percent favorable and 26 percent unfavorable. Review of earlier polls in Market Opinion Research Poll, April 1986, prepared for Friends of Bill Janklow, polling data found in Janklow Papers, Box 13. In July 1998, after three four-year terms and a multitude of controversial decisions and issues, when Janklow was running for a fourth term, his approval rating among all voters was 71 percent favorable and 19 percent unfavorable (McLaughlin poll, July 1998, box 13, Janklow Staff Papers).

56. The 2020 population of the Albany-Schenectady-Troy metropolitan statistical area (MSA), the sixty-third largest MSA in the United States, is 12,529 higher than the 2020 population of the entire state of South Dakota. www.census.gov.

57. Venhuizen, *Governors*, pp. 232, 255; Venhuizen, "Governor Andrew Lee," Trail of Governors, https://trailofgovernors.com/governor-andrew-e-lee/; See entries in Biographical Directory of the United States Congress: Noem, https://bioguideretro.congress.gov/Home/MemberDetails?memIndex=N000184; Knowles, https://bioguideretro.congress.gov/Home/MemberDetails?memIndex=K000293. Kelley, https://bioguideretro.congress.gov/Home/MemberDetails?memIndex=000060; Kyle, https://bioguideretro.congress.gov/Home/MemberDetails?memIndex=000353; Mundt, https://bioguideretro.congress.gov/Home/MemberDetails?memIndex=M001078. Volk: http://www.fyi-dakota.com/index.php/biographies/dave-volk.

58. Number of Native American tribes in South Dakota, https://sdstate.edu/office-diversity-inclusion-equity-access/south-dakota-tribes.

59. South Dakota political bodies, https://southdakota.hometownlocator.com/counties/; https://ballotpedia.org/List_of_school_districts_in_South_Dakota.

60. South Dakota elected statewide offices, https://ballotpedia.org/South_Dakota_state_executive_offices.

61. California elected statewide offices, www.census.gov; https://ballotpedia.org/California_state_executive_offices.

62. New York elected statewide offices, www.census.gov; https://ballotpedia.org/New_York_state_executive_offices.

63. Degrees of separation among South Dakotans, https://exploringyourmind.com/the-six-degrees-of-separation-theory/

64. On W. W. Taylor's corruption, see John Andrews, "Treachery in the Treasury," *South Dakota Magazine*, 30 Dec. 2014.

65. On corruption among recent Illinois governors, see "4 of Illinois' last 7 governors went to prison," *Daily Journal* (Kankakee, Ill.), 30 Jan. 2013.

66. On corruption among Louisiana politicians, see Tim Morris, "The most corrupt state? Louisiana owns it: Opinion," *New Orleans Times-Picayune*, 25 July 2017.

MICHAEL A. CARD

10 | THE POLITICS OF THE SOUTH DAKOTA BUDGET PROCESS

• • •

The budget of a government organization is its most important policy document.[1] For a state government, the budget is likely the most significant legislation to pass through the legislature in any year, though often the most ignored. The General Appropriations Act (also called "general bill") is part of the overall financial plan required of the governor, which appropriates authority to expend monies to meet the ordinary expenses of the executive, legislative and judicial departments of the state; the current expenses of state institutions; interest on the public debt; and expenditures for public schools.[2] Its passage affects the lives of everyone in South Dakota. While this volume focuses on the political culture of South Dakota, this chapter examines those aspects of the dominant political culture that developed the tax policies that determine how revenue is raised to fund the state's operations.

South Dakota political scientist Robert Burns notes, "Where a state gets its money and where it spends it, is a reflection of its values." He continues, citizens need "to search within themselves and see the way in which it [the state of South Dakota] generates revenue, how it taxes, who it taxes, what level it taxes and how much tax revenue is generated and then see if it meets with their personal value system."[3] Some individuals believe they are the best judge of what to do with their money, and, at its extreme, some believe that "taxation is stealing." Others insist that the "good life" is possible only if the government promotes the public welfare over individual interests. Most taxpayers would probably like it both ways—low taxes and a wide variety of public services.[4]

Budgeting for revenues and expenses is inherently "political" in the sense that politics is about having "a say in . . . how the government is organized, or what its policies will be."[5] Developing a budget means, first of all, making choices about the amount of revenue expected to be received, which then determines the level of expenditures which can be funded from that level of revenues, which, in turn, determines the size and scope of state government. This brings up the question of what level of government is appropriate and what means should be chosen to fund that level of government. First, this chapter addresses the primary political factors influencing what level of government is appropriate, measured by conceptions of political culture. It then turns to a discussion of how the primary means are chosen to fund that level of service, and whether those means meet the criteria for a good tax system.

The political culture perspective in political science posits that public policies and budget outputs are not only based on political and economic factors, but also reflect a state's historical and cultural forces.[6] While many have decried its salience in explaining behavior, several studies on the linkage between political culture and expenditures have found independent effects on total state and local spending in the 1990s, even after controlling for commonly cited economic, political, and demographic variables.[7] Popular press studies have also noted relationships. Scholar Joel Garreau claims that North America is culturally heterogeneous, consisting of nine qualitatively distinct areas.[8] Colin Woodward notes that the United States is a federation comprised of the whole or part of eleven regional cultures, some of which truly do not see eye to eye with one another.[9] Woodward posits that some of these eleven are distinct in that each has its own common culture, ethnic origin, language, historical experience, artifacts, and symbols. Scholar Daniel Elazar's classification of political subcultures in the American states is political science's most well-known definition of political culture as "the particular pattern of orientation to political action in which each political system is embedded."[10]

Elazar identified the three American state political subcultures as moralistic, individualistic, or traditionalistic, or a state might have some combination of these cultures, depending on historic interplays among religious and ethnic groups, settlements, and resource deployments within a state. Elazar traces these categories to differences in immigrant groups that tended to congregate in their own settlements, frequently migrated together, and shared common political ideals. The culture of a specific city or state mirrors the cultural geography of settlement and migration, carrying with it views about government, bureaucracy, and politics. More recently, studies have mostly verified the durability of Elazar's insights, including more than a hundred empirical studies that address Elazar's conceptualizations or slight variations, with most confirming Elazar's thesis. Elazar's state classification system has been shown to be superior in explaining some public policy outputs, such as Aid to Families with Dependent Children payments, local government revenues, welfare expenditures, and tax burdens.[11]

The empirical evidence links moralistic political cultures with lower local government spending and higher state government spending.[12] Individualistic political cultures were connected with higher local government and lower state government expenditures.[13] Other studies have positively associated party competition, higher voter turnout, and party relevance in elections with moralistic political cultures. Individualistic political cultures tend to have and spend more on staffing for their legislative and gubernatorial administrations, while traditionalistic states tend to have lower tax efforts and tax capacity, be more dependent on federal assistance, and have lower debt levels.[14]

In moralistic cultures, government is considered a legitimate instrument for promoting public welfare. In contrast to the moralism that characterized the Puritan settlements of the New England region, the mid-Atlantic reflected an emphasis on individual pursuits in religious tolerance, pluralism, and a preference for limited government. Tolerance and acceptance of differences is consistent with Quaker values, prevalent in the mid-Atlantic states, and contrasting with the "puritanical" norms of New England. Locations Elazar associates with individualistic political cultures conceive democratic government as a marketplace, instituted for utilitarian reasons to handle functions demanded by the people it serves. Government intervention into private activities was to be restricted to the minimum necessary to keep the marketplace functional. The migration patterns that populated the South replicated norms of the "landed gentry" of Europe. Elazar posited that settlers adopted a traditionalistic culture that viewed government as a means of maintaining the existing social order. Landowners assumed a dominant role in the political process in this culture. The values of this subculture dominated the old South and over time spread westwards across the south.

Elazar classifies South Dakota as a mix of moralistic and individualistic political cultures—moralistic to the northeast and individualistic in the west and a combination of the two in the southeast.[15] The Euro-

American settlement of southeast South Dakota was largely composed of post-Civil War Union army veterans and their families.[16] However, in the late 1930s, with the end of the Progressive Era, that individualistic culture became and largely remains the dominant political culture.

Conservativism continues to characterize most South Dakotans, as it has throughout the state's history.[17] Delegates to the state's constitutional conventions were interested in limiting the power of the legislature, the governor, the courts, and the influence of corporations while maintaining individual liberties.[18] To combat the excesses of corporate influences on the governor and legislature, state constitution writers placed checks and balances on all three branches of government. The constitution limited the governor by electing rather than appointing many officials and by requiring senate confirmation for such appointments, with governing boards for each agency receiving appropriations directly from the legislature.[19] Short terms of office were also required to hold officials accountable to the citizenry.

Writing during the Progressive Era, George Smith and Clark Young noted regarding the moralistic political culture, "In society, many things must be done that the individual could not accomplish alone." They developed a short list of developments citizens deemed essential at the time of their writing: roads and bridges built and maintained, schools established and maintained, streets built and maintained, safe water and sewerages built and maintained. They concluded that "government is to secure for the individual that which he could not possibly obtain for himself alone."[20] They also expected regulation of "so-called 'natural monopolies'" and expansion of demand into wider and wider fields. This would be paid for by taxation, described as "the right of government to demand from each person under its jurisdiction such a part of the total expenditures as shall be just and right; but it is a right that should be exercised only in the interests of all." The clear allusion is that unequal distribution of benefits is a dangerous form of oppression and tyranny, and that government could prevent or restrict this tyranny. More toward the end of the Progressive Era, Professor E. P. Crossen noted the upward trend of taxation. Crossen noted,

> The cost of government, particularly the cost of state and local government, is influenced by the habits and standards of living of the people supporting the government and by the degree of

> self-control and intelligence used by them in voting on matters of public expenditure. A considerable part of the rise of taxes represents a cost of providing improved facilities and additional services which either were thought unattainable or were not considered necessary twenty years ago.[21]

Crossen continued by describing the citizens' demands for increased educational attainment by the state's youth, the increasing complexity of society, the increased use of the automobile creating a need for improved roads, community pride creating a need for civic buildings, the state and local provision of services formerly considered private businesses such as lighting and telephone systems, the state loaning of money for farmlands, a state cement plant and coal mine, and so on. He could have added hail insurance, the penitentiary selling twine, Governor McMaster ordering the sale of gasoline from county highway shops to combat alleged price gouging by oil companies, and several other state-owned enterprises consonant with the moralistic political classification, deemed "necessary" as South Dakotans wanted to provide comparable services such as those available to citizens of states in existence for a much longer period of time. Crossen also noted that the problems of taxation were not only their high level, but also one of incidence—upon whom the cost of a tax falls:

> The problem of taxes is not altogether one of higher or low taxes period. It is also a problem of equitable distribution of the tax burden and of the relation between the improvements and services desired and the ability of the state to afford such improvements and services.[22]

Moralistic political cultures tend to be expansive in their concept of government. Individuals who hold this moralistic political framework view government as the instrument of good, and view politics as the mechanism for solving disputes, competitive in terms of ideas, with many elections, high voter turnout, and political parties that are appropriately focused on issues and principles, including paying one's "fair share." Individualistic political cultures tend to view government as a marketplace—a means to respond efficiently to citizen demands through encouragement of private initiative and efforts to improve the marketplace. Government activity in economic development is favored, but unlike the moralistic political culture which favors direct governmental action, individualistic political cultures focus on enhancing the business community. It is rather evident that these two political cultures compete and are often in conflict, perhaps serving as fracture points in dominant political parties. The traditionalistic political culture is more concerned with maintaining social order. Society is more hierarchical, with low voter turnout and participation as elites are viewed as having the right to dominate politics. These elites identify members of their group whose "right to govern" stems from their social ties and family membership. Like individualistic political cultures, political participants expect to benefit personally from the activity, though not necessarily by direct gain. As one might expect, the objects of government expenditures are also predicted to vary by political culture of the dominant coalition.

There are many revenue sources authorized by the legislature to finance activities designed to meet the needs and goals of the state as identified by the governor and the legislature. These sources consist of a variety of taxes, trust funds, reserve funds, grants from private entities and the federal government, and "agency funds." The criteria to evaluate revenue sources includes adequacy to generate revenue to sustain public services in a stable manner and grow at a pace that keeps up with the cost of services the government provides, simple enough for citizens to understand, benefits accruing to individuals, especially nonresidents, should involve contributions of their fair share to support those services, "efficiency" in that the tax system does not create incentives for making decisions counterproductive to the state's economy, and balance among the types of taxes levied.[23]

South Dakota has been recognized as a good if not great place to do business. In 2020, the Tax Foundation ranked South Dakota as the second-best state in which to do business, largely because of its first-place ranking in areas of low corporate and low individual taxes.[24] However, even with this favorable ranking, the state ranks thirty-third in sales and use taxes, twentieth in property taxes, and forty-second in unemployment (or reemployment) insurance taxes.

The Institute for Taxation and Economic Policy (ITEP), an organization that focuses its efforts on analysis of tax and economic policy and proposals in terms of how they shape equitable tax systems, reveals how taxes affect both public revenues as well as the people in the state.[25] ITEP ranks South Dakota as having the fourth most regressive tax system in the nation, meaning that lower income individuals in the state pay a higher percentage of their income in taxes for property, sales, use, and excise taxes than do higher income individuals. In contrast to the Tax Foundation, ITEP's ranking does not seem to consider additional criteria to evaluate state tax systems other than "vertical equity" ("fairness" determined by taxes as a percentage of personal or family income). The Tax Foundation uses a broader set of criteria for its analysis: "tax adequacy" (providing enough revenue to meet the basic needs of society), "stability" (consistency and predictability in the tax code with stable revenue), "simplicity" (a system that enables taxpayers and tax remitters to easily comply with tax laws and ease for the government to administer and enforce), "transparency" (enabling taxpayers to be able to plainly determine what they must pay and when they must pay it as well as avoiding hidden tax burdens and ensuring full and open consideration of proposed changes to the tax code), "neutrality" (taxes neither encourage nor discourage personal or business decisions), and "horizontal equity" (ensuring that taxpayers in similar situations pay similar amounts in taxes).[26] One other criteria is "tax incidence" (determining who bears the economic cost of a tax between producers and consumers or among various class segments of a population).

The South Dakota tax system in 2021 paralleled the typical taxes found in other states with the notable exceptions of the lack of a personal income tax or a corporate income tax, and the existence of a contractor's excise tax.[27] Other relatively small but significant revenue sources included lottery taxes and fees, insurance company tax, unclaimed property receipts, tobacco taxes, bank franchise tax, miscellaneous excise taxes and fees including cigarettes, alcohol, and motor fuel and vehicle taxes. One-time windfalls (receipts) are also a source of revenue.[28]

South Dakota's budget heavily relies on federal funds, although the percentage of federal revenue used to support state expenditures decreased from 47.8 percent in 2010 to 35.9 percent in 2021. Federal funds have been greater than state general funds appropriations since 2000, though the state funds have been increasing in dollar amounts in each of these last eleven years, as of this writing.

Table 1. Legislative Appropriations by Funding Category, FY2011–2022

Fiscal year	*General Funds*	*Federal Funds*	*Other funds*	*Total*
2011	$1,145,662,738	$1,963,509,180	$998,519,418	$4,107,691,336
2012	1,150,867,146	1,857,203,151	1,024,674,756	4,032,7745,053
2013	1,232,361,618	1,754,950,330	1,068,340,191	4,055,652,139
2014	1,293,068,278	1,643,807,414	1,130,054,687	4,277,236,722
2015	1,372,395,933	1,679,576,551	1,225,264,238	4,277,236,722
2016	1,417,040,757	1,663,511,722	1,240,272,297	4,320,824,826
2017	1,554,021,368	1,651,067,371	1,377,780,256	4,582,868,995
2018	1,591,226,544	1,643,804,785	1,357,707,611	4,592,738,940
2019	1,607,249,152	1,705,999,448	1,390,009,997	4,703,258,597
2020	1,686,448,082	1,847,335,160	1,437,019,922	4,970,803,164
2021	1,734,513,310	1,769,897,110	1,419,515,498	4,923,925,918
2022	1,818,313,439	1,834,400,340	1,451,012,100	5,103,725,879

As recently as fiscal year (FY) 2021, general funds (mostly sales tax) amounted to $1.735 billion, authority for agencies and institutions to expend funds received from the federal government was $1.77 billion, and "other funds" amounted to $1.420 billion. For fiscal year 2022, the legislature authorized and appropriated $1.631 billions in general funds, gave authority to spend federal funds of $1.821 billion, and gave authority to spend other funds of $1.4538 billion. State general funds in 1999 were greater than federal funds authorized by the legislature to be spent on state activities through the general appropriations bill; federal funds have been greater than state general fund appropriations since the 2000 fiscal year.[29]

Most recently, in FY21 and FY22, the state received significant funds from various federal coronavirus relief acts, including the Families First Coronavirus Response Act (FFCRA), which allocated about $64.92 million to South Dakota; the Coronavirus Aid, Relief, and Economic Security Act (CARES Act) gave about $6.88 billion; the Paycheck Protection Program and Health Care Enhancement Act (PPPHCEA) allocated about $63.18 million the Consolidated Appropriations Act, 2021 (P.L. 116-260) allocated about $647.82 million to South Dakota; and the American Rescue Plan Act (ARPA) provided about $3.42 billion. In total, South Dakota has received $11.08 billion in Coronavirus-related funds as of 16 June 2021.[30] This stimulus money has gone or will go to either South Dakota agencies or local governments, organizations, and citizens.[31] Since some of these funds have not been appropriated, they may be spent up to 2026. Still, even without these windfalls, South Dakota is one of the nation's most federally dependent for resources to support the state government and its institutions, even though its fiscal stability in 2020 was quite strong, especially compared to surrounding states.

Table 2 displays the state-federal "Balance of Payments," representing the balance of cash inflows and cash outflows between the state and its residents and the federal government. Positive numbers represent net cash inflows from the federal government and negative numbers represent net cash outflows from the state to the federal government. Positive numbers represent the balance of payments from the federal government to South Dakota, after subtracting South Dakota's and South Dakotans' payments to the federal government. The figures in the bottom row reflect the net federal spending distributed to a state (expenditures) less the amount paid to the federal government by a state's residents and businesses (receipts). The net gain reflects expenditures the state does not have to provide to receive "services," notwithstanding that some of these services might not be provided because of the cost to the state. In terms of comparison with neighboring states, Minnesota ranks forty-sixth in terms of receiving the most funds per capita from the federal government, while South Dakota ranks thirty-third in terms of all state balance of payments with the federal government. In comparison to its bordering states, South Dakota trails only Montana and Wyoming, each with significantly larger tracts of federally owned land; both states exceed South Dakota's and South Dakotan's receipts from the federal government. It is interesting to note that this trend began with Governor Tom Berry, a Democrat who held office from 1933 to 1937. To Berry, "common sense" and "personal responsibility" were more important than any economist's ideas about taxes. Berry also served as the State Relief Director; he made several trips to Washington, where, upon leaving office, he quipped, "the only time I left Pierre was to go to Washington to try to get more aid for the people."[32] Berry used federal money to supplement the state's

Table 2. Per Capita Expenditures and Receipts from the Federal Government to States Surrounding South Dakota, 2019[39]

Per capita amounts by transfer funds category (rank)

IA (35)	*MN (46)*	*MT (17)*	*NE (40)*	*ND (34)*	*SD (33)*	*WY (26)*	*US Average Across States*
Direct Payments							
$7,530	$7,033	$8,633	$7,481	$6,617	$7,819	$7,847	$7,672
Grants							
$1,942	$2,218	$2,915	$1,522	$2,670	$1,864	$4,450	$2,145
Contracts							
$469	$723	$663	$431	$1,159	$1,090	$318	$1,706
Wages							
$309	$350	$1,010	$753	$1,324	$1,072	$1,271	$833
Individual Income Tax							
-$3,657	-$5,366	-$3,617	-$3,873	-$4,592	-$4,088	-$5,523	-$5,161
Social Insurance Taxes							
-$4,106	-$4,235	-$4371	-$4,693	-$4,356	-$3,739	-$3,739	-$3,739
Corporate income Taxes							
-$642	-$718	-$657	-$714	-$759	-$784	-$984	-$694
Excise Taxes							
-$353	-$313	-$356	-$344	-$456	-$366	-$501	-$30
Other taxes							
$0	$28	$0	-$166	$0	$0	-$0	-$50
Total per capita balance of payments							
$1,492	-$336	$4,221	$397	$1,607	$2,037	$2,796	$2,412

meager Depression-era resources, a tradition that has apparently continued. Still, in the twenty-first century, the state has much more ability to raise resources above the Depression-era level.

Property taxes have been the primary source of funds for school districts, counties, municipalities, and other units of local government since statehood. As noted earlier, the state ended its property tax levy with the enactment of the gross receipts income tax and an ore tax in

1933. Counties are responsible for property tax assessment, collection, and distribution, subject to state laws administered by the Department of Revenue, providing a higher degree of horizontal equity (individuals with similar income and assets should pay the same amount in taxes). The property tax provides for a degree of local control over the tax rate and over the total taxes collected. In 2020, school districts received 55.9 percent of the property taxes paid ($807 million) while counties received 26.7 percent of property taxes paid ($386 million) and municipalities received 13.5 percent ($195 million), with the tiny remainder split between townships and special assessments.[33] State aid to K-12 education spending has increased, largely because of the 2016 addition of nearly one-half of one percent sales tax, mostly earmarked to increase teacher salaries. However, the tax limitation measure that significantly revised the school funding formula also capped growth on property taxes at 3 percent or the rate of inflation, whichever is less, or the amount of tax on the value of new construction added to the property tax rolls. This "cap" on taxes collected has limited increases in school district spending to the percentage increase in the consumer price index, and by the increases in the assessed value of new construction in the district in the prior year. School district spending could also be limited if the legislature were to amend the statute specifying the "per-student" allocation to reduce the amount which the legislature set and appropriated in a previous year to account for reductions in overall state revenues. This would mean districts have fewer resources to expend. Large, accumulated surpluses also reduce state aid contributions.

Property is taxed at rates corresponding to the classification of property types. South Dakota has a default property tax rate for all property, taxed at the highest levy, which is often called "commercial" although it is actually everything that's not classified as "agricultural" or "owner-occupied housing." Agricultural property gets a special, lower rate. Owner-occupied homes also get a lower rate.[34] Special assessments and utilities assessed by a local government to pay for property-specific and neighborhood projects constitute the final categories.

The South Dakota Legislature has enacted two independent systems that limit the growth of property taxes. The first is the state aid to education payments system. These payments effectively reduce property taxes for schools that would otherwise be paid by property owners.

The second system is the cap placed on the property taxes collected by all levels of local government. These caps limit the local governments' property tax collections to the amount they collected the previous year, plus small increases for inflation based on the consumer price index and new construction within the taxing jurisdiction.[35]

Property taxes are likely the most despised tax administered by a government since property owners must make two payments a year, and owning significant amounts of property means two significant payments, each and every year.[36] Other dissatisfaction depends on a distinction between statutory liability to pay the tax and "tax incidence"—the latter reflects who bears the economic cost of paying the tax. Non-owner-occupied housing or rental housing is classified as commercial property and taxed at a higher rate. Since rental housing is usually occupied by lower-income residents, and the residents see the property tax included into the rental payments they pay their landlord, the property tax incidence falls on the renter. For instance, owner-occupied taxes calculated as the percentage of a property's assessed market value that is to be paid in taxes was 1.32 percent in 2020, while commercial property was taxed at an effective rate of 1.65 percent of the assessed value of the property.[37]

As South Dakota's average population increases in age, more individuals have limited opportunity to increase their earnings to cover the cost of increasing property taxes. To reduce the taxes paid by certain classifications of citizens whose ability to pay is constrained, the legislature created "circuit breakers"— a term used to reduce the property taxes due for low-income elderly and disabled individuals to match the taxpayer's ability to pay the property tax (increasing vertical equity or progressivity of the tax) than would otherwise exist. These circuit breakers help make the property tax "fairer" in that the tax is more closely aligned with the taxpayer's ability to pay. The legislature tasked the Department of Revenue with a "senior freeze program" that freezes property value assessments for qualifying individuals over the age of sixty-five. To qualify, the applicant must have owned his or her home for at least one year, the value of the property must be under $202,943, and the applicant's income cannot exceed $29,565 for a single-member household or $36,957 for a household with more than one member.

Figure 1 indicates that there is a significant disparity in the property

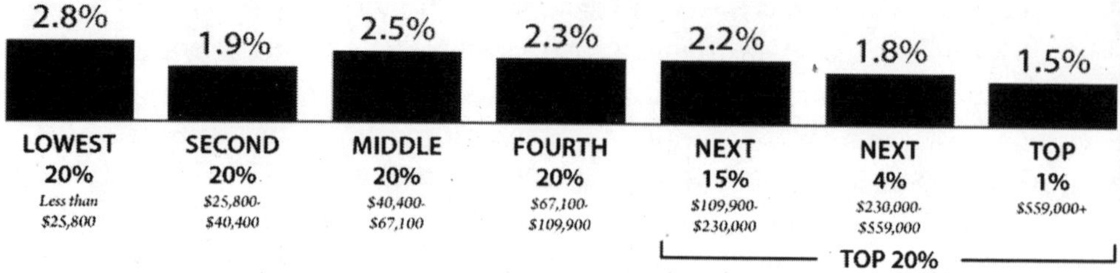

Figure 1. Institute for Taxation and Economic Policy (ITEP) Calculations of Property Taxes in South Dakota as a Share of Family Income by Quintile

taxes paid by the lowest versus highest income quintiles. The tax is more fair than it would have been without the circuit-breakers, which are not included in ITEP's analysis.

In the 1994 election, Initiated Measure 1, or Dakota 1 as it was called, nearly passed. If it had passed, it would have reduced property tax collections, leaving school districts critically short of funds to operate, and some argued, required a significant change to the state's tax structure. Newly elected third term governor, William (Bill) Janklow ran for office in the same election, proclaiming himself to be a problem-solver with a track record reflecting using both conservative and populist ideas to address the problems of the state.[38] Janklow went through the challenges involved in working with the legislature to reduce property taxes to find the money to pay for those reductions by engaging in a process to reduce the number of state employees and to reorganize the state government for efficiencies. The threat was diffused as there have been few realistic attempts to institute an income tax since that effort to indirectly force an income tax.

The burden of residential property tax falls more heavily on non-owner-occupied rental housing. This is because real estate used for non-owner-occupied housing is valued at higher rates than most other property due to cash flows from rental payments increasing the value of the property. This makes rental housing property subject to higher rates levied on commercial property. Further, landowners transfer the tax incidence of rental property to renters, although the legal requirement to pay the tax remains with the property owner. As renters are more likely to be lower income, the property tax continues to be relatively regressive, though the circuit breakers make for a smaller percentage than other regressive taxes.

Disputes over the appropriate assessment still occur, though the training and computerized records have reduced legitimate claims to a lack of horizontal equity. Since property is hard to hide, there is little tax avoidance. While the size of the tax base may differ based on the size of the taxing jurisdiction, the assessment in one year and the tax bill the next keep revenue relatively stable and tax-neutral once assessments have been made. The size of the tax base establishes tax adequacy. Still, the counties face significant costs in assessing property, and movements to value the property on the productive capacity of the property reflect a more individualistic political culture.

At least up to 2021, there is no personal or corporate state-sanctioned income tax in South Dakota. However, there was a form of an active income tax from 1933 to 1940, and an inactive one from 1940 through 1967, although the tax rate table was deleted in 1941.[39] Forty-two states levy individual income taxes, with forty-one taxing wage and salary income, while New Hampshire taxes only dividend and interest income. That leaves eight states with no state authorized individual income tax: Alaska, Florida, Nevada, South Dakota, Tennessee, Texas, Washington, and Wyoming.[40] Recent attempts to enact an income tax or to conduct a serious review of tax policy have failed to gain traction in the legislature.[41]

In 1935, the South Dakota Legislature enacted Governor Berry's proposal for a two percent sales tax to provide revenue upon the failure of his 1933 gross receipts tax to generate sufficient revenue "for support of the state government and its existing public institutions."[42] The sales tax rate was increased to 3 percent in 1937, to 4 percent in 1969, and to four and 4.5 percent in 2016 when an additional 0.5 percent tax was added to transfer monies to school districts to increase teacher pay, with a small portion going to technical school instructor pay and the balance to provide property tax relief.

The state imposes a tax on the gross receipts from selling, leasing, and renting tangible personal property and the sale of [most] services. A use tax of the same rate as the sales tax is imposed on goods and services that are used, stored, or consumed in South Dakota upon which the state's sales tax was not paid. The state's general fund, used for "support of state government and its existing public institutions" is fueled at the rate of 62 percent by the sales tax, with the sales, use, and contractor's excise tax together constituting 69.9 percent of the general fund.[43] The sales and use tax covers food, clothing, and other necessities. The lowest 20 percent of South Dakotans in terms of income pay 11.2 percent of their income in total state and local taxes, including 8.4 percent for the sales tax. The breadth of the sales tax makes the total tax less regressive than the total tax burden. "Everybody pays something," as South Dakota has one of the nation's broadest sales tax bases; taxes are collected on most services, including those provided by professionals. This makes what would be an otherwise very regressive tax (violating the principle of taxation based on a person's ability to pay) slightly less regressive. In a contrary move, the legislature has exempted from the sales and use tax certain transactions that results in reduced tax revenue.[44]

These exemptions from state sales and use tax, outlined in the December version of the *Governor's Budget Summary Book* for the past several years, represent a revenue loss as the exemptions created by statute result from items not subject to sales and use taxes, and other taxes.[45] Tax exemptions are created to provide incentives for engaging in activities that would benefit the development of industry, the commonwealth, or certain categories of beneficiaries. The exemptions for agriculture were estimated at over $580 million in sales taxes foregone. Exemptions provided for healthcare are estimated at a loss of $315 million, governments $186 million, and business expenses $248 million. The Bureau of Finance and Management estimates sales tax exemptions for FY 2022 of $1.45 billion, 75 percent of the total general fund revenue used to support state government and its existing institutions.[46]

These exemptions make the sales and use tax more regressive, as these exemptions represent taxes unlikely to be levied against the members of lowest income groups but likely to benefit higher income individuals and families as the sales on these goods and services are exempt from taxation. Further, by inclusion in the tax code, they are not regularly reviewed as a budget item, decreasing tax transparency. If these exemptions were eliminated from the tax code, additional funds would be available to meet the state's goals. Farm Bureau lobbyists have argued that exempting these items is appropriate because if taxes were to be levied on these items or services, they would increase the cost of production, which would be passed on to South Dakota taxpayers.[47] Still others argue that goods and services exempted from sales

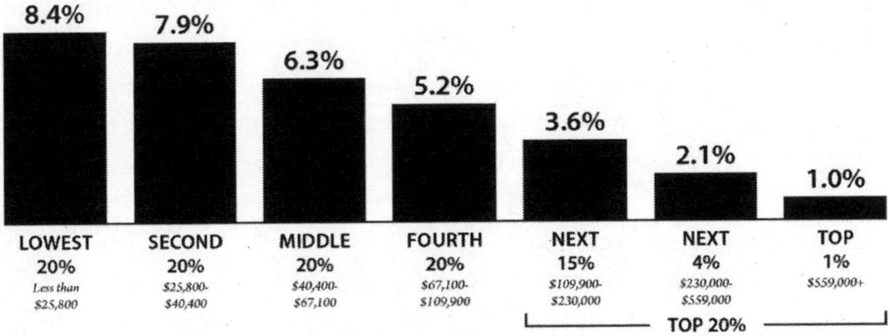

Figure 2. ITEP Calculation of Sales, Use and Excise Taxes in South Dakota as a Percentage of Family Income

tax through the Wayfair Decision and delivered out of state would see these taxes be "exported" to taxpayers in other states.[48] The incidence of taxes on medical equipment and services, unless exempted, would be passed onto South Dakota residents. Insurance companies, which also pay medical costs, would increase rates to maintain their profits or create a surplus for nonprofit health care organizations. These tax exemptions on agricultural and health care goods and services support the political culture of a small-town agrarian social order identified as a core component of a traditionalistic political culture.[49] While many people think that we are missing a great amount of potential revenue, many exemptions are business expenses and production inputs that very few states tax. More sales and tax exemptions might be granted to incentivize businesses to locate in South Dakota as the tax on business inputs is essentially a tax on capital.[50] Sifting through these competing values requires considerable patience and wisdom.[51]

The Department of Revenue collects and then distributes about $430 million to cities, tribes, and a few other entities, which levy 1 or 2 percent, in addition to the 4.5 percent state sales or use tax for the municipal sales or use tax.[52] Cities can also levy a 1 percent tax on the gross receipts of sales of alcoholic beverages, lodging and accommodations, admissions to amusements including athletic and cultural events (1 percent), with the additional percent colloquially referred to as a "bed, booze, and board tax." The state also collects sales taxes on businesses situated on tribal trust land imposed by the state's tribal governments upon a memorandum of agreement between the state and the tribe, and the state distributed $12.4 million to the appropriate tribal governments.

To lessen the impact and regressivity of the sales and use taxes, similar to the justification surrounding property tax "circuit breakers," the state has a sales tax rebate for eligible residents. Eligible applicants must be state residents for all of the calendar year; be sixty-five years old on or before the first day of the tax year or have a disability in that year; and have incomes of less than $12,880 for a single person or less than $17,420 for a multiple-person household. That is, nearly all fit in the lowest income quintile, making the sales tax slightly more progressive. This suggests that eliminating the sales tax on food or having a broader set of eligibility criteria for the sales tax rebate would greatly reduce the regressivity of the sales tax.

In 1979, South Dakota enacted a contractor's excise tax, a tax levied on specific goods or services, in this case, a 2 percent tax levied on the gross receipts of all prime construction contractors. This involves materials and labor on improvements to real property, with the tax evidence then passed along to the purchaser of those goods and services. This results in a problem economists call "pyramiding." Simply put, pyramiding involves paying taxes on revenue for which you have already paid taxes. The legislature has reduced this for projects other than utilities construction projects where subcontractors are not taxed in addition to the tax levied on prime contractors.[53]

South Dakota has remained largely dependent on sales and use taxes for general fund revenues since 1935. From 2009 to 2020, 73.1 percent of the state's general fund was based on sales, use, and excise taxes.[54] South Dakota's sales and use taxes are the highest in the surrounding states (see Table 3). Iowa's state and local sales and use taxes are at the national median (an equal number of states are higher and lower than Iowa's 3.34 percent).

The most recent significant attempt to remove the sales tax from food was 2004's Initiated Measure 1, defeated 123,210 votes to 255,855. David Owen, President and Chief Lobbyist of Commerce and Industry of South Dakota, testified in the hearing for the 2021 Senate Bill 104 to remove the tax on food, that the state with support from many stakeholders put in place a policy to provide food tax relief by providing refunds on food taxes paid by low income individuals to respond to the concerns raised by the initiative.[55] In 2009, the eligibility for food-tax refunds was changed to exclude households that were income-eligible to receive Supplemental Nutrition Assistance Program (SNAP) benefits, reducing the number of South Dakotans who received refunds from 42,161 to 726 in FY2010.[56]

The bills to exempt the sales tax on food are usually defeated at the bill's first hearing, such as 2019's HB 1238 and 2021's Senate Bill 104, eliminating the sales tax on certain food items. State Economist Mark Quasney argued that South Dakota has a relatively low sales and use tax rate, based on the premise that everyone pays a little—"their fair share."[57] Quasney noted, under this reasoning, exempting food from the sales tax would mean the sales tax would be levied on discretionary items, the reason the sales tax was instituted in 1935. Opponents argued that eliminating the sales tax on food would reduce tax receipts by $70 million and, since everyone purchases food, it would make sales tax revenues less stable, creating financial uncertainty for the state.[58] That stability results from taxes falling on lower income residents who pay a higher percentage of their income on sales taxes for food items than do higher income individuals. The individualistic political culture—asserting that individuals are responsible for themselves—supports this policy decision.

South Dakota taxes many types of goods and services under its tax codes. This has enabled the sales and use tax collections to remain relatively stable over the years, through the last two recessions (December 2007 to June 2009 and February 2020 to April 2020). As the state's economy shifts in gross domestic product (GDP)—total dollar value of all goods and services produced by an economy over a specific period—from sales of goods to sales of services, especially financial services, South Dakota's sales and use tax policy has remained a reliable source of income.

This reliability violates the vertical equity principle: that people pay taxes according to their ability to pay. Lower income individuals should pay lower effective rates of tax ("effective" is defined as percentage of income paid in taxes or a particular tax). As the burden or incidence of sales and use taxes decreases as a percentage of income rises, the stability in general fund revenue has been provided by lower income taxpayers.

If we compare the property tax, individual income tax, and the total sales, use and excise tax data from the Tax Policy Center for the fifty states as a percentage (share) of personal income, we see support for the assertion that South Dakota is a low tax state: it ranks forty-third among all states in total tax burden (aggregated taxes paid as a share of aggregated personal income) for a rate of 7.4 percent of personal income. South Dakota's Gini coefficient ranks it as the eighth most equal state, similar to most states bordering South Dakota.[59]

Table 3 shows the total tax burden as a percentage of income for states surrounding South Dakota and for property, income, and sales and excise taxes. By reviewing the tax structures of the surrounding states for these three taxes, we can see significant differences. Minnesota, rated by Elazar as a moralistic political culture state with one large metropolitan area and three smaller ones (including the Fargo-Moorhead area) has the highest overall tax burden.[60] Iowa, also classified as a moralistic political culture state with two large and two medium-sized metropolitan areas has as a bordering state the second highest overall tax burden. Nebraska, classified by Elazar as a combination moralistic-individualistic state with one large and one medium-sized metropolitan area, ranks higher in terms of taxes per capita than do North Dakota, Montana, South Dakota, or Wyoming. Elazar ranks North Dakota as a moralistic state, with one metropolitan area shared with Minnesota, but with intermittent high revenues from oilfield revenues. North Dakota also ranks lower than Minnesota, Iowa, or Nebraska because of its low individual income tax burden. Montana, which Elazar classifies as moralistic and individualistic, has seven small metropolitan areas, and its total tax burden ranks relatively low because of its low sales and excise tax burden. Wyoming has a substantially lower total tax burden than the other states because it has no state individual income tax burden and a significantly lower sales and excise tax burden than other border states, save Minnesota and Montana. South Dakota, classified by Elazar as having moralistic and individualistic political cultures, ranks lower than all of its border states, save Wyoming (which Elazar rates as an individualistic political culture) in total tax burden. However, South Dakota has a higher than median state property tax and sales and excise as a percentage of income, benefitting from its lack of a personal or effective corporate income tax.

Montana, North Dakota, and Wyoming have benefitted in the recent past from having economies largely dependent on mineral extrac-

Table 3. 2020 Tax Burdens for Total Tax, Property Tax, Sales and Use Excise Taxes, and Individual Income Tax for States Surrounding South Dakota[67]

Total Tax Burden Rank (1=Highest)	*State*	*Total Tax Burden (%)*	*Property Tax Burden (%)*	*Property Tax Burden Rank*	*Individual Income Tax Burden (%)*	*Individual Income Tax Burden Rank*	*Total Sales & Excise Tax Burden (%)*	*Total Sales & Excise Tax Burden Rank*
6	MN	9.99%	2.86%	23	3.68%	5	2.45%	20
13	IA	9.26%	3.39%	14	2.53%	18	3.34%	25
14	NE	9.01%	3.77%	10	2.30%	26	2.94%	36
38	ND	7.81%	2.97%	21	0.87%	41	3.97%	13
40	MT	7.45%	3.59%	12	2.58%	16	1.28%	47
43	SD	7.37%	3.02%	19	0.00%	44	4.35%	8
48	WY	6.14%	3.33%	15	0.00%	44	2.81%	40
	Median rate	8.34% MI & WA	2.8%	MS	2.41% VT		3.34% (IA)	

Note: The tax burden percentage is the tax burden as a percentage of income.

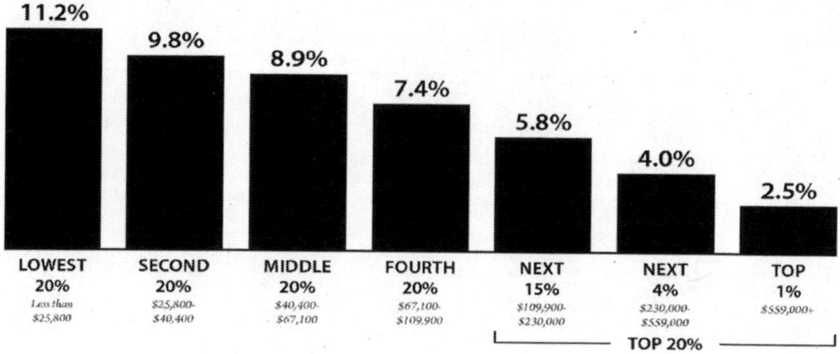

Figure 3. ITEP Calculation of South Dakota Sales, Use, and Contractor's Excise Tax Distribution as a Percent of Family Income

tion, but these states have more recently experienced greatly reduced tax revenue from that source.

While South Dakota's total tax burden is relatively low, the effect of South Dakota's low taxes is that they fall disproportionately on those least able to afford them. Figure 3 compares the share of family income by income quintile paid in these taxes. The overall tax structure with respect to property, excise, and sales and use taxes is regressive, meaning the lowest income groups pay a higher percentage of their income in sales and property taxes than do higher income groupings.[61]

Many South Dakotans are proud to live in a "low tax state" and the data support that claim. Its *per capita* state taxes are among the lowest in the nation, ranking between thirty-seventh (using Tax Foundation calculations based on family income) and forty-third (based on ITEP data based on personal income). Either way, South Dakotans pay 7.4 percent of their income in taxes based on household income (ITEP data) and 9.1 percent based on personal income (Tax Foundation data). South Dakota has a 13.2 percent lower tax burden than the U.S. average.[62] South Dakota has a lower per capita state-local tax burden than all of its surrounding states except Wyoming.[63] Likewise, taxpayers in Minnesota have a 44 percent higher per capita tax burden than do South Dakotans. So, while taxes are low, lower income individuals and families pay a higher percentage of their income in taxes than do wealthier individuals and families. South Dakotans do pay lower taxes overall, but that facet is not part of the economic analysis of the effectiveness of tax systems.

South Dakota's voter initiative (Amendment C) in 2001 repealed the intergenerational wealth transfer tax, better known as the inheritance tax. This tax was one of the most progressive taxes devised and implemented. The inheritance tax was usually paid by those in the highest income quintiles. Its repeal made the overall tax system slightly more regressive.

In considering any reforms of the tax code, a moralistic political culture would assert, much as earlier progressives noted, that each should pay according to his or her ability to pay.[64] Citizens attempting to uphold the moralistic political culture may ask members of legislative bodies, "Who will pay more or less in taxes as a result of this situation, or tax changes?" South Dakota's sales-tax driven general fund depends on having a broad base allowing relatively low tax burdens. The regressivity of the tax burden indicates that a more progressive tax policy would have higher income individuals and families paying a higher rate. However, figure 3 reveals that the lowest quintile of families pays a percentage of their income over twice that paid by the highest income earns (20 percent of the state's families). This current situation is clearly not based on one's ability to pay, suggesting that the individualistic political culture is indeed dominant in the tax structure.

According to legislative rule (Joint Rule 7–11.1), the Joint Committee on Appropriations must make its revenue estimates or general fund revenue targets on no later than the twenty-third legislative day. These estimates of revenue collection have been the basis for determining the state's spending to facilitate growth and development and determining what is not to be funded. The Bureau of Finance and Management and the Legislative Research Council make presentations to the Joint Appropriations Committee, which then adopts budget authority and appropriation levels. Reversions (unspent general fund appropriations) are common, averaging $18.9 million in the past five years ((FY) 2017–2021), and are deposited in the state's two budget reserve funds. Keeping government spending at low levels is a core principle of the increasingly dominant individualistic political culture. Even in Governor Berry's term (1933–1937), he vowed to obtain as much federal money for the state as possible, enabling the state to provide services that it could not otherwise offer. In 2021 and 2022, federal money enables to state to stockpile resources for a "rainy day." The Volcker Alliance notes that South Dakota has adequate reserves, and has a statutory limitation on the level of those funds.[65] However, the Alliance suggests having a statutory definition for when reserves are to be used, effectively defining when it is "raining." The farm debt crises experienced in South Dakota and its neighboring states combined with specific crises such as that from the 1980s and legislators' collective memory of debt from the Rural Credit program have kept the state from borrowing against its trust funds and other sources of cash.[66]

This mindset has also enabled South Dakota's pension system to be fully funded, a feat that only one or two other states can claim. These efforts to create financial cushions for emergencies may have led to depositing more monies into trust funds than circumstances would require. This policy preference has enabled the state to maintain low taxes and, as a result, provide a relatively low level of services. This preference also suggests that revenue estimates drive the budget system or require creative financing to plan for revenues to meet planned expenses. The low tax system prevents provision of higher levels of services which might enable greater success toward achieving the state's goals. Such a system could result in less income inequality, or a more equitable distribution of taxes according to one's ability to pay. Opponents argue that everybody pays a little, and everybody pays something. That generalization leaves out the details and lacks transparency. What is lost is the moralistic notion that one should pay taxes according to one's ability to pay one's "fair share": what is just and right.[67]

The rationale usually given is one of conservation of capital. The state's dependence on the agricultural economy with its resultant commodity pricing is similar to neighbor states, which are also at least partially dependent on commodity prices. Further, neighbors Montana, North Dakota, Wyoming, and, to a lesser extent, Minnesota, also suffer from the "extraction economy," where taxes are levied against coal, oil, natural gas and other minerals such as copper and iron, and as a result, are similar position to agriculture in being dependent on world price levels.

The environmental threats faced by the state create conservativism in all things financial. Such a presumption also leads citizens to resist changing the policy *status quo*. Such conservativism has not changed dramatically since the road to recovery from rural credits began in the 1940s.[68] South Dakotans tend to vote for Republican candidates and have a focus on preserving agriculture while at the same time recognizing the challenges to small-town culture and its local institutions and ethnic traditions.[69] Still, South Dakota is becoming less dependent on agriculture as population shifts to its two economic centers, Sioux Falls and Rapid City, which are growing in diverse ways.

While South Dakota's roots are in the agriculture industry, by 2020, the financial services industry had greatly expanded (27.5 percent of GDP). Meanwhile, the mainstays of the state's GDP remained government and government enterprises (11.0 percent of GDP), education, healthcare and social assistance (10.1 percent of GDP), retail trade (6.8 percent of GDP), agriculture, forestry and fishing and hunting (6.8 percent of GDP), and all others (37.8 percent of GDP).[70] South Dakotans will continue relying on the immortal heritage of its populist past, electing politicians with outsized personalities, and accepting slower growth in the economy. As more rural communities face significant youth out-migration, indirectly threatening ethnic settlement patterns, the state will spend much of its scarce resources preserving the status quo. As a result, the population outside the two major economic and cultural hubs is projected to become more isolated and cultural battles for state resources between the larger communities and the smaller towns intensify.

The future contours of South Dakota's political culture are likely to face more turbulence as the state shifts from an agrarian economy based on a small-town culture to larger, corporate farms (including family-owned corporations) and an expanding financial and information-services economy centered in the state's more densely populated areas. In 2019, U.S. Secretary of Agriculture Sonny Perdue noted to Minnesota farmers, go big or just go: "In America the big get bigger and the small go out [of business]. I don't think in America we, or any small business, we have a guaranteed income or guaranteed profitability."[71]

The requirements for enhancing the state's development are changing. According to 2020 Census Bureau figures, thirty-three of South Dakota's sixty-six counties lost population between 2010 and 2020.[72] According to estimates for 2021, child population is estimated to grow at 7.1 percent, compared to a total increase of 8.9 percent over the 2010 to 2020 decade.[73] South Dakotas are living longer, importing older residents, giving birth to fewer children, or some combination of these.

A relatively high percentage of South Dakota's youth (as well as those from its bordering states) have traditionally left the state, representing a social culture similar to the moralistic political culture.[74] Young people in their late twenties and early thirties, the years when young adults make a decision on where to raise their families, must see a chance for economic opportunity and jobs with living wages. Family ties may trump economic situations, but only for a while.

These aspects of political culture still play out in state-level revenue forecasting. The amount of revenues projected set a cap on the budget, both enforced by two constitutional provisions: the recent balanced budget requirement and the hammer of enforcement set by Article XI, which requires the legislature to institute a statewide property tax to balance the budget to cover shortfalls at the end of the fiscal year: "And whenever it shall appear that such ordinary expenses shall exceed the income of the state for such year, the Legislature shall provide for levying a tax for the ensuing year, sufficient, with other sources of income, to pay the deficiency of the preceding year, together with the estimated expenses of such ensuing year."

One cannot faithfully argue that current and previous governors and the legislature are not interested in developing and protecting the state's human capital. Over one-half of the state's budget is devoted to K-12 education, technical education, and higher education. About 11 percent is allocated for traditional government services in the 2022 fiscal year.[75] Yet, without jobs or wages that compare to those available elsewhere, South Dakota's youth, especially those more tolerant of new experiences (descriptive of the moralistic political culture), are likely to continue to exit the state.

With the increasing dominance of the individualistic political culture, there seems to be a great desire for the legislature to focus on social issues to enforce individual responsibility, "keep outsiders out," and maintain the social order or institute social controls legislating societal norms.[76] Our perceptions shape our reality. We act based on our perceptions, including the practice of choosing outcomes of policies that we ask our governments to enact. A changing culture is more likely to influence our politics than the other way around.

NOTES

1. Irene S. Rubin, *The Politics of Public Budgeting: Getting and Spending, Borrowing and Balancing* (Washington, D.C.: CQ Press, 2010); ITEP South Dakota Budget and Policy Project, "South Dakota Budget Primer: A Guide to the South Dakota Budget Process," 14 Jan. 2013, https://itep.org/south-dakota-budget-and-policy-project-south-dakota-budget-primer/; Aaron Wildavsky and Naomi Caiden, *The New Politics of the Budgetary Process*, 3rd ed. (New York: Longman, 1997).

2. Constitution of South Dakota, article XII, section 2.

3. KELO Interview with Robert Burns, Professor of Political Science at South Dakota State University, 17 Feb. 2011, http://www.keloland.com/_video/_videoplayer_embed.cfm?VideoFile=021711values. The video was not available as of 31 Dec. 2019.

4. J. G. Peters, "Trends in state expenditures and revenue," in *Nebraska Government & Politics*, ed. R.D. Miewald (Lincoln: University of Nebraska Press, 1984), p. 163.

5. Theodore J. Lowi, Benjamin Ginsberg, Kenneth Shepsie, and Stephen Ansolabehere, *American Government: Power and Purpose*, 15th ed. (New York: W. W. Norton, 2019).

6. Aaron Wildavsky, "A Cultural Theory of Expenditure Growth and (Un)balanced Budgets," *Journal of Public Economics* 28 (Dec. 1985): 349–57.

7. Steven G. Koven and Christopher Mausolff, "The Influence of Political Culture on State Budgets: Another Look at Elazar's Formulation," *The American Review of Public Administration* 32 (Mar. 2002): 66.

8. Joel Garreau, *The Nine Nations of North America* (Boston: Houghton Mifflin, 1996).

9. Colin Woodward, *American Nations: A History of the Eleven Rival Regional Cultures of North America* (New York: Penguin, 2011).

10. Daniel J. Elazar, *American Federalism: A View from the States*, 2nd Edition (New York: Thomas Crowell, 1984), pp. 100–101.

11. Joel Lieske, "Regional Subcultures of the United States," *The Journal of Politics* 55 (Nov. 1993): 888–913.

12. David Young Miller, "The Impact of Political Culture on Patterns of State and Local Government Expenditures," *Publius: The Journal of Federalism* 21 (Spring 1991: 83–100.

13. Ibid., 87.

14. David R. Morgan and Sheilah S. Watson, "Political Culture, Political System Characteristics, and Public Policies Among the American States, "*Publius: The Journal of Federalism* 21 (Spring 1991): 44–45.

15. Daniel J. Elazar, "Political Culture on the Plains," *Western Historical Quarterly* 11 (July 1980): 261–83.

16. Jon K. Lauck, *Prairie Republic: The Political Culture of Dakota Territory, 1879–1889* (Norman: University of Oklahoma Press, 2010), p. 281.

17. Michael A. Card, "Historical Musings: Comments on Lauck, Miller & Hogan's Contours of South Dakota Political Culture," *South Dakota History* 36 (Fall 2006): 322–28.

18. John D. Hicks, *The Constitutions of the Northwest States* (Lincoln: University Studies of the University of Nebraska, 1925), pp. 1–2.

19. Francis Newton Thorpe, "Recent Constitution-Making in the United States." *The Annals of the American Academy of Political and Social Science* 2 (Nov. 1891): 1–57. See also, Hicks, *The Constitutions of the Northwest States.*

20. George M Smith and Clark M. Young, *History and Government of South Dakota and the Government of the United States* (New York: American Book Co., 1912), pp. 94–95.

21. E. P. Crossen, "Taxation and Public Finance in South Dakota," *Bulletins* 232 (1928): 76.

22. Ibid., 4.

23. Joy Smolniski, *South Dakota Budget Primer* (Sioux Falls: South Dakota Budget and Policy Project, 2010).

24. Jared Walczak and Janelle Cammenga, "State Business Tax Climate Index," Tax Foundation, 21 Oct. 2020, https://taxfoundation.org/2021-state-business-tax-climate-index/#Changes.

25. Institute on Taxation and Economic Policy, "Mission and History," https://itep.org/about/.

26. Tax Foundation, "Principles," https://taxfoundation.org/principles/; ITEP, "Tax Principles: Building Blocks of a Sound Tax System," https://itep.org/tax-principles-building-block-of-a-sound-tax-system/.

27. James A. Papke, *Tax Policy Alternatives for the State of South Dakota, Report of the Tax Consultant: Dr. James A. Papke* (Pierre: n.p., 1968), p. 53. South Dakota Council for Tax Decision, *A Modern Tax System for South Dakota* (Pierre: Council for Tax Decision, 1971): Frederick D. Stocker, *The South Dakota Revenue Structure: An Agenda for Modernization and Diversification* (Pierre: National Education Association and South Dakota Education Association, 1987), p. 40.

28. State of South Dakota, *Budget in Brief*, Fiscal Year 2002, pp. 1–7.

29. South Dakota Legislative Research Council, "Statistical Comparison, 2021, https://mylrc.sdlegislature.gov/api/Documents/Statistical%20Comparison/127113.pdf.

30. South Dakota Special Appropriations Committee, "COVID-19 Stimulus to South Dakota," https://mylrc.sdlegislature.gov/api/Documents/220704.pdf.

31. Ibid.

32. Joseph V. Ryan, "Tom Berry," in *Over a Century of Leadership: South Dakota*

Territorial and State Governors, ed. Lynwood Oyos (Sioux Falls: Center for Western Studies, 1987), pp. 129, 131.

33. South Dakota Department of Revenue (SDDR), *2020 Annual Report*, Appendix C, https://dor.sd.gov/media/dppd3hjk/2020-print-annual-report.pdf.

34. Tonnes Vanhuizen, personal communication, July 2021.

35. SDDR, *2020 Annual Report*, p. 28.

36. Robert Lee, Ronald Johnson, and Philip Joyce, *Public Budgeting Systems*, 10th ed. (Burlington, Mass.: Jones & Bartlett Learning, 2020), p. x.

37. SDDR, *2020 Annual Report*, p. 26.

38. Emily O. Wanless, "Understanding South Dakota's Political Culture through the 1994 Election of Governor Bill Janklow," in *Plains Political Tradition: Essays on South Dakota Political Culture*, Vol. 3, ed. Jon K. Lauck, John E. Miller, and Paula M. Nelson (Pierre: South Dakota Historical Society Press, 2018), pp. 210–31.

39. Section 57.2801, "Income Tax Levy and Computation" was repealed by Section 1, Chapter 295, Laws of 1943, Senate Bill 41. This was confirmed by *SDCL*, Vol. 1, p. 966.

40. Katherine Loughead, "State Individual Income Tax Rates and Brackets for 2021," Tax Foundation, 17 Feb. 2021, https://taxfoundation.org/publications/state-individual-income-tax-rates-and-brackets/.

41. Most recent was HB 1163 in 2019, in which democratic lawmakers sponsored a bill to establish a tax revenue task force to study tax revenue in the state. It was deferred to the 41st legislative day, 8–4 on 31 Jan. 2019, https://sdlegislature.gov/Session/Bill/9937.

42. South Dakota Constitution, article III, section 1.

43. Ibid.

44. John Mikesell, *Fiscal Administration: Anlyasis and applications for the Public Sector* (Boston: Cengage Learning, 2018. Page 639 cites Minnesota statutes, section 270C.11, subdivision 6 (1).

45. State of South Dakota, *Budget in Brief*, Fiscal Year 2022, 8 Dec. 2021.

46. Ibid., pp. 19–23. See also, Bart Pfankuch, "S.D. Sales tax breaks: consumers pay; big businesses get exemptions," *Sioux Falls Argus Leader*, 8 Mar. 2018.

47. Ibid.

48. South Dakota V. Wayfair, Inc., 138 S. Ct. 2080 (2018).

49. Jon K. Lauck, John E. Miller, and Ed Hogan, "Historical Musings: The Contours of South Dakota Political Culture," *South Dakota History* 34 (Summer 2004): 157–78.

50. Personal communication with Ray Ring, 2 Sept. 2021.

51. M. W. Wehle, Aidan Davis, Carl Davis, Matt Gardner, Lisa Christensen Gee, and Dylan Grundman, "Who Pays? A Distributional Analysis of the Tax Systems in all 50 States," 6th ed., ITEP, 2018, https://itep.org/whopays/.

52. SDDR, *2020 Annual Report*, p. 12.

53. South Dakota, *Budget in Brief*, Fiscal Year 2020, p. 5.

54. SDDR, *2009 Annual Report*, p. 11; *2020 Annual Report*, p. 11.

55. "South Dakota Budget Primer," p. 4, cites the 2010 Department of Social Services Annual Report as the source of this data.

56. Ibid., p. 4 cites the 2010 Department of Social Services Annual report for this claim.

57. Mark Quasney, State Economist, testimony before Senate Taxation Committee, on Senate bill 104, beginning at 50:40, https://sdpb.sd.gov/SDPBPodcast/2021/sta15.mp3#t=972.

58. Danielle Ferguson, "Economists: Eliminating sales tax on food would aid low-income families in South Dakota," *South Dakota News Watch*, 7 June 2021, https://www.sdnewswatch.org/stories/economists-eliminating-sales-tax-on-food-would-aid-low-income-families-in-south-dakota/.

59. Wikipedia, "List of U.S. states by Gini coefficient." Gini is the measure of inequality of incomes and sometimes wealth across individuals. Gini is calculated from Census Bureau data, and retrieved from https://en.wikipedia.org/wiki/List_of_U.S._states_by_Gini_coefficient

60. Elazar, *American Federalism*, p. 117

61. Wehle et al., "Who Pays?"

62. Erica York and Jared Walczak, "State and Local Tax Burdens, Calendar Year 2019," Tax Foundation, 18 Mar. 2021, https://taxfoundation.org/publications/state-local-tax-burden-rankings/#Years

63. Ibid.

64. Gilbert C. Fite, "South Dakota's Rural Credit System: A Venture in State Socialism, 1917–1946" *Agricultural History* 21 (Oct. 1947): 239–49.

65. The Volcker Alliance, "Truth and Integrity in State Budgeting," 2 Nov. 2017, https://www.volckeralliance.org/truth-and-integrity-state-budgeting.

66. Fite, "South Dakota's Rural Credit System"; Gilbert C. Fite, "Failure on The Last Frontier: A Family Chronicle," *Western Historical Quarterly* 18 (Jan. 1987): 4–14.

67. Smith and Young, *History and Government*, p. 95.

68. Lauck et al., "Historical Musings: Contours."

69. Ibid.

70. Statista Research Department, "Real GDP of the Federal State of South Dakota from 2000 to 2020," 19 Apr. 2021, https://www.statista.com/statistics/188129/gdp-of-the-us-federal-state-of-south-dakota-since-1997/#statisticContainer.

71. Todd Richmond, "Trump farm secretary: No guarantee small dairy farms will survive," *AP*, 1 Oct. 2019. See also, Editorial Board, "Sonny Perdue to farmers," *Minneapolis Star-Tribune*, 4 Oct. 2019.

72. U.S. Census Bureau, "2020 Population and Housing State Data," 12 Aug. 2021, https://www.census.gov/library/visualizations/interactive/2020-population-and-housing-state-data.html

73. Tim Anderson, "Demographic Truths and Consequences for the Midwest," Council of State Governments: Midwest, July 2021, https:/csgmidwest.org/demographic-truths-and-consequences-for-the-midwest.

74. The recent texts regarding rural brain drain include L Patrick J. Carr and Maria J. Kefalas, *Hollowing out the Middle: The Rural Brain Drain and What it Means for America* (Boston: Beacon Press, 2009); Ross Benes, *Rural Rebellion: How Nebraska Became a Republican Stronghold* (Lawrence: University of Kansas Press, 2021); Robert Wuthnow, *The Left Behind: Decline and Rage in Small-Town America* (Princeton: Princeton University Press, 2018); State Historical Society of North Dakota, *Governing North Dakota, 2015–2017* (Bismarck: State Historical Society of North Dakota, 2015). The social culture research closely aligned with movement of young people out of state can be followed in J. E. Harrington, and M. J. Gelfand, "Tightness-Looseness across the 50 United States," *PNAS* Vol. 111, no. 22: 7990–95.

75. State of South Dakota, *Budget in Brief*, Fiscal Year 2022, p. 62.

76. Harrington and Gelfand, "Tightness-looseness," 7990–95.

Contributors

Justin Blessinger is a Professor of English at Dakota State University, where he has taught since 2003. His research interests are broad and run from accessible technology to history to the poet T.S. Eliot. His office is the same one used by General Beadle in the early years of the university. He lives with his wife and two children in Madison, South Dakota.

Michael Card, a native of Timber Lake, South Dakota, is an associate professor of public policy and administration at the University of South Dakota. Card earned his B.S. and M.P.A. from the University of South Dakota and his Ph.D. from the Ohio State University. Card teaches in the areas of state and local governments as well as public and nonprofit budgeting and financial management, human resource management, and strategic leadership of public and nonprofit organizations. Card has authored articles and book chapters on leadership, public policy, competitive strategy for nonprofit organizations, strategic management for public and nonprofit organizations, and South Dakota's state government and Midwestern politics. He served as Midwest regional editor for the *Political Encyclopedia of the U.S. States and Regions* and wrote a piece in *South Dakota History* on South Dakota's political culture and potential for future growth.

Marshall Damgaard is the author of *The South Dakota State Capitol: The First Century*, published by the South Dakota Historical Society Press. He also researched and wrote "Closing Time: A Twenty-Five Year Retrospective on the Life and Death of the University of South Dakota at Springfield" in the Fall 2009 edition of *South Dakota History*. He worked in various capacities for Republican governor Bill Janklow for thirty-two years and also served as executive director of the Public Utilities Commission for over five years. He taught undergraduate political science courses at the University of South Dakota for nine years and is now on the graduate history faculty at USD. He currently serves on the State Historical Society Board of Trustees.

Sean J. Flynn is professor of history at Dakota Wesleyan University and former president of the South Dakota State Historical Society

Board of Trustees. He earned his B.A. degree at South Dakota State University and his M.A. and Ph.D. at Texas Tech University. Professor Flynn is the author of *Without Reservation: Benjamin Reifel and American Indian Acculturation* (South Dakota Historical Society Press, 2018). His research interests include the career of U.S. senator Karl E. Mundt and the effects of federal Indian policy on North Dakota and South Dakota since World War II.

Paul Higbee was born in Iowa but grew up in South Dakota. He earned a bachelor's degree at Black Hills State University and an advanced degree in Communication Arts at the University of Notre Dame. He was an educator at Black Hills Special Services Cooperative and Technology and Innovation in Education for thirty-eight years. He scripted civics and history television programming for students, broadcast by South Dakota Public Television. In 1992, Higbee became *South Dakota Magazine*'s Black Hills correspondent and columnist. He is the author of two book-length biographies, profiling South Dakota governor Tom Berry and World War II B-25 pilot Don Smith. In 2001, Higbee was the Governor's History Award recipient. He lives in Spearfish with his wife, Janet.

Randi Ramsden studied American history, literature, and culture in Germany and at the University of Wisconsin-Madison. She earned her M.A. in American Studies from Johannes Gutenberg University in Mainz, Germany. Her scholarly interests include American newspaper history, digital humanities, and the civil rights movement. Her article "Shaping Identity: The History of German-Language Newspapers in Wisconsin" was published in the Fall 2016 issue of the *Wisconsin Magazine of History*. Before joining the Max Kade Institute for German American Studies at the University of Wisconsin-Madison, she managed the Wisconsin National Digital Newspaper Program at the Wisconsin Historical Society for five years.

Gregory S. Rose is dean and director of the Ohio State University at Marion and associate professor of geography. His bachelor's degrees in geography and history are from Valparaiso University in Indiana and his master's and doctorate degrees in geography are from Michigan State University. His research area is the nineteenth-century Midwest. He has researched and published on birthplace origins, previous residences, and Midwestern migration destinations of domestic and foreign immigrant populations using census nativity data and genealogical records, migrants' cultural impacts on the Midwest, the region's historical economic development, and definitions of the Midwest according to cultural elements, vernacular perceptions, agricultural areas, and environmental factors.

Tonnis H. Venhuizen is an Armour native. He earned his B.S. in history and political science from South Dakota State University and his J.D. from the University of South Dakota School of Law, where he was an editor of the *South Dakota Law Review*. A former chief of staff to Governor Dennis Daugaard and Governor Kristi Noem, Venhuizen is a member of the South Dakota Board of Regents. Venhuizen serves on the board of the Trail of Governors Foundation, which is erecting life-size bronze statues of every former South Dakota governor throughout the city of Pierre. In 2014, Venhuizen's essay "Leaders in the Land of Infinite Variety: A Collective Portrait of South Dakota's Governors" was included in *The Plains Political Tradition*, Vol. 2. He edited and annotated the autobiography of Governor W. J. Bulow, excerpts of which were published in *South Dakota History* in Spring 2021.

Daryl A. Webb grew up in South Dakota and earned his bachelor's degree from Northern State University in Aberdeen, South Dakota. After college, Webb worked in museums in South Dakota and Nebraska, researching and designing exhibits. Following his museum career, Webb returned to school and earned his Ph.D. in history at Marquette University. Webb has taught at Cardinal Stritch University since 2007.

Paul Wilson is a political consultant specializing in television advertising. Mr. Wilson received his undergraduate degree in public administration and his master's degree in journalism from the University of Missouri at Columbia. Prior to forming his own firm, Mr. Wilson worked for ten years as Vice President of Bailey Deardourff & Associates in Washington D.C., one of the first such firms in the country. Wilson has two grown children, five grandchildren, and is married to Marjorie Kline. In addition to his political work, Mr. Wilson is President of the Kathy Wilson Foundation, which he established in memory of his first wife. The Foundation is dedicated to helping children with special needs at the preschool age.

Index

Page numbers in *italics* refer to illustrations and photographs; those followed by *map, n, f* or *t* refer to maps, notes, figures or tables

Abdnor, James: background and family, 204–5, 206, 212; Congressional challenges, 174, 182–83, 186, 187, 207; political career, 9, 205–6, 207, 211
Abdnor, Mary (Wehby), 204, 206
Abdnor, Samuel Joseph, 204
Aberdeen, S.Dak., 43–44
Abolitionists, 63–67, 68map, 69, 71–72
Abortion, 218n40
Abourezk, Charles Thomas, 206
Abourezk, James, 9, 202, 205, 206–8, 212
Abourezk, Juliana ("Lena"), 206
Abourezk, Sanaa, 208
Acheson, Dean, 141, 142
Adams, Dwight, 172, 173
African Americans: civil rights legislation, 163–64; hostility toward, 66; population statistics (1870–1890), 16–17
Agency funds, 227
Agrarian conservatism, 3, 97, 99, 112, 237, 244–45
Agricultural Adjustment Administration (AAA), 131
Agricultural policy: under Benson, 162; commodity pricing, 244; and economic decline, 77, 78, 92, 103, 110, 182; of Mickelson, 192–93; Norbeck's reforms, 81, 82–83, 87; shift to corporate farms, 245; taxes and exemptions, 111, 232, 236, 237. *See also* Farmers and farming
Aid to Families with Dependent Children, 224
Alabama, 17
Alaska, 235
Alcoholic beverages, 48, 111, 202
Alexander I, 40
Alpha Nu literary society, 60, 64, 66, 67
Alt-Arcis, Russia, 41
American-Arab Anti-Discrimination Committee, 208
American Indian Movement (AIM), 210
American Indian Policy Review Commission (AIPRC), 208
American Indians: and Case, 159–60, 163, 167n44; flooding of reservation lands, 159–60; Mickelson's "Year of Reconciliation," 197; population statistics (1860–1890), 14–16, 15t; Reifel as first in Congress, 204; tribal taxes, 237–38. *See also specific tribes and reservations*
Americanization, 39, 45–46, 54–55
American Rescue Plan Act (ARPA), 230
Anderson, Andrew S., 100, 102
Anderson, John, 203
Anderson, Myrtle, 203
Annapolis, Ind., 69
Ann Arbor, Mich., 64, 65, 67, 68map
Anti-Communism: McCarthy hearings, 160–61; of Mundt, 7–8, 127, 128–29, 130, 142, 161

Anti-German sentiment, 44, 49, 55
Anti-Semitism, 129
Appropriations, state, 108–9, 228–30, 229t, 243
Army Corps of Engineers, 158, 159
Ashley, James, 67
Assimilation, 39
Austrian immigrants, 21t, 22, 47

Bailey Deardourff & Associates, 170
Banking: financial services industry, 245; franchise tax, 228; rural credit program, 84, 85, 92, 97, 103, 111, 243; state management of, 92; trusts, 78, 244
Banks, Nathaniel P., 65
Baptists, 29
Bavaria, Germany, immigrants from, 30
Beadle, James Ward, 64, 69
Beadle, John, 62, 69
Beadle, William Henry Harrison, 6, 60–67, 68map, 69, 71–76; as abolitionist, 61, 63–67, 68map, 69, 71-72; autobiographical writings, 62, 63–65, 73–74; Dakota State University ties, 6, 60, 61, 72; early years, 61, 62–63, 67; family, 61, 62–63, 64, 69, 71; military service and training, 62–63; statue of, 60; as surveyor general, 6, 60, 61, 73; temperament, 60–61, 72
Beadle Co., S.Dak., 26map, 28, 61
Bear Butte, S.Dak., 156
Beer, 48, 202
Benson, Ezra Taft, 162
Bentley, Elizabeth, 130
Beresford, S.Dak., 7
Berry, Cynthia, 201
Berry, E. Y., 207
Berry, Faye, 201
Berry, Lorena, 201
Berry, Thomas M., 7, 97, 118, 201–2; background and family, 201; Bulow on, 110–11, 114; as governor, 111–14, 117, 152, 202, 212, 230–31, 235, 243; U.S. Senate bid, 114, 115, 116–17
Birds, conservation of, 90
Black Elk Peak, 91
Black Hills: Chinese immigrants in, 17; conservation in, 90–92, 192; mining, 32, 151, 153–54, 192; nineteenth-century settlement in, 17, 24, 32; tourism, 91, 151
Black Hills National Cemetery, 156
Black Sea German immigrants, 28, 40, 42, 54
Blessinger, Justin: chapter by, 60–76; referenced, 6, 253
Bloomingdale, Ind., 69, 71
Boating, 158–59
Boe, Nils, 212
Bohemian immigrants, 21t, 22, 32
Bon Homme Co., S.Dak., 29, 30, 31, 32, 40, 42
Boom Decade, 13, 23, 24
Boreman, S.Dak., 30
Bottum, Joseph, 164
Brady, Tom, 207
Breckinridge, John, 66
Brooke, Edward, 208
Brookings Co., S.Dak., 16, 26map, 31, 172, 197
Brown Co., S.Dak., 25, 26map, 30, 31, 32
Brule Co., S.Dak., 25, 26map, 32
Bryan, William Jennings, 80, 98
Budget process, 222–46; balanced budget, 7, 108, 117, 246; and citizens' values, 222, 237; historical and cultural forces affecting, 223–27; revenue process, 243–46;

revenue sources, 227–43, 229t, 231t. *See also* Taxes; Tax policy
Buffalo Co., S.Dak., 20, 25, 26map
"Bull Moose" campaign, 99
Bulow, Sarah, *107*
Bulow, William J., 6–7, 97 *101, 107*; autobiography, 120–21n21; on Berry, 110–11, 114; candidacy, 100, 102, 103, 105–6, 116–17; early years and education, 103–4, 121n31; on FDR, 114–15, 116, 117; as Governor, 106–10, 118; as a Jeffersonian Democrat, 7, 97, 112, 116, 117, 118; Mundt's tribute to, 118; as U.S. Senator, 110, 112–13, 116, 118, 153
Bureaucracy, 127–28
Bureau of Indian Affairs. *See* United States Bureau of Indian Affairs
Bureau of Reclamation, 158
Burke, Charles H., 99, 120n13
Burning Breast, Lucy, 202
Burns, Robert, 222
Bushfield, Harlan J., 115, 117
Business: commercial property tax, 233; support for, 227; tax incentives, 236, 237
Butikofer, Hermann, 44
Butte, Mont., 79
Byrne, Frank M., 81, 99

Califano, Joseph, 163
Campbell Co., S.Dak., 29, 31, 54
"Camp fever," 63
Canadian immigrants: American Indian, 15; geographic distribution of, 26map, 31–32; population counts, 12, 18, 18t, 19, 20, 21t, 22, 23
Capitalism, 77, 82, 84, 85
Card, Michael: chapter by, 222; referenced, 9, 253
Carlson, Robert, 218n40
Carnegie, Andrew, 78
Carter, Jimmy, 209
Case, Francis H., 6, 8, 115; civil rights views, 163–64; in Congress, 8, 149, 159, 160–62, 166n22; death, 164; early years and family, 148, 150–51, 153; flood control, 158–60; highway funding, 163; labor bills, 156–57; LBJ on, 151, 164; on McCarthy, 160–61; military service and installations, 151, 155, 156; mining positions, 153–54; natural gas incident, 161–62; on the New Deal, 151–52; temperament, 150–51, 157
Case, Herbert, 148
Case, Mary, 148
Case, Myrle, 153
Case Labor Bill (HR 5262), 156–57
Catherine the Great, 40
Catholicism, 42, 208, 209, 212, 218n40
Cattle industry, 149, 165n9
Cement plants, 77, 83, 84, 85, 92, 97, 226
Census (1850–1890): African Americans categorized in, 16–17; American Indians categorized in, 14–16, 15t; Chinese immigrants listed in, 17–18; Euro-American immigrant geographic distribution, 23–34, 26maps, 27map; Euro-American immigrant origins, 13, 18–23, 18t, 21t, 28–29; nativity data, 13, 29
Census (2020), 245–46
Chaffee, John, 173
Challenger space shuttle, 183
Chambers, Whittaker, 7, 130–41; alias, 135, 136; Hiss relationship, 132–40; physical appearance, 132, 133, 136; reflection on Hiss case, 140–41
Charles Mix Co., S.Dak., 16, 17

Chemawa Indian School (Salem Indian Training School), 72
Cherner Motor Company, 138
Chernobyl disaster, 183
Cheyenne River Indian Reservation, 15t
Chinese immigrants, 16, 17–18
Christian Family Movement, 208
Christopherson, C. A. ("Charley"), 104, 110
Citibank, 180, 181
Citizen participation, 2
Civic buildings, 226
Civil rights, 163–64
Civil Rights Act of 1957, 164
Civil War: Beadle's service in, 6, 61, 62; Case and LBJ's ancestors in, 150; and South Dakota political culture, 3; veterans as surveyors, 61–62
Clark Co., S.Dak., 31
"Clashing Dynasties" (Gawalt), 66
Clausen, Clyde, 193
Clay Co., S.Dak, 25, 26map, 28, 32
Coal mines, 77, 84, 85, 92, 111, 226
Codington Co., S.Dak., 31, 32
Cold War, 129
Commerce and industry of South Dakota, 238
Commodity prices, 103, 244
Communism: Communist Party of the United States (CPUSA), 128, 130, 134, 135; espionage activities, 129, 130, 131; Hiss's ties to, 131, 134, 135, 137–38, 139; and the Mundt-Nixon Bill, 130; and New Dealers, 128, 160
Competition, economic, 77, 82, 84, 85
Condon, Robert, 130
Conservatism: of Bulow, 106, 108, 109; dominance of, 3, 7, 9–10, 117, 225, 244–45; of Gunderson, 97, 100, 102; of Gurney, 113, 115; of Mundt, 118, 127, 128; of Norbeck, 6, 78, 82, 92–93, 99
"The Contours of South Dakota Political Culture" (Lauck, Miller, and Hogan), 2
Contractor's excise tax, 228, 235, 238
Coolidge, Calvin, 99, 102, 109, 120n17, 204
Cooperatives, farmers, 79, 82
Corinth, Miss., siege of, 63
Coronavirus Aid, Relief, and Economic Security Act (CARES Act), 229
Coronavirus relief funds, 229–30
Corporate tax, 227, 228
Corruption, 213
Corson Co., S.Dak., 30
Country Life Movement, 87–90
Coursey, O. W., 64
Court packing plan, 7, 114–15
"Cowboys of 1902," 110
CPUSA (Communist Party of the United States), 128, 130, 134, 135
Crawford, Coe I., 81, 98, 99, 214n4
Crime, 191–92
Cronin, John, 133
Crosley, George, 135, 136
Crossen, E. P., 225–26
Crow Creek Indian Reservation, 15t, 16
Curtiss, George William, 65
Custer Chronicle, 151
Custer Co., S.Dak., 30
Custer State Park, 77, 90–91, 102, 109
Cutcheon, B.M., 66
Czech immigrants, 3, 32

Daily Press and Dakotaian, 41
Dakota 1, 234
Dakota Farmers' Leader, 43

Dakota Freie Presse, 41–44, 49, 54–55
Dakota Herold, 47
Dakota State University, 6, 60, 61, 72
Dakota Territory: Beadle's influence on and appointments in, 6, 61–62, 72–74; county divisions, 20–21; establishment and lure of, 14, 19; Republican Party's dominance in, 3; settlement (*See* Immigrants and immigration; Population, nineteenth century); surveying in, 61–62
Dakota Wesleyan University, 150
Dallas Morning News, 156
Damgaard, Marshall: chapter by, 199–221; referenced, 9, 253
Dams, 149, 158–60
Danbom, David, 78
Danish immigrants, 21t, 22, 32, 33
Daschle, Thomas A.: Catholicism of, 212, 218n40; Congressional races, 179, 183, 185, 186, 205; liberalism of, 93; Mickelson support, 194–95; political career, 186
Davison Co., S.Dak., 26map, 28
Day Co., S.Dak., 25, 26map, 30, 31
"The Days of Auld Lang Syne" (Beadle), 65
Deadwood, S.Dak., 17, 32
Debs, Eugene, 79
Debt, 108, 224
Democratic Congressional Campaign Committee, 154
Democratic National Convention (1936), 112
Democratic Party: ascendancy and fall of, 97–99, 105–10, 115, 116–17, 207; Berry in, 110–13, 201–2; Bulow as first Democratic governor, 6–7, 106–10; in the German-language press, 51–52; and LBJ, 150, 152, 154–55, 158, 160, 161, 164–65; McGovern's rebuilding of, 162, 165; Populist fusion with, 98; weakness of, 3–4, 98
Demuth, Hans, 45, 47–48
Denholm, Frank, 207
Department of Motor Vehicles (DMV), 138
Deuel Co., S.Dak., 25, 26map, 31
Deutscher Herold, 49, 50, 52, 55
Dies, Martin, 128, 129
Dies Committee, 128, 129
Disabled individuals, 233, 238
District Fifty-Seven, 201
District Twenty-Nine, 205
Door-to-door canvassing, 174, 178
Dougherty, Bill, 207, 209, 212
Drifting Goose (Yanktonais Indian), 73–74
Drug abuse, 191–92
Dust Bowl, 202
Dutch immigrants, 3
Dwight D. Eisenhower National System of Interstate and Defense Highways, 163

East River, S.Dak., 2, 24, 153–54, 174
Economic policy: balanced budget, 7, 108, 117, 246; Berry's budget cuts, 111; conservative reforms of Norbeck, 3, 6, 7, 9, 77–78, 80–82, 87–90, 92–93; extraction economies, 244; fiscal conservatism of Gunderson, Bulow, and Berry, 100, 102–3, 108–9, 111, 118; future directions, 245–46; of Mickelson, 186–87, 189–90, 191, 193–95; New Deal programs, 7–8, 111–13, 118. *See also* Agricultural policy; Budget process; Tax policy

Edmunds Co., S.Dak., 54
Education: Berry's cuts in, 111; curriculum reforms, 89–90; GDP percentage, 245; Mickelson's SDEA endorsement, 193–94; progressive reforms of, 81; public lands in support of, 60, 62; rural, Norbeck's reforms for, 77, 88–90, 92; tax revenues for, 226, 231, 232–33. *See also* Schools; Teachers
Egalitarianism, 2, 9
Egan, George, 81
Eisenhower, Dwight D., 126, 160, 162
Elazar, Daniel, 223–24, 240
Elderly, 188, 233, 238
Elections, state: (1889–1914), 98; (1908), 51–54; (1918), 84; (1924), 100, 102; (1926), 3, 6–7, 105–6; (1986), 181–82, 182t, 183–85, 184t, 185t, 199; (1990), 188, 190–91, 195–96; (1994), 187
Elections, U.S.: (1896), 98; (1898), 48; (1900), 49; (1912), 99; (1914), 99; (1924), 102; (1932), 110; (1938), 115; (1942), 116–17; (1948), 158; (1956), 162; (1962), 164; (1986), 182–83, 185–86; (2004), 1–2
Elevators, 79, 83, 84, 85
Elitism, 227
Ellermann, Herman, 42–43, 49
Ellsworth Air Force Base, 156
Elrod, Samuel H., 98
Embezzlement, 103
Employment: Mickelson on, 186–87, 189–90, 191, 193–94; unemployment insurance, 202
Engel, John, 159
English immigrants, 18t, 21t, 22, 31, 32
Environmental conservation: Mickelson on, 192; Norbeck's contributions to, 77, 78, 82, 90–92
Episcopal Hare Vocational School, 203
Ernst, Joni, 198n8
Espionage, 129, 130, 131, 140, 141, 142
Espionage Act, 55
Eureka Co., S.Dak., 41
Eureka Independent, 50, 51
Eureka Post, 50–55, *53*
Everett, Edward, 65
Expenditures: in the budget process, 222–23, 224; comparisons with neighboring states, 230, 231t; and federal funding, 228, 229t, 230, 231t; and political subcultures, 224, 225–26, 227
Extraction economies, 244

Fall River Co., S.Dak., 17
Families First Coronavirus Response Act (FFCRA), 229
Farm Bureau, 236
Farmers Alliance, 79
Farmers and farming, 2, 3; Case and LBJ's background in, 148–49; cooperatives, 79, 82; curriculum for, 89–90; farm crisis, 97, 105, 110, 175, 182, 192, 244; GDP percentage, 245; irrigation, 149, 159; itinerant farm workers, 79, 80; Mickelson's campaign targeting, 176–79, 188–89, 193; Nonpartisan League's recruitment of, 80; threats to competition of, 77, 78–79, 82. *See also* Agricultural policy; Rural areas; Water resources
Farrar, Frank, 207, 209, 212
Farrell, John A., 135
Federal Bureau of Investigation (FBI): and the Condon investigation, 130; and Hiss trial, 133, 139
Federal funding, 224, 228–32, 229t, 243

Federal Power Commission, 161
Federal Theater and Writers Project, 128
Financial services industry, 245
First District, 104, 115, 127, 207
Fischer, John H., 52
Fishing and hunting culture, 90, 158–59, 180–81, 245
Flinn & Lutgen, 50, 54
Flint, Mich., 79
Flood Control Act of 1944, 158–59
Florida, 235
Flour mills, 85
Flynn, Sean J.: chapter by, 126–47; referenced, 7, 8, 253–54
Food and Drug Commission, 83
Food sales tax, 238–39
Ford Model A. (automobile), 135, 136, 137–38
Forestry, 91, 245
Fort Laramie Treaty, 14
Fort Meade, S.Dak., 156
Fosheim, Oscar, 115
Foss, Joe, 212
Fox, William F., 61–62
Fraktur typeface, 46–47
Francois Martin, 51
Freedmen's Bureau, 6, 61
Free speech, 65, 87
French Canadian immigrants, 18
French immigrants, 18t, 19, 21t, 22
Fried, Richard M., 141

Gamble family (John, Robert, and Ralph), 200
Garner, John Nance, 114
Garreau, Joel, 223
Gasoline retail market, 97, 102–3, 226
Gawalt, Gerard W., 66
GDP (gross domestic product), 239, 245
General Appropriations Act, 222
German immigrants: Americanization of, 39, 45–46; and census nativity data, 29–31; discrimination against, 44, 49, 55; economic role of, 54; geographic distribution of, 28–31; influence of, 2–3, 5–6, 34, 39, 54; lack of common national identity, 46; population counts, 18t, 19, 21t, 22, 23; provinces represented by, 29–30; Republican affiliation of, 42–43; in Russia, 40
German-language newspapers, 39–59; and Americanization, 39, 45–46, 54–55; *Dakota Freie Presse*, 41–44, 49, 54–55; decline of, 54–55; *Deutscher Herold*, 49, 50, 52; and ethnic identity, 39, 40, 41, 43, 44–47, 52; *Eureka Post*, 50–55, *53*; Fraktur typeface in, 46–47; industrialization of, 49–50; *Nachrichten-Herold*, 43; political campaign ads in, 52–54, *53*; political views in, 42–43, 47–49, 52; subscription counts, 44, 49, 54; *Süd Dakota Nachrichten*, 44–45, 47, 48–49; *Süd-Dakota Nachrichten und Herold*, 47–49
German Russian immigrants: and census nativity data, 28–31; geographic distribution of, 28–31, 54; influence of, 2–3, 5–6, 39, 54; newspapers catering to, 41–43, 44, 50, 51, 54–55; population counts, 28–30, 33; religious affiliations, 29, 40, 42; rivalry between Black Sea and Volga Germans, 42; Russian settlement history, 40
Gestring, Sheila, 10
Giago, Tim, 197
Giedt, Theodore, 50–51

Gini coefficient ranking, 240, 250n59
Gold rush towns, 17, 24, 32
Gold standard, 153
Governor's Budget Summary Book, 236
Grannis, Samuel, 150
Grant Co., S.Dak., 25, 26map, 27map, 30, 31
Grants, 227
Graves, Myrle, 151
Great Depression, 3, 7, 110, 113, 152, 202
Great Sioux Reservation, 14
Greely, Horace, 65
Green, Warren, 110, 111, 201
Gregory Co., S.Dak., 16
Griffing, Josephine, 65
Grigsby, Melvin, 200, 212
Grigsby family (Sioux, John, and George), 200
Gross domestic product (GDP), 239, 245
Gunderson, Carl, 97, 100, 102, 105–6
Gurney, Chan, 113, 115, 155, 159

Hackemer, Kurt, 10, 61–62
Hadley, Alfred, 71
Hadley, Frank H., 71
Hadley, Newton, 71
Hail insurance programs, 80, 85, 92, 111, 226
Haines, N.Dak., coal mine, 85
Halberstam, David, 132, 134, 139
Halleen, Shirley, 196t
Hand Co., S.Dak., 25, 26map
Hanover, Germany, immigrants from, 30
Hansen, Lowell, 171, 172, 175, 180–81, 182t
Hanson Co., S.Dak., 26map, 28, 32
Harding, Warren G., 99
Harris-Fulbright Bill, 161
Harvard University, 203
Healthcare, 236, 237, 245
Hearst, George, 154
Heart disease, 149, 164, 165
Heidepriem, Scott, 129
"Heimat" (homeland), 47, 51
Hendricks, Robert, 160, 161
Herseth, Lars (R. Lars), 183, 184t, 185, 186, 187, 189–90, 209
Herseth, Lorna (Buntrock), 199, 214n1
Herseth, Mark, 199
Herseth, Ralph, 199, 214n1, 214n4
Herseth, Stephanie, 199, 212, 214,
Herseth political family, 9, 199, 212
Higbee, Paul: chapter by, 148–69; referenced, 8, 254
High-income residents, 234, 234f, 236
Highways. *See* Roads and highways
Hildebrandt, Fred H., 115.153
Hirsch, Robert, 207
Hiss, Alger: biography, 131; Chambers relationship, 132–40; Communist ties, 131, 134, 135, 137–38, 139; indictment and conviction, 130, 140; physical appearance, 132–33; testimony, 133–34, 135–37
Hiss trial: Chambers testimony, 7, 130–41; coverage of, 136; Mundt's role in, 7–8, 126–27, 130, 132, 133–35, 136–42; and New Dealers, 126–27, 130, 131, 133, 140–42; Nixon's role in, 126, 130, 131, 132, 133–36, 139; verdict, 140–41
Hitchcock, Herbert, 113, 115, 153
Hogan, Ed, 1; "The Contours of South Dakota Political Culture" (with Lauck and Miller), 2
Holcomb, Thomas, 155

Holt Co., S.Dak., 201
Holum, Kenneth, 162
Homestake Gold Mine, 111, 115, 153–54
Hoover, Herbert, 110
Hosmer Co., S.Dak., 41
Hot Springs Star, 151
House Committee on Un-American Affairs (HUAC): Bentley's appearance before, 130; Dies Committee, 128; Mundt's presence on, 129–30, 131–32, 133–35, 136–37, 138–42; Nixon's role on, 126, 130, 131, 132, 133–36, 139. *See also* Hiss, Alger, trial
House Foreign Affairs Committee, 129
House Naval Affairs Committee, 155
House Ways and Means Committee Hearing Room, 131
Hughes Co., S.Dak., 16, 17
Hungarian immigrants, 209, 219n47
Hunting and fishing culture, 90, 158–59, 180–81
Hutchinson Co., S.Dak., 29, 30, 31, 40
Hutterites, 29, 40, 42
Hydroelectric plants, 85, 91, 92; Case's development of, 149, 158; LBJ's development of, 149

Illinois: corruption in, 213; immigrants from, 4, 18t, 19, 21t, 22, 23, 32, 33; settlement, 14, 33
Immigrants and immigration: and assimilation, 39; Boom Decade, 13, 23, 24; definition of "immigrants," 23; ethnic clustering of, 30–31; geographic distribution of, 23–34, 26maps, 27map; German-language press on nativism of, 49; influence of, 2–5, 33–34, 39, 223; origins of, 2–3, 4–5, 12–14, 17–23, 18t, 21t. *See also* Census (1850–1890); *specific ethnic, national, and regional groups*
Income tax: creation of, in the 1930s, 10, 111, 202, 235; current lack of, 228, 231, 231t, 234, 235; Mickelson's opposition to, 180, 187, 189–90; in states surrounding South Dakota, 235, 239–42, 241t
Indiana: immigrants from, 18t, 21t, 32, 33; Indiana Volunteers, 62–63; settlement, 14, 33
Indiana Magazine of History, 66
Indian Child Welfare Act (ICWA), 208
Indian Citizenship Act of 1924, 204
Indigenous peoples of the Americas. *See* American Indians; *specific tribes*
Individualistic political cultures. *See* Political cultures, individualistic
Industrialization, 49–50, 78
Industrial Workers of the World (IWW), 6, 79–80, 85, 86–87
Information-services economy, 245
Inheritance tax, 243
Initiated Measure 1, 234, 238
Inland America, 126–127
Institute for Taxation and Economic Policy (ITEP), 227–28, 234t, 242f
Interstate Highway System, 163
Interventionism, 116–17
Iowa, 4; immigrants from, 17, 18t, 19, 21t, 22, 23, 33; immigrants' geographic distribution, 26map, 28; settlement, 13, 14, 33; taxation, 231t, 240, 241t
Irish Immigrants: geographic distribution of, 31, 32; population counts, 3, 18, 18t, 19, 21t, 22

Irrigation, 149, 159
Isolationism: of Bulow, 7, 116, 118; of Mundt, 128
Itinerant farm workers, 79, 80
IWW (Industrial Workers of the World), 6, 79–80, 85, 86–87

Janklow, Arthur, 209
Janklow, LouElla, 209
Janklow, Mary Dean (Thom), 209
Janklow, William, 4, 9, 212, 213, 219n52; and Abourezk, 206; background and family, 209–10; Congressional term and resignation, 186, 211; as governor, 171, 174, 175, 180–81, 186, 211, 220n55, 234; and Hansen, 180–81; legal career, 210; Mickelson support, 187; U.S. Senate challenge, 182–83, 186, 187
Janklow Archival Project, 219n47
Japanese immigrants, 16, 17
Jefferson, S.Dak., 32
Jefferson, Thomas, 78
Jeffersonianism, 7, 97, 112, 116, 117, 118
Jeffries, George, 121n31
Jensen, Leslie, 113, 115, 116
Jewish population, 219n47
Job growth, 186–87, 189, 191, 193–94
Johnson, Edwin S., 99
Johnson, Lady Bird, 153, 164
Johnson, Lyndon B., 8, 149; ballot controversy, 158; on Case, 151, 164; early years and family, 149, 152–53; liberalism of, 152; on McCarthy, 161; military service, 155–56; oil and gas advocacy, 154–55, 161–62; presidency, 164–65; space program support, 162–63; temperament, 150
Johnson, Sam Ealy, Sr, 150
Jones, Buell F., 109
Judd, Walter, 133
Judicial Procedures Reform Bill of 1937, 114

Kelley, John Edward, 212
Kennebec, S.Dak., 204
Kennedy, Edward, 208
Kennedy, John F., 208
Kentucky immigrants, 17, 33
Kingsbury Co., S.Dak., 26map, 28, 32
Kirby, Joe, 104, 121n31
Kittridge, Alfred B., 98
Kneip, Bernice (Pederson), 208
Kneip, Frank, 208
Kneip, Nancy (Pankey), 208
Kneip, Richard, 152, 183, 186, 207, 208–9, 212
Knights of the Golden Circle, 66
Knowland, William, 160
Knowles, Freeman Tulley, 212
Kranz, Dave, 185
Ku Klux Klan (KKK), 66
Kundert, Alice, 170–71, 172, 182t
Kyle, James Henderson, 79, 212

Labor: anti-union labor bills, 149, 154, 156–57; Mickelson and Hansen on, 175
La Follette, Robert, 97, 102
Lake Co., S.Dak., 31, 61
Lake Traverse Indian Reservation, 15t
Lakota Sioux Indians, 202
Lakota Times, 197
Landon, Alfred M., 113
Lange, Dorothea, 127
Latham, Earl, 128
Lauck, Jon K.: introduction by, 1–11; referenced, 1, 126–27; "The Contours of South Dakota Political Culture" (with Miller and Hogan), 2

Lawrence Co., S.Dak., 17, 26map, 28, 30, 32
Lawson, Michael L., 159
Lead, S.Dak., 17
Lebanese immigrants, 204, 205, 206
Lee, Andrew E., 98, 105, 212
Lee, John, 72
Lend-Lease Program, 129
Liberals and liberalism, 97, 128–29. *See also* New Deal; Progressivism
Liberty Township, Ind., 61
Life (magazine), 130
Limited government, 2, 7, 224, 225
Lincoln, Abraham, 66
Lincoln Co., S.Dak., 25, 26map, 28, 32, 41
Linotype, 50
Local government revenues, 224, 226
Lodi, Ind., 69
Loen, Vernon, 203
Loriks, Emil, 115, 127
Lottery tax, 228
Louisiana, corruption in, 213
Lowe, Barrett, 62, 67
Lower Brule Indian Reservation, 15t, 16
Low-income residents, 233–34, 234f, 236, 238, 239, 241t, 242
Lutgen, Michael, 50
Lutheran Germans, 29, 40, 42

McCarran Act, 130
McCarthy, Joseph, 160–61
McClure, P. F., 98
McCook Co., S.Dak., 26map, 28, 31
McDowell, John, 131
McGovern, George, 4, 9; and anti-Catholicism, 218n40; and Case, 149, 150, 164; Congressional races, 162, 205, 207, 208; and Democratic Party, 162, 165; and LBJ, 149, 165; liberalism of, 93
McGregor, James, 203
McKinley, William, 49
McMaster, William H., 97, 99, 102, 103, 110, 226
McNary-Haugen bill, 120n17
McNeil, Marshall, 156
McPherson, Harry, 163
McPherson Co., S.Dak., 29, 31, 54
McPherson County Herald, 51
Madison, S.Dak., 72
Madison Normal School (Dakota State University), 6, 60, 61, 72
Maine immigrants, 18, 18t
Manfred, Frederick, 2
Marketplace, government as a, 224, 226–27
Market Strategies Polling, 184–85, 184t, 195, 196t
Marshall Co., S.Dak., 25, 26map
Martin, Eben, 120
Marxists and Marxism: Dies's hatred for, 128; New Dealers associated with, 127, 132
Massachusetts immigrants, 18t
Meade Co., S.Dak., 17
Mellette, Arthur C., 98
Mellette Co., S.Dak., 30, 201
Mennonites, 29, 40, 42
Métis immigrants, 18
Meyer, Paul B., 44
Meyer, S.Dak., 30
Michigan: immigrants from, 18t, 19, 21t, 32; settlement, 14
Michigan Alumnus, 63, 65
Mickelson, George S.: background and family, 8, 171, 173, 190, 197, 199, 214n4; death, 187, 197; demeanor, 171, 172, 175, 183
Mickelson, George S., campaign, 6,

8–9, 171–97, 199, 200; agricultural outreach, 176–79, 188–89; on American Indians, 197; Citibank hunting trip, 180–81; on crime, 191–92; economic policies, 186–88, 189–90, 191, 193–95; general election, 183–90; polls, 184–85, 184t, 191, 193, 195, 196t; primary race, 171–83, 182t; reelection, 190–96
Mickelson, George S., campaign ads: *Agriculture,* 193; *Blue Ribbon Cow,* 177; *Business Climate,* 189–90; *Close,* 190, 194; *Colleagues,* 179; *Day One,* 194; *Don't Have to be a Farmer,* 188–89; *Environment,* 192; *Fight for Farmers,* 179; *Golden Seniors,* 188; *I'm not a farmer,* 176–77; *Income Tax Friend,* 187; *Misleading Opponent,* 180; *New Jobs,* 191; *Prison,* 191–92; *Ready to be Your Governor,* 177–78; *Samuelson No Plan,* 195; *Vision,* 193; *Wages Up,* 186–87; *Weather is Tough Here,* 178; *Where the Ducks Are,* 181
Mickelson, George T., 8, 173, 199, 214n1, 214n4
Mickelson, Linda, 178, 190, 197
Mickelson, Madge (Turner), 214n1
Mickelson, Mark, 199, 214n2
Mickelson political family, 199, 212
Mid-Atlantic states, 224
Midwest (U.S. region): immigrants from, 2, 4, 5, 12, 33–34 (*See also specific states*); liberal derision of, 126–27, 128, 133, 142; Mundt as a representative of, 127, 133
Miller, John E., 1–2, 10, 106; "The Contours of South Dakota Political Culture" (with Lauck and Hogan), 2
Miller, Walter Dale, 186, 187, 193, 196t
Milwaukee, Wisc., 79
Mining, 17, 24, 32, 151, 153–54, 192, 226, 244
Minneapolis Tribune, 183
Minnehaha Co., S.Dak., 17, 25, 26map, 28, 30, 31, 32, 174
Minnesota, 4; African Americans from, 17; immigrants from, 19, 20, 21t, 22, 23, 26map, 31, 33; settlement, 13, 14, 33; statehood, 19; taxation, 230, 231t, 240, 241t, 242, 244
Minnesota Territory: American Indian population, 15; immigrant population in (1850), 18–19, 18t
Minuteman missile launch facilities, 163, 168n69
Missile launch facilities, 163
Missouri immigrants, 18t, 19
Missouri River, dams developed in, 158
Mitchell Capital (newspaper), 80
Mob violence, 64–65
Monopolies and trusts, 77, 78–79, 80–83
Montana, 14, 230, 231t, 240, 241t, 244
Moody Co., S.Dak., 16, 26map, 28, 31, 32
Moore, Leonard J., 66
Moralistic political cultures. *See* Political cultures, moralistic
Morgan, Ted, 128
Morgenthaler Linotype Company, 50
Morris, Roger, 126
Mount Rushmore, 92, 102, 109
Mundt, Karl E.: anti-Communism of, 127, 128–29, 135; on Bulow, 118; foreign policy views, 129; Hiss's ridiculing of, 133–34; Hiss trial involvement, 7–8, 126–27,

130, 132, 133–35, 136–42; New Deal opposition, 127–28; in U.S. Congress, 7, 115, 116, 117, 127, 155, 207, 208, 212
Mundt, Mary, 134, 135
Mundt-Nixon Bill, 130
Murphy, Maurice, 66
Mydland, Gordon, 206

Nachrichten. See Süd Dakota Nachrichten
Nachrichten-Herold, 43
National Bureau of Standards, 130
National Capitol Planning Commission, 204
National Conference on Catholic Welfare, 133
National Park Service, 204
National Statuary Hall, U.S. Capitol, 60
National Union Company, 45
National Youth Administration, 152, 155
Native Americans. *See* American Indians; *specific tribes*
Nativism, 49
Natural resources, conservation of. *See* Environmental conservation
Nebraska, 14, 231t, 241t
Nelson, Paula: introduction by, 1–11
Nevada, 235
New Deal: Case's views of, 151; and the Hiss Case, 126–27, 130, 131, 133, 140–42; LBJ's support of, 152; opposition to policies of, 7–8, 111–13, 127–29; South Dakotans' support for, 152
New England, 224
New Hampshire, 235
Newspapers, German-language. *See* German-language newspapers
Newsweek, 157
New York Daily Post, 160
New York immigrants: geographic distribution of, 26map, 28, 33; population counts, 12, 18, 18t, 19, 20, 21t, 22, 23, 33
New York Times, 1, 139
Nimitz, Chester, 155
Nixon, Richard: election, 208; in the Hiss trial, 126, 131, 132, 133–36, 139; Mundt-Nixon Bill, 130
Noem, Kristi, 212
Nonpartisan League (NPL), 6, 80, 85–87
Nonpartisanship, 7
Norbeck, Peter, 3, 6, 7, 9, 77–93; agricultural reforms, 81, 82–83; conservation programs, 77, 78, 82, 90–92; as conservative reformer, 6, 78, 82, 92–93, 99, 120n13; death, 113, 114, 115–16, 153; as Governor, 82–91, 99, 103; Gunderson's break with, 102–3, 106; rural programs, 87–90; Socialist opposition, 85–87; state ownership initiatives, 77–78, 83–85; as U.S. senator, 91–92, 97, 99, 109, 120n17
Normal training programs, 89
Norris, George W., 97
North Dakota: Dakota Territory and, 14; Nonpartisan League in, 6, 80; population in 1889, 14; taxation, 231t, 240, 241t, 244
Northwestern University, 151
Northwest Ordinance, 62
Norwegian immigrants: geographic distribution of, 25, 26map, 33; population counts, 18t, 19–20, 21–22, 21t, 23
NPL (Nonpartisan League), 6, 80, 85–87

O'Donnell, John, 160
Ohio: immigrants from, 18–19, 18t, 19, 21t, 22, 23, 33; settlement, 14, 33
Oil and gas industry, 154–55, 161–62, 226
Ore tax, 111, 202, 231
Owen, David, 238

Pacifism, 40
Packing houses, 79, 85
Parke Co., Ind., 66, 67, 69, 72
Parks, 77, 90–91
Paycheck Protection Program and Health Care Enhancement Act (PPPHCEA), 229
Pearl Harbor attack, 116, 129, 155
Pearson, Drew, 162
Pennington Co., S.Dak., 17, 26map, 28, 32, 174
Pennsylvania immigrants, 18t, 19, 21t, 22, 33
Pension system, 244
People's Party, 200
Perdue, Sonny, 245
Peterson, Robert, 113
Pettigrew, Richard F., 9, 98
Peurifoy, John, 135
Pheasant hunting, 90
Phillips, Wendell, 65
Pick, Lewis, 159
Pick-Sloan Plan, 158–60
Pierre, S.Dak., 17
Pierre Weekly Free Press, 87
Pillsbury, Parker, 65
Pine Ridge Indian Reservation, 15t, 110, 203
The Plow That Broke the Plains (film), 127
Police force, 86, 87
Political culture: and the budget process, 9–10, 222–46; characteristics and features, 4; conservative and Republican dominance in, 2–4, 7, 9–10, 117, 225; defined, 223; Elazar's subcultures, 223–27; and the German-language press, 5–6, 48–49; immigrants' influence on, 2–5, 33–34, 39, 223, 224–25; and *The Plains Political Tradition* series, 1–2; political families, 9, 199–201, 212–13; political leaders, 6–9, 201–13. *See also* Budget process; German-language newspapers; Immigrants and immigration; *names of individual political leaders;* Population, nineteenth century
Political cultures, individualistic: dominance of, 246; features, 10, 223, 224, 226, 227, 243; and moralistic cultures, 224; and taxes, 235, 239, 240, 241t; Zelinsky on, 12
Political cultures, moralistic: features, 10, 223–24, 226–27; and individualistic cultures, 224–25, 227; and progressivism, 9, 225–26; and taxes, 10, 240, 241t, 243, 244; and youth, 246; Zelinsky on, 12
Political cultures, traditionalistic, 223, 227, 237
Political parties, culture and, 224, 226
Population, nineteenth century, 12–38; African Americans, 16–17; American Indians, 14–16, 15t; Boom Decade, 13, 23, 24; Canadian immigrants, 18, 19, 23; Chinese immigrants, 17–18; Euro-American immigrants' distribution, 23–34, 26maps, 27map; Euro-American immigrants' influence, 2–3, 4–5, 33–34, 224–25; Euro-American

immigrants' origins, 12–14, 17–23, 18t, 21t, 22, 23, 24; historical sources for, 23; Minnesota Territory, 18–19, 18t. *See also specific ethnic, national, and regional groups*
Population, twenty-first century, 245–46
Populism: of Abourezk, 207; Democratic-Populist fusion, 98; and German immigrants, 43; heritage of, 3, 9, 245; Populist Party, 3, 79
Porter, Jack, 158
Postal savings banks, 79
Pound, Jamie, 173
Powderly, Terence V., 49
Pragmatism, 10
Prchal, Edward, 116
Press, German-language. *See* German-language newspapers
Prison population, 15
Progressive Era, 9, 80–81, 98–99, 225–26
Progressivism: Country Life Movement, 87–90; demise of, 100, 97, 99, 111; Gunderson's antagonism toward, 106; of McMaster, 97; Norbeck's reforms, 3, 6, 7, 9, 77–78, 80–82, 87–90, 92–93, 120n13
Prohibition, 48, 52, *53*, 53–54
Property: landowners, 224, 234; property tax, 10, 111, 231–35, 239–42, 241t, 246; state-run, 62; valuation, 103, 235
Protestant Germans, 43
Protests, 79–80, 86–87
Prussian immigrants, 30
Public ownership: abandonment and failure of, 92; Norbeck's development of, 77–78, 83–85; Populist Party on, 79; progressives on, 80
Public services, 225–27
Public virtue, 2
Puritanism, 224
Pyle, Gladys, 124n82
Pyle, John, 200
Pyle, Mamie Shields, 200
Pyle, May, 200
Pyle, Nellie, 200

Quakers: as abolitionists, 64, 66, 67, 68map, 69, 72; and political values, 224
Quasney, Mark, 239
Quinke, Bernhard, 41

Racism, 18, 66–67, 129
Radicalism, 79
Railroads, 78, 79, 81, 83, 86
Raisin Institute, 67
Ramsden, Randi: chapter by, 39–59; referenced, 5, 254
Ranching, 2
Rankin, John, 129, 134
Rapid City, S.Dak., 17, 85
Rapid City Daily Journal, 151
Rapid City Journal, 86
Rayburn, Sam, 152
Reagan, Ronald, 186, 205
Red Shirts, 66
Reeves, Thomas C., 133, 140
Regulation, governmental, 83
Reifel, Alice (Johnson), 203
Reifel, Benjamin (Wiyaka Wanjila), 167n44, 202–4, 207, 212
Reifel, William ("Shorty"), 202
Religion: anti-Catholicism, 208, 218n40; of German and German Russian immigrants, 29, 40, 42

Remele, Larry, 92
Rental housing, 234
Republicanism, 2–3, 10. *See also* Conservatism
Republican Party: Abdnor in, 205; Case's rebuilding of, 152, 153, 155, 159, 166n22; conservatism returned in, 116; Democratic Party's challenge to, 97–99, 105–10, 115; dominance of, 3–4, 98, 105–10, 115, 117, 244–45; German-language newspapers' ties to, 42–43, 51–52; Mickelson supported by, 185; opposition in India, 66; progressivism in, 7–8, 80, 81, 97, 98, 99, 115–16 (*See also* Progressivism)
Reserve funds, 227
Reston, James, 139
Retail trade, 245
Revenues, local, 224, 226
Revenue sources: federal, 224, 228–32, 229t, 243; local, 224, 226, 231, 233; state, 224, 226, 230; state-federal balance of payments, 230, 231t. *See also* Taxes; Tax policy
Right-to-work laws, 175
Ritter, Karl, 52
Roads and highways: Case's funding for, 163; under Norbeck, 81, 85, 88, 91, 92; and taxes, 225, 226
Roberts, Clint, 171, 172, 174, 175, 176, 182t
Rockefeller, John D., 78
Roe, Orvin Jarper, 51
Roman Catholics, 29
Ronayne, M. O., 51
Roosevelt, Franklin D., 7, 8, 97, 111–13, 118; administration, 127, 128, 131, 132, 141–42, 160; court packing plan, 114–15; and World War II, 116, 117, 155, 156. *See also* New Deal
Roosevelt, Theodore, 99; conservative reform of, 6, 80, 98; death of, 99
Roscoe Co., S.Dak., 41
Rose, Greg S.: chapter by, 12–38; referenced, 4, 5, 254–55
Rosebud Indian Reservation, 15t, 16, 110, 202, 206, 210
Rosen, William, 138
Rounds, M. Michael ("Mike"), 212, 218n40
Rural areas: Country Life Movement, 87–90; credit programs, 84, 85, 92, 97, 103, 111, 244; Norbeck's reforms for, 77–78, 81, 84–85, 87–93; urban-rural divide, 89–90, 245
Russian German immigrants. *See* German Russian immigrants
Russian Immigrants, 18t, 20, 21t, 22, 23, 28, 31
Russian Orthodox Church, 40

Salaries and wages, 186–87, 193–94
Salem Indian Training School (Chemawa Indian school), 72
Sales tax, 10, 111, 235–42, 237f, 241t, 243
Sallet, Friedrich, 42, 43–44, 49, 55
Samp, Rolly, 210, 211
Samuelson, Bob L., 190–91, 193–95, 196t
Sanborn/Miner Co., S.Dak., 26map, 28, 31, 32
Sande, Kermit, 210
Sandlin, Stephanie Herseth, 199, 212, 214n2
Scandinavian Immigrants, 3, 4–5, 33. *See also* Danish immigrants; Norwegian immigrants; Swedish immigrants
Schafer, Joseph, 72
Schenectady, N.Y., 79

Schools: funding, 60, 62, 89, 231, 232–33, 234; rural, under Norbeck, 88–90
Scott, Randy, 211
Scottish immigrants, 21t, 22, 32
Second District, 115, 149, 153, 156, 157, 158, 171, 207
Segregation, 163, 164
Senate Public Works Committee, 163
Senior citizens, 188, 233, 238
Settlers and settlement. *See* Census (1850-1890); Immigrants and immigration; Population, nineteenth century
Sevareid, Eric, 152
Shackman, Grace, 67
Sharpe, Merrell Q., 129, 200
Siebert, Wilbur H., 68map, 69, 71map, 71
Silver Star medal, 155–56
Sioux Falls, S.Dak., 17; Bulow in, 104, 121n31; *Nachrichten* in, 43, 45; political leaders from, 9
Sioux Falls Daily Argus-Leader, 86, 92, 100; on Mickelson, 185, 196; on Mundt and the Hiss trial, 141–42; on Roberts, 175
Sioux Indians, 2, 14, 204
Six Crises (Nixon), 126
Slavery: Beadle's anti-slavery views, 63–64, 72; pro-slavery groups, 66–67. *See also* Abolitionists
Smith, George, 225
Smith-Hughes Act, 90
Social assistance services, 245
Socialism and socialists: early twentieth century rise of, 79; Norbeck's response to, 77–78, 82, 85–86
Sons of Liberty, 66
South (U.S. region): immigration from, 17, 33; segregation in, 163, 164; traditionalist culture of, 224
South Dakota Alliance, 79
South Dakota Bureau of Finance and Management, 236, 243
South Dakota constitution, 225
South Dakota Department of Revenue, 233, 237
South Dakota Education Association, 193–94
South Dakota Farmers Union, 80, 83, 153–54
South Dakota Food and Drug Commission, 83
South Dakota Highway Department, 88
South Dakota History, 2
South Dakota Home Guard, 87
South Dakota Memorial Art Center, 204
South Dakota Office of Mine Inspectors, 83
South Dakota Outstanding Young Farmer award, 205
South Dakota Railroad Commission, 83
South Dakota School of Mines, 206
South Dakota State Legislature: Abdnor in, 205; appropriations, 108–9, 228–30, 229t, 243; under Berry, 7, 110–13, 235; budget process, 9–10, 222–46; under Bulow, 6–7, 106–10; under Byrne, 81; under Crawford, 81; Democratic Party ascendancy and fall, 7, 110, 115, 116–17, 207; family legacies in, 199–200; food tax bills, 238–39; under Gunderson, 102–3, 108; Mickelson endorsements, 179–80; under Norbeck, 77, 81–92; Populist Party in, 79; Republican

dominance of, 3, 106–10, 115; Samuelson's record in, 195
South Dakota State Planning Commission, 112
South Dakota State University, 1, 203, 208
South Dakota State University Agricultural Extension Service, 23
South Dakota Young Republicans, 205
Southern Dakota Railway, 40
Southwest Texas State Teachers College, 151
Soviet Union: Cold War, 129; espionage, 8, 129, 130, 131, 140, 141, 142; U.S. cooperation with, 129
Space program, 162–63, 183
Spearfish, S.Dak., 156
Spindletop well, 154
Spink Co., S.Dak., 30, 31, 32
Srstka, William, 210
Stanley Co., S.Dak., 16
Statehood (South Dakota), 14, 20–21, 98
State-run enterprises. *See* Public ownership
Steeper, Fred, 195
Stevensen, Coke, 158
St. John's University, 208
Stock yards, 79, 85
Stofferahn, Ken, 183, 186
Stokes, Thomas, 157
Strategic Arms Reduction Treaty, 163
Stripling, Robert, 126, 131, 133
Strip mining, 192
Sturgis, S.Dak., 17
Süd Dakota Nachrichten, 44–45, *45,* 47, 48–49
Süd-Dakota Nachrichten und Herold, 47–49
Suffrage, woman, 48, 200
Sully Co., S.Dak., 17
Superior Oil Company, 161
Supplemental Nutrition Assistance Program (SNAP), 239
Swedish immigrants: geographic distribution of, 25, 26map, 33; population counts, 18t, 19–20, 21, 21t, 22, 23
Switzerland, 47
Sylvan Lake, 91

Taft, William Howard, 99
Taft-Hartley Bill, 157
Tanenhaus, Sam, 136
Tauzin, Billy, 213
Taxes: and American Indians' census designations, 14–16, 15t; bank franchise tax, 228; Berry's raising of, 111; contractor's excise tax, 228, 235, 238; corporate tax, 227, 228; gasoline tax, 111; income tax (*See* Income tax); industrial profits tax, 154; inheritance tax, 243; insurance company tax, 228; lottery tax, 228; ore tax, 111, 202, 231; per capita, 108; property tax, 10, 111, 231–35, 239–42, 241t, 246; sales tax, 10, 111, 235–42, 237f, 241t, 242f, 243; sales tax on food, 238–39; tobacco tax, 228; use tax, 235–37, 237f, 238, 241t, 242f
Tax Foundation, 227–28, 242
Tax policy, 222–46; and business, 227, 236; circuit breakers, 233, 234; for cities, 237; comparisons with neighboring states, 238–42, 241t; and GDP shifts, 239, 245; and income level, 233–34, 234f, 236, 238, 239, 241t, 242; and individualistic cultures, 235, 239, 240, 241t; and moralistic cultures, 10, 240, 241t, 243, 244;

Norbeck's reforms, 81; per capita state taxes, 242; progressive, 238, 243; pyramiding, 238; ranking and criteria, 227–28; rebates, 238; regressivity, 234, 236, 238, 242, 243; state comparisons, 238; tax burdens, 238–42, 241t; tax exemptions, 236–37; tax incidence, 233; and traditionalist cultures, 224, 237; for tribes, 236, 237; vertical equity principle, 239–40
Tax Policy Center, 239
Taylor, Bayard, 65
Taylor, Claudia (Lady Bird Johnson), 153
Taylor, W. W., 213
Teachers: Mickelson's support of, 193–94; Norbeck's program for, 89; tax revenues for, 235
Telephone systems, 226
Television: campaign ads (*See* Mickelson, George S., campaign ads); Hiss-Chambers hearings, 136; McCarthy hearings ban, 161; Sioux Falls stations, 181–82
Tennessee, 235; African American immigrants from, 17Terre Haute, Ind., 66
Texas, 235; cattle industry, 149, 165n9; immigrants from, 17; LBJ's ties to, 149, 150; oil and gas industry, 154–55, 161–62
Thomas, Harvey, 71
Thomas, Parnell, 131, 138
"Three Hundred Fighting Regiments" (Fox), 61–62
Thune, John, 9, 206
Time, 130, 150
Tobacco tax, 228
Tobin, James, 65
Todd Co., S.Dak., 30
Tolerance, 224
Tourism, 91
Traditionalistic political cultures. *See* Political cultures, traditionalistic
Treason. *See* Hiss trial
Treaty of Yankton, 14
Truman, Harry S., 130, 134, 135, 140, 157; administration, 133, 160
Trust funds, 227
Trusts. *See* Monopolies and trusts
Tucker, Lavinia, 69, 71, 73n22
Turner Co., S.Dak., 27map, 29, 30, 31, 32; German immigrants in, 40, 41
Turnipseed, A. G., 103, 104
Typhoid, 63

Ukraine, Germans from, 28
Underground Railroad, 64, 66, 67, 68map, 69, 70map, 71map, 71
The Underground Railroad from Slavery to Freedom (Siebert), 68map, 69, 71map
"The Underground Railroad in Ann Arbor" (Shackman), 67
Unemployment insurance, 202
Union Co., S.Dak., 25, 26map, 28, 31–32
United States Army, 155–56
United States Bureau of Indian Affairs, 15, 203, 204
United States Census. *See* Census (1850-1890); Census (2020)
United States Congress, 1, 7, 102, 104, 108; 1924 election, 102; Abdnor in, 205–6; Bulow in, 110, 112; Case in, 8, 149, 159, 160–62; Democrat from S.Dak. elected to, 99; LBJ in, 149, 150, 152, 153, 154–56, 157–58, 160–64; McGovern in, 162; Mundt in, 7–8; Norbeck in, 91–92, 97, 99; Populist Party in, 79; Smith-

Hughes Act, 90. *See also* House Committee on Un-American Affairs (HUAC)
United States Department of Commerce, 130
United States Department of State, 133, 135, 140, 141
United States Department of the Interior, 91
United States Information and Education Exchange Act, 129
United States Navy, 155–56
United States Small Business Administration, 205
United States Supreme Court, 114
United States War Department, 91
University of Michigan: *Alpha Nu* literary society, 60, 64, 66, 67; Beadle at, 60, 62, 63, 64, 66, 67; Bulow's admission to, 103–4
University of Nebraska, 204
University of South Dakota, 10, 206, 210, 219n47
Urban-rural divide, 89–90, 245
Use tax, 235–37, 237f, 238, 239, 241t, 242f
Ustrud, Hans, 111, 202
Utley, H. M., 66

"Vaterland" (Fatherland), 47, 51
Venhuizen, Tonnis H.: chapter by, 97–125; referenced, 3, 6–7, 255
"Venona" counterintelligence project, 142
Vermont immigrants, 18t, 19
Vessey, Robert S., 98
Veterans Administration Hospital, 156
Vietnam War, 165
Virginia immigrants, 17, 33
Voice of America, 129
Volcker Alliance, 243–44
Volga German immigrants, 40, 42
Volk, Dave, 212
Voting: Case's stuffed ballot controversy, 162; LBJ's ballot controversy, 158; voter turnout, 224, 226, 227; voting rights, 163–64

Wabash Riflemen, 63
Wages, 186–87, 193–94
Walworth Co., S.Dak., 29, 31, 54
Ware, Harold, 131, 132
Ware Group, 131, 133
Warehouses, 79
Washington (state), 235
Washington Post, 132
Water resources, 85, 91, 92, 148–49, 158–60
Watkins, Arthur, 160
Wayfair Decision, 237
Weapons, concealed, 86
Webb, Daryl A.: chapter by, 77–96; referenced, 3, 6, 255
Weinstein, Allen, 141
Welfare expenditures, 224
Welsh immigrants, 21t, 22, 31, 32
Wenzlaff, Johann Christian, 41–42
Wenzlaff, Salomon, 42
Westling, Elmer, 100
West River (S.Dak. region), 2, 174
West Virginia, 17
White League, 66
Wicker, Tom, 135
Wildlife, conservation of. *See* Environmental conservation
Wilkenson. Todd, 197
Wilson, Paul: about, 8, 170–71, 255; chapter by, 170–98
Wilson, Woodrow, 80, 99, 151

Wine licensing, 202
Wisconsin, 4; immigrants, geographic distribution of, 25, 26map, 27; immigrants, population counts, 17, 18, 18t, 19, 20, 21t, 22, 23, 33; settlement, 14, 33
Wiyaka Wanjila. *See* Reifel, Benjamin (Wiyaka Wanjila)
Women: first S.Dak. woman in U.S. House, 199; first S.Dak. woman in U.S. Senate, 124n82, 200; suffrage movement, 48, 200
Wood, John, 131
Woodward, Colin, 223
Workmen's compensation law, 83
World War I: and anti-German sentiment, 55; Socialists deemed un-American during, 86–87
World War II: and Bulow's isolationism, 7; entry, 116, 155; LBJ in, 155–56; military building projects in South Dakota, 156–57
Woster, Kevin, 196
Wurttemberg, Germany, immigrants from, 30
Wyoming, 14, 230, 231t, 235, 240, 241t, 242, 244

Yankton, S.Dak., 17, 40–41, 83
Yanktonais Indians, 71, 72
Yankton Co., S.Dak., 17, 25, 26map, 29, 30, 31, 32, 40–41
Yankton Indian Reservation, 15t, 16
Yankton Press and Union and Dakotaian, 40
Yellowstone National Park, 91
Young, Clark, 225
Youth, 246

Zelinksy, Wilbur, 12